# Debates in Criminal Justice

This innovative new book recognises that, while criminal justice studies is a core component of all criminology/criminal justice undergraduate degrees, it can be a confusing, overwhelming and a relatively dry topic despite its importance. Taking an original approach, this book sets out a series of ten key dilemmas – presented as debates – designed to provide students with a clear framework within which to develop their knowledge and analysis in a way that is both effective and an enjoyable learning experience. It is also designed for use by lecturers, who can structure a core unit of their courses around it.

*Debates in Criminal Justice* provides a new and dynamic framework for learning, making considerable use of the other already available academic key texts, press articles, web sources and more.

**Tom Ellis** is Principal Lecturer in Criminology at the Institute of Criminal Justice Studies, University of Portsmouth, UK.

**Steve Savage** is Professor of Criminology and Director of the Institute of Criminal Justice Studies, University of Portsmouth, UK.

# Debates in Criminal Justice
## Key themes and issues

## Edited by Tom Ellis and Steve Savage

Routledge
Taylor & Francis Group

LONDON AND NEW YORK

First published 2012
by Routledge
2 Park Square, Milton Park, Abingdon, Oxon OX14 4RN

Simultaneously published in the USA and Canada
by Routledge
711 Third Avenue, New York, NY 10017

*Routledge is an imprint of the Taylor & Francis Group, an informa business*

*British Library Cataloguing in Publication Data*
A catalogue record for this book is available from the British Library

*Library of Congress Cataloging in Publication Data*
Debates in criminal justice / edited by Tom Ellis and Steve Savage.
    p. cm.
  1. Criminology.  I. Ellis, Tom.  II. Savage, Steve.
HV6024.D43 2011
364–dc22

                                                    2011009037

ISBN: 978-0-415-44590-0 (hbk)
ISBN: 978-0-415-44591-7 (pbk)
ISBN: 978-0-203-80448-3 (ebk)

Typeset in 10/12pt Sabon
by Graphicraft Limited, Hong Kong

Printed and bound in Great Britain by
TJ International Ltd, Padstow, Cornwall

For Claire, for all those extra hours

# Contents

# List of contributors

**Tom Ellis** is a Principal Lecturer at the Institute of Criminal Justice Studies (ICJS) at the University of Portsmouth. His areas of research and publication include: Japanese criminal justice; youth justice; prisons; and also race, diversity and criminal justice, where he sits on the Ministry of Justice's Race Statistics Advisory Board. Until 1999, he worked for the Home Office Research, Development and Statistics Directorate and also had a two-year spell with the UN at UNICRI, based in Rome. Tom is also an external member of the Child Exploitation and Online Protection Centre (CEOP) Research Panel.

**Steve Savage** is Professor of Criminology and Director of the Institute of Criminal Justice Studies, which he founded in 1992. After doctoral research on sociological theory, his research interests focused on the politics of social policy, and subsequently the politics of criminal justice and policing. Recent research has included studies of police governance and police reform, campaigns against miscarriages of justice, crime and illegal immigration, and more recently, the independent investigation of complaints against the police.

**Diana Bretherick**, a former barrister, is a senior lecturer in ICJS and her areas of expertise are: homicide; cultural criminology; representations of crime and criminals in literature, film and TV; crime and the news media; and history of popular criminology.

**Mark Button** is Reader in Criminology and Associate Head Curriculum in ICJS and has recently founded the Centre for Counter Fraud Studies of which he is Director. He is also Head of Secretariat for the national Counter Fraud Professional Accreditation Board. Mark has written a number of books and articles on counter fraud and private policing issues. Before joining ICJS, he was a Research Assistant to the Rt Hon Bruce George MP, specialising in policing, security and home affairs issues.

**Jane Creaton** is a Principal Lecturer in Criminal Law and Criminal Justice in ICJS. Her areas of expertise include vulnerable witnesses, expert evidence and the legal profession but her current research interests focus on professional doctorates and academic writing practices in criminology.

**Les Johnston** is a (recently retired) Professor of Criminology in ICJS. His research interests and publications include: security governance; public, commercial and citizen-based policing; risk and security management; and social and political theory.

**Chris Lewis** is visiting professor in ICJS. His varied career includes working as Home Office Chief Statistician and Assistant Director of Research 1986–2003 and as consultant on justice statistics for the World Bank, UNODC and the African Development Bank 2004–11. Research and teaching includes: gun crime; equality and diversity; criminal justice statistics; prosecutions and sentencing; violent crime; covert operation; and offender programmes in custody. He is also a Trustee of Kainos Community which runs prison and community programmes for offenders.

**Mike Nash** is Professor of Criminology and Head of Department in ICJS. He has published extensively on public protection issues, including a number of single and joint authored texts. His current research interests concern inter-agency relationships and culture change under the public protection umbrella. He is currently planning to extend this work with a colleague to explore emerging public protection processes in South Korea.

**Francis Pakes** qualified in psychology in his native Netherlands and completed his PhD with Leiden University in 2001. He has worked in ICJS since 1998. Francis has authored, co-authored or edited several books, including: *Comparative criminal justice*; *Community justice: Issues for probation and criminal justice*; *Psychology and crime*; and *Criminal psychology*.

**Daniel Silverstone** is a Principal Lecturer in criminology at London Metropolitan University. His research interests and publications are in the areas of: organised crime; drugs and the night-time economy; and illegal firearms use.

**Jacki Tapley** is Programme Head for one of the largest suite of undergraduate criminology degrees in the UK. Her work focuses on victimology, the role of victims in the criminal justice system and criminal justice responses to victims. Prior to coming to ICJS in 2000 Jacki was a Probation Officer in Dorset. She is a member of the Dorset Criminal Justice Board consultative committee which focuses on the different agencies' responsibilities towards victims and the implementation of policies and legislation.

**Andy Williams** is a Principal Lecturer in Forensic Criminology in ICJS. His main areas of research and publication are: sexual offenders; forensic evidence; crime scene behaviour; offender profiling; moral panics, paedophilia and public protection. He is co-author of *The Anatomy of Serious Further Offences* (Oxford University Press, 2008) and co-edited *The Handbook of Public Protection* (Willan, 2010).

# Introduction

From the 1990s onward, criminal justice legislation, policy and organisation have changed at an incredible pace in England and Wales compared with previous decades. This has been matched by a huge growth in what is written about criminal justice, by academics and by others, most notably journalists, who are able to publish much more quickly, but perhaps to different requirements and standards of evidence.

This book does not therefore seek to replace other existing texts and sources, but, rather, to assist in studying them effectively and teaching criminal justice within a framework that is both appealing and interesting to students and staff alike. We have used and developed the debate format for over 10 years and it has been very successful and popular in achieving its learning outcomes in what is potentially a very dry, though necessary, key area within criminological studies.

> NB It is important to note that the authors have, for the most part, argued from relatively extreme positions. They have acted as devil's advocates in order to comply with the format demanded by a debate approach. Therefore, it is important to bear in mind that the views presented should not be taken as the actual views of those authors.

This book will not give you 'the answers'. It will identify the key questions within each topic and give you the means to find the sources so that you will be able to answer them in a balanced and logical way. The book contains ten carefully, though contrastingly constructed, debates that are designed to provide the student with a clear basic framework within which they can develop their knowledge and analysis of key criminal justice dilemmas and issues.

The debate format is familiar to most through the approach most often taken in press, radio and other media, and even in student debating societies. As such, the book allows students to start from a level that they are more familiar with and to progress beyond this so that they understand the limits of 'for and against' approaches in academic study. Some of the chapters are therefore developed beyond the debate format in order to help students to progress to the higher levels of critical thinking required as they progress through their courses. For instance, Chapter 5, on restorative and retributive justice approaches, uses established arguments between these two approaches as a way of progressing to understanding and applying all of the key philosophies of punishment.

If used well, this book should enable students to understand the key underpinning concepts to criminal justice, such as 'What is criminal justice for?' or 'Why is punishment necessary?' For each issue, we also provide you with further reading, further questions to ask yourself, and further answers to seek within your additional reading. **It is essential, therefore, that you use the book as intended, and complete your additional reading, to gain the full benefit of its design.** Most assessments will require more than a simple recapitulation of the debates contained here. These debates necessarily overlap and assessments are likely to require you to use materials from at least two different chapters in order to ensure that you integrate your learning.

The content is not exhaustive, but we have picked what we think are a good mix of key issues and contemporary dilemmas which are based on the authors' fields of study. We have also endeavoured to include a number of 'jump off points' for those who wish to deepen their studies in a particular area, perhaps when thinking about a dissertation topic.

The book is split into two parts. **Part 1** is more conceptual and based on key *themes* that form the basis of criminal justice studies. For instance, by debating the arguments for crime control or due process, the first debate is a device for introducing the different models of criminal justice. It also requires you to read further and decide for yourself whether models need to be developed in a different way to provide an explanation of what criminal justice *should* be for and what it actually *does*. Similarly, arguments for and against whether imprisonment 'works', lead to questions about how success or failure of punishment *can* be measured and/or *should* be measured, and whether these measures are determined by which philosophical standpoint is used.

**Part 2** of the unit presents *issues* in criminal justice, two of which ('legalisation of drugs' and 'capital punishment') have been selected based on long running areas of debate within criminology and criminal justice, while others are of more recent contemporary concern.

As noted, each debate is approached and delivered in a different way. We hope that this variation in approach allows your learning to stay fresh. What is common to all of the debates are the indications of the additional work you need to carry out in order to underpin your learning fully.

Finally, this is an easy book to use, but it is not designed for lazy scholarship. It is not intended as a reference source that should be cited in itself, but as a way of structuring your reading of the key sources referred to in the text. Referring only to this book, or simply quoting from it, shows that the student has not done some of their own expected 'spadework' and it will be easy for tutors to spot this. That said, it does make it as easy as possible to decide on which sources you should read.

---

### Academic and non-academic sources

In many of the debates, extensive use has been made of press and other web-based sources. These are included in order to provide you with a richer source of materials and should mainly be used to illustrate the issues derived from the required academic reading. However, you should be clear that such sources are *not* usually peer reviewed and should therefore not be used *instead* of academic sources. 'A hierarchy of evidence' is provided at the end of Chapter 1 to help you decide on the relative value of the sources.

---

The book has been developed as the basis of both campus-based and distance learning modules, with students ranging from full-time undergraduates to police and probation officers. The book is also designed as an introductory text for Master's students who have no prior experience of criminal justice, or who need to refresh their knowledge. Tutors should therefore find it easy to adapt it to particular courses and integrate additional materials. We hope you enjoy reading it as much as we enjoyed producing it.

Tom Ellis and Steve Savage

September 2011

## Online resources

This book is supported by online resources that can be found at:

<http://www.debatesincriminaljustice.com/>

This is intended, first, for use by students as a way of using the links provided in some chapters to access the key sources more effectively in an e-learning environment. It is also intended for use by lecturers who wish to build or adapt a course around the book and related materials. Suggested module/course outlines, typical assessments and updates are provided. Exemplar on-line chapters are provided here to aid students and staff alike and, depending on demand, further resources and new debates chapters may be added.

# Part 1
# Themes in criminal justice

# 1 Crime control or due process?

*Tom Ellis and Mike Nash*

## Introduction

What is criminal justice for? How does criminal justice function? This first, relatively simple chapter, starts by outlining the key features of a crime control model from the type of perspective that those who often advocate it adopt. You will find this type of argument most commonly in popular newspapers and media, but also to some extent among criminal justice professionals who work in agencies tasked with crime control, such as the police. This approach is then criticised and an argument is made that the due process model is the one on which criminal justice should be based. This view tends to be popular among academics and also those criminal justice professionals involved in the court process itself, such as probation officers. Having established the oldest framework for models of criminal justice, in the final section of this chapter, we broaden the focus to include other models and explanations. As we note throughout the text, it is important for you to use the debate format as the framework from which to develop your understanding and it is important to use the final section, and the additional reading suggested there, to gain a full understanding of the key issues. By the end of working through this chapter, you will therefore: be familiar with the key **models of criminal justice**, be able to distinguish between them, and will have developed a critical understanding of their uses.

For those of you who have already covered the basic structure of criminal justice in England and Wales, and relationships between the various agencies involved, it would be better at this point to read:

- Newburn, T. (2007) *Criminology*. Cullompton: Willan, pp. 542–57.

An alternative, but now somewhat dated source is:

- White, R.C.A. (2002) 'The structure and organization of criminal justice in England and Wales: an overview'. In M. McConville and G. Wilson (eds) *The Handbook of Criminal Justice Process*. Oxford: Oxford University Press, pp. 5–21.

A more basic but up-to-date source is:

- Blake, C., Sheldon, B. and Williams, P. (2010) *Policing and Criminal Justice*. Exeter: Learning Matters Ltd, <http://www.learningmatters. co.uk>

The latter book has the advantage of being written since the division of responsibilities between the Home Office and the newly created Ministry of Justice has made the picture a little more complex. If you need to understand this in more detail, the following sources will be very useful:

- Ministry of Justice (2009) 'Business Model'. London: Ministry of Justice, <http://www.justice.gov.uk/publications/ministry-of-justice-business-model-2009.htm>

The first 21 pages are a useful exposition of what the MoJ says it is for and how it will go about it.

- Ministry of Justice Corporate Plan 2009–11. London: Ministry of Justice, <http://www.justice.gov.uk/publications/docs/corporate-plan-2009-11.pdf>

## In support of crime control

It is hard to find much support (as opposed to critiques) among academic criminologists for a crime control approach, perhaps because their livelihoods depend on significant levels of crime! However, a crime control approach is very well supported in the popular press, particularly tabloid newspapers, which after all form the bulk of what the public reads. It seems clear that the current criminal justice process was designed for the much lower level of crime that existed in the past and is too bureaucratic, time-consuming and inefficient to deal effectively with the sheer volume of crime that now exists. If a law-abiding member of the public becomes a victim of crime, they find themselves lost in a legal process that values the rights of the suspects above the rights of those who have been wronged.

### Crime control – a popular press example?

Your house is reduced to a wreck. Your family treasures are trashed, your doors and windows broken, your money and valuables stolen . . . You may never again feel at ease in your own home.

Only the victims can fully understand the shock and misery of being burgled . . . For that reason, prison has always been considered the appropriate penalty. No longer. A drug addict who committed 18 break-ins over seven months walked grinning from court.

The message could hardly be more damaging. The fact is that burglars are hardly ever caught.

Now, even the ones who are caught won't be jailed. It is almost as if they are being encouraged to rob [sic].

Lord Woolf says he wants to reduce overcrowding and that prison does nothing to reform burglars.

In a Britain where police so seldom manage to catch thieves, where witness intimidation is almost routine and where the legal system increasingly seems impervious to common sense, Lord Woolf has confirmed his reputation as a man more concerned about the welfare of criminals than the plight of their victims.

(*Daily Mail*, Saturday, 21 December 2002, p. 12)

It is clear that there is a frustration here with a system that is designed to ensure the rights of the offenders, but is not really concerned about the victims.

---

### More examples

- 'Ex-New York cop sacked from probation service for putting public safety first', *Daily Mail*, 5 June 2006, <http://www.dailymail.co.uk/news/article-389092/Ex-New-York-cop-sacked-probation-service-putting-public-safety-first.html>

See also:

- 'Convicts who have killed on probation', *Daily Mail*, <http://www.dailymail.co.uk/legacygallery/gallery-7656/Convicts-killed-probation.html?selectedImage=67179>

This will also be relevant when reading the chapter on victims' rights and suspects' rights.

---

The overwhelming idea is that criminal justice should have **crime control** as its main aim.

### *What is crime control?*

The **crime control model** is about focusing the purpose of the criminal justice process on the demands of the majority of citizens who are law-abiding. Under these conditions, criminal justice is about the efficient control of crime.

### Task

- Read: Davies, M., Croall, H. and Tyrer, J. (2010) *Criminal Justice: An Introduction to the Criminal Justice System in England and Wales* (4th edn). London: Longman, Chapter 1.

Limit your reading to these two models at this point. Another basic introductory text that can be used is:

- Smart, U. (2006) *Criminal Justice*. London: Sage, Part Two, pp. 15–134.

Essentially there should be a unified or 'joined up' criminal justice **system**, where all parts of the system work in harmony to reduce or prevent crime and to apprehend, prosecute, convict and punish most, or all, of those who offend. In this way, the public are protected by reduction of crime, and effective detection and prosecution of those who do offend.

This model of justice accepts that there will be a few aberrant cases where the innocent are convicted, but this is justified by the utilitarian notion that crime control overwhelmingly achieves the greater good for the majority (see Chapter 5 on restorative and retributive justice and the other philosophies of punishment).

### Task

How do we decide what is an acceptably small number of cases in which innocent people are wrongly convicted?

- Read: 'The scales of injustice' by Michael Naughton, *Observer*, 28 July 2002 <http://observer.guardian.co.uk/crimedebate/story/0,12079,764137,00.html>

Make notes for and against the crime control approach. You will also find a useful set of sources for further illustrative examples at the following website:

- <http://www.innocent.org.uk/misc/articles.html>

Inevitably, this system demands a high level of informal fact-finding, or, in other words, the case is dealt with outside of the formal court setting as much as possible. While the notion of due process presumes that the criminal courts will play a major role in examining the evidence and determining innocence or guilt, Skolnick's 1966 classic text (*Justice Without Trial*. New York: Wiley) outlines the way in which the police make many decisions about whether to proceed with arrest and the processes beyond that without the intervention of the courts.

**Task**

The up-to-date intricacies of this process in England and Wales are well summarised and argued in the following book:

- Cape, E. and Young R.P. (eds) (2008) *Regulating Policing: The Police and Criminal Evidence Act 1984, Past, Present and Future.* Portland, OR: Hart Publishing.

Ensure you are clear about why the Police and Criminal Evidence Act was necessary and note down how this might relate to notions of crime control and due process.

You should also ensure you read the chapter by Young on what he calls the 'summarisation of justice' and make notes on the extent to which you think this marks a shift toward a crime control model.

See also:

- '"Police Justice" now deal with more crimes than the courts'. *Guardian*, 30 November 2007, <http://www.guardian.co.uk/politics/2007/nov/30/ukcrime.law>

The crime control model relies on:

- presumption of guilt – in contrast to the formal judicial process;
- recognition that victims should have more rights than the accused;
- belief that prison and other punishment must be unpleasant in order to work (**deterrence**);
- belief that sentences must be long to protect the public (**incapacitation**); and
- belief that keeping **order** on the street is more important than following the letter of the **law**.

**Task**

Make notes at this point on what you think the differences are between 'law' and 'order' and whether you think it is easy to strike the
right balance.

Have a read of Skolnick and, if you wish to pursue this area in
more depth, a good starting point is:

● Rosenfeld, Richard, Fornango, Robert, and Rengifo, Andres F.
(2007) 'The impact of order-maintenance policing on New York
City homicide and robbery rates: 1988–2001'. *Criminology*,
45(2) 355–84.

Refine your notes on the basis of your reading.

### The rights of the public and crime control

A crime control model is preferable for the majority of relatively powerless,
law-abiding citizens, so that they can exercise their rights to walk the streets,
relax in their own homes and leave their vehicles and/or businesses without the fear of crime and victimisation. It also means that most offenders
will be caught, unlike under the current system where the detection and
clear-up rates are extremely poor. Offenders will be seen to be punished
(see Chapter 5, restorative justice and retribution and the other philosophies
of punishment). Crime control will also ensure that: the public are protected
from future victimisation by the same offender; members of the public will
know when offenders are released; and offenders will know that they are
being monitored so that they cannot offend again (see Chapter 10 on sex
offender notification).

### Round up of crime control

The crime control model ensures that a civilised society can protect all of its
citizens from victimisation by criminals. Those convicted, or even acquitted,
of previous crimes, should remain as suspects for future crimes and, if
arrested and found guilty again, they will receive much harsher sentences.
The model rightly assumes that offenders' rights are less important than
victims' rights and that justice is for the majority of law-abiding citizens,
not for the minority of repeat offenders.

# In support of due process

## Context

The highly politicised nature of crime causation and crime control means that great care needs to be taken with the administration of justice. It is a foolish person who believes that 'the law' stands outside of external influences, independent and aloof from pressure. These influences are invariably more vocal from the punitive side of the debate. It is much easier to stand up for the rights of victims than the rights of offenders and it will certainly gain more popular and media support.

Supporters of due process may well find themselves in a minority, labelled as being on the offender's side, a bleeding heart that will be taken for granted. Crime control supporters on the other hand have the seeming weight of moral authority behind them. Offenders, by transgressing against other (innocent) people, lose the right to protection and, indeed, more rights should be given to the state in order to bring offenders to justice. This desire is so strong that mistakes will be forgiven, for the needs of the majority outweigh those of the minority.

It is not surprising, however, to realise that it is likely that criminal justice processes will oscillate between due process and crime control. For example, a change of government may significantly alter the type of legislation passed, offering more or fewer rights to suspects and defendants. Equally, even without a political or legislative change, the interpretation of legislation may change, in particular perhaps with harsher sentencing occurring more frequently. This may be in direct response to notorious cases receiving widespread media attention.

The issue here is: should the way we deal with offenders (or even suspects) be subject to such vagaries, or should we ensure that the law is neutral, objective and fair to all involved? This debate is about values, which to a large extent reflect how we wish to live in society. It is an important debate.

## Task

Do 'tougher' crime control policies achieve their aim of lower crime?

Read the following and make notes:

- Kovandzic, Thomislav V., Sloan, John J., III and Vieraitis, Lynne M. (2004) '"Striking Out" as Crime Reduction Policy: The Impact of "Three Strikes" Laws on Crime Rates in US Cities'. *Justice Quarterly*, 21(2), 207–39.

### What is due process?

In simple terms it could be said that a pure due process approach is one that sees the rights of those entering the criminal justice process protected. It aims to ensure that those who are innocent of crimes are acquitted, and are given every assistance to make this situation happen. It places the onus of establishing guilt on the state, which is of course regarded as much more powerful than the individual. Herbert Packer established these models, and in so doing he was not describing an absolute but a theoretical construct, with values determining the process of justice. In other words, someone would not one day stand up and say we are going to have a due process or crime control system of justice. It was more how justice would be administered along a continuum between these two positions.

A pure due process approach aims to curb the powers of the powerful state and its agents. For example, a number of rights would be given to the suspect and a series of hurdles placed in the way of professionals working within criminal justice to ensure fairness to the weaker party.

Most texts now rely on summaries of Packer's original text, but you may wish to check the original:

- Packer, H.L. (1968) *The Limits of Criminal Sanctions*. Stanford, CA: Stanford University Press.

These rights may vary over time but often will be concerned with basic physical comforts. For example, there will be rules governing the length of time a person can be interviewed without a break for rest or food. There will be rules governing how interviews should be conducted, with audio and video taping to ensure that suspects are not bullied, beaten or threatened into making a confession. This may sound the stuff of totalitarian regimes, but was a facet of criminal justice in the UK not so long ago. In early 2006 a UK TV series, *Life on Mars*, presented just such a message: a Detective Inspector from 2006 suddenly, as a result of an accident, found himself living and working in the 1970s. Aside from the complete lack of forensic support, the most striking aspect of the programme was the way in which suspects were treated. Arrest was on the flimsiest of evidence. Once in police custody suspects were often shouted at, pushed, punched, tricked and generally ill-treated until a confession was forthcoming. A colleague who was a police officer at the time says that the programme is frighteningly real in its depiction of the period.

**Task**

- Read: Reiner, R. (1997) In M. Maguire, R. Morgan and R. Reiner (eds) *The Oxford Handbook of Criminology* (2nd edn). Oxford: Oxford University Press, Chapter 28.

This neatly summarises the history of the way in which police 'backstage' practices were progressively combated by increasingly restrictive legislation (especially the Police and Criminal Evidence Act 1984, which is covered yet further below) in an attempt to bring practice into line with the formal requirements of the law, i.e., a move toward a due process model.

### Confession and due process

The centrality of the confession perhaps lies at the heart of the problems experienced in criminal justice processes. An admission of guilt forecloses the investigation and shortens the trial. It may lead to an early release from police detention and, indeed, a confession may result in a reduced sentence. The admission of guilt therefore has many benefits for both 'sides' and it is for this reason that it needs rules around it which protect the vulnerable. It is not too much of a stretch of the imagination to see that certain suspects would be very susceptible to pressure in a police station.

**Task**

See, for instance, a summary of the case of Stefan Kiszko:

- 'Stark reminder of how an innocent man can be railroaded into spending years in jail', *Guardian*, 11 November 2006: <http://www.guardian.co.uk/uk/2006/nov/11/ukcrime.duncancampbell>

Or the case of Paul Blackburn:

- 'Appeal victory after 25 years' jail', *Guardian*, 26 May 2005: <http://www.guardian.co.uk/uk_news/story/0,1492263,00.html>

The young, the elderly or those suffering from any form of mental illness might all admit to crimes they have not committed. Even those concerned about getting home to children, or even to pets, might be persuaded of their guilt if it helped them get out of a police station more quickly. Equally, promises of lighter sentences could prove tempting, especially to those facing custody for the first time. It is for this reason that a basic premise of justice in this country has been 'innocent until proven guilty'. The onus is on the state to prove guilt, rather than the defendant to prove innocence. Hence the traditional right to silence afforded to suspects who should not be put into a position to incriminate themselves. However, this right was somewhat compromised by the Criminal Justice and Public Order Act (CJPOA) 1994, which allowed adverse influences to be drawn from silence in the following circumstances:

- failure to mention a fact when under caution before charge which is later relied on in your defence;
- failure to mention a fact that it would have been reasonable to mention at the time;
- failure to account for objects, substances or marks found on your person in the place you were arrested; and
- failure after your arrest to account for your presence at a place at or about the time the offence is alleged to have been committed.

It still remains the case that these negative inferences cannot be drawn if the suspect was not given the opportunity to consult a solicitor prior to being questioned or charged. This alteration to the right of silence shows how 'pure' models of justice are unlikely to exist, but reaffirms the notion of a sliding scale or continuum, along which actions, policies and legislation can move. In this instance, the movement was towards a crime control model.

## Task

Why might innocent people be vulnerable to such miscarriages of justice?

Read the following two articles:

- Kassin, Saul M. (2005) 'On the psychology of confessions: does *innocence* put *innocents* at risk?' *American Psychologist*, 60(3), 215–28.
- Macfarlane, Bruce (2006) 'Convicting the innocent: a triple failure of the justice system'. *Manitoba Law Journal*, 31(3), 403–87.

What does this area of research tell us about the balance between crime control and due process?

*Due process – a reflection of how we want to be treated ourselves?*

As indicated above, it is easy to fall behind the crime control bandwagon. Low clear-up rates by police officers, apparently lenient sentencing and further crimes by those on bail (or even those who should have been deported after serving their sentence) all offer evidence that we have gone too far in being fair to offenders. An approach that would toughen up the response to offenders is fine when it is going to be applied to 'the other', that personification of crime represented by images we all hold in our heads. But what if 'the other' is yourself or one of your relatives? Most of us want a system of fair play, one that treats people equally and gives them a chance. The ultimate crime control model does not do this.

### Task

Think about the 'law-abiding minority' of the crime control perspective. Is this more about 'order' than it is about 'law'?

Read Blair's pledge to wage war on crime: is he really only focused on certain types of crime that relate more to public order and visible crimes?

- 'Blair pledge to wage new crime war'. *Observer*, 10 November 2002, <http://observer.guardian.co.uk/crimedebate/story/0,837315,00. html>

Also read one of the following sources:

- Karstedt, S. and Farrall, S. (2007) 'Law-abiding majority? The everyday crimes of the middle classes'. Briefing 3 June 2007. Centre for Crime and Justice Studies, <http://www.crimeandjustice. org.uk/opus45/Law_abiding_Majority_FINAL_VERSION.pdf>
- Karstedt, S. and Farrall, S. (2006) 'The moral economy of everyday crime: markets, consumers and citizens'. *British Journal of Criminology*, 46(6), pp. 1011–36, <http://bjc.oxfordjournals.org/cgi/content/full/46/6/1011>

What does this say about the purpose of criminal justice and in whose interests it functions?

### Study skills note

Which of the above two sources will give you the best summary and which will be the most authoritative to cite? If you are unsure, you should ask your tutor!

## Crime control: results rather than rights

A crime control model will prioritise results over everything. Results in this context mean admissions and convictions: the solving of the crime. In a true crime control model it would matter less even if the wrong person were convicted: the case would have been solved. Faith in the process of **law and order** would be maintained and criminals would fear committing crime in the future.

---

**Task**

Read the following account of a 'rape' case:

- 'The guilty go free', *Guardian*, 9 October 2005, <http://observer. guardian.co.uk/comment/story/0,1588270,00.html>

To what extent is the tension between crime control and due process a necessary part of the criminal justice process?

Who are the victims here?

To what extent has the results focus skewed the investigation of the truth?

You can also link this approach to the materials in Chapter 3 on adversarial and inquisitorial justice.

---

Think through the following possible scenarios and ask yourself which one you would want to be in, or not? In a full crime control model it is likely that no-one would be informed of your arrest and detention in the police station. It is possible that a long and unnecessary car journey would be taken so that you could be 'spoken to' in the back seat. Once in the police station you might suffer emotional or even physical abuse and you might be lied to and tricked into a confession. You could be denied legal advice and possibly food and rest. You might be faced with charges that bear no relationship to any crimes you may have committed, in the hope of persuading you to accept lower charges. Evidence against you might be falsified or planted. All of these scenarios come towards the outer limits of a crime control model, but most if not all have had their place in the history of British criminal justice.

## Due process: protecting your rights

If you do find yourself in custody you will have a number of rights, which are enshrined in the Police and Criminal Evidence Act (PACE) 1984 – codes C and D in particular. As well as those rights already mentioned, you would be entitled to the use of an appropriate adult if necessary, or an interpreter. You should be formally risk-assessed for self-harm and receive any medical attention that might be required. However, these rights can be fragile at times of political tension or media scrutiny of particular cases or of notorious crimes. For example, the right to free legal advice and private discussion with a solicitor can be delayed for up to 36 hours in certain instances (such as in serious arrestable offences to assist in the recovery of property). Similarly, the maximum period of detention without charge (24 hours) can be extended up to 96 hours either at the direction of a Superintendent or, later, of the court.

---

**Task**

Have a look at the current developments in reviewing and using PACE in practice at:

- <http://police.homeoffice.gov.uk/operational-policing/powers-pace-codes/pace-code-intro/>

Make notes on the extent to which there is an apparent tension between due process demands and operational requirements.
   You can also look at how police powers are recorded as used in:

- 'Police powers and procedures England and Wales 2007/08', <http://www.homeoffice.gov.uk/rds/pdfs09/hosb0709.pdf>

Where books or articles mention statistical sources, always check whether a more up-to-date publication is available on the relevant government websites and use these. Once a book is over a year old, the 'recent' figures cited are usually out of date and you should get used to finding out for yourself and updating where necessary.

---

The debate concerning the detention period for suspected terrorists reflects how certain crimes or outrages can trigger rapid proposals for legislative change. The government had proposed extending the existing 14-day detention period to 90 days, a proposal voted out by the Commons and substituted with 28 days. In this case, despite the public outrage over extremely serious incidents, this measure was regarded as a step too far. That said, there is nothing to stop the government persisting and gaining more support in the event of further incidents. The continuum between crime control and due process is, then, one that sees a good deal of movement, demonstrating that neither position is fixed and is susceptible in many ways to how safe the public feels itself to be.

---

**Task**

Is a society that feels unsafe more likely to accept or demand a system that is closer to crime control?

Have a look at the articles, including the introduction, and especially Barbara Hudson's final article 'Justice in a Time of Terror' in the special issue 'Criminology and the War on Terror' of the *British Journal of Criminology* 49(5) 2009 <http://bjc.oxfordjournals.org/>
    Have a read of a reaction nearer the time of a terror attack by a prominent defence lawyer:

- 'The police are not our rulers. This is the politics of fear'. *Independent*, 6 November 2005, <http://www.independent.co.uk/opinion/commentators/michael-mansfield-the-police-are-not-our-rulers-this-is-the-politics-of-fear-514086.html>

Make a note on the difference in approach between the journalistic and academic style and content.

---

*Summary*

Crime control measures appeal to popular and populist sentiment. They suggest a quick and effective response to the problem of crime and wrap this in a shroud of protecting the innocent and vulnerable. In many ways this is perfectly understandable. Yet it is these same people who would want all the rights currently available if they, or their family, found themselves detained in a police station.

---

**Task**

One way of considering this is the police's use of 'due process' arguments in order to protect themselves; see, for instance:

- 'Few speeding police get fined', *Guardian*, 27 December 2005, <http://www.guardian.co.uk/uk_news/story/0,1673952,00.html>
- 'Acquittal of 159mph officer overturned', *Guardian*, 1 February 2006, <http://www.guardian.co.uk/crime/article/0,1699713,00.html>

Due process is about values and decent behaviour. It may at times lead to guilty people being acquitted, a position that is undoubtedly unsatisfactory. But if this leads to better investigation of the case and irrefutable evidence, then so much the better. Conviction and potential loss of liberty should not result from undue pressure on suspects or false evidence. It should not result from bribes or trickery. The values enshrined in criminal justice systems should reflect those of the society in which we want to live, and any civilised society should be concerned with the rights of all its citizens rather than a certain section of them.

**Task**

Read the following:

- <www.innocent.org.uk/cases/guildford4/#the%20grauniad>
- 'We were victims too', *Observer*, 7 July 2002, <http://observer.guardian.co.uk/crimedebate/story/0,12079,750770,00.html>
- 'The case of Sally Clarke', *The Times*, 17 March 2007, <http://www.timesonline.co.uk/tol/news/uk/article1528451.ece>

What is the outcome of the results-driven 'crime control' approach in terms of:

- The cost to the taxpayer?
- The punishment of the people who committed the crime?
- The victims' families?
- The families of those who were falsely found guilty?

Consolidate your learning further by reading:

- Grounds, Adrian T. (2005) 'Understanding the Effects of Wrongful Imprisonment'. In Tonry, Michael (ed.) *Crime and Justice: A Review of Research*, Vol. 32. Chicago, IL: University of Chicago Press.

**NB Remember, press articles should be used to illustrate issues from your academic reading, but not as a replacement for them.**

## Thinking beyond crime control and due process

Table 1.1 summarises the key differences between the due process and crime control models of criminal justice.

As noted, the two models debated here, although apparently exclusive, tend to operate as ends of a continuum, with most justice systems appearing

*Table 1.1* Key differences between due process and crime control models

| Due process | Crime control |
|---|---|
| Guarantees rights of suspects | Conviction of the guilty the priority |
| Series of obstacles and hurdles | Confession a priority |
| Controls on police powers | Extensive powers for the police |
| Complicated criminal process | Speedy conviction – a 'conveyor belt' |
| Tolerates acquittal of the guilty | Tolerates conviction of the innocent |

at various points along the line. The English system in some ways has been characterised by a move from crime control to due process over the last 15–20 years, particularly in relation to some areas of police powers (for example, powers relating to the detention and questioning of suspects). The debate at present, however, appears to be focusing on the question of whether the balance has shifted too far in the direction of protecting the defendant and whether we need to move further in the direction of securing convictions. New Labour's stance on being 'tough on crime' (and not just 'tough on the causes of crime') looked very much oriented this way, and carried many of the hallmarks of a shift back to **crime control**.

---

**Further study**

If you wish to pursue the politics of law and order further:

- For a useful potted history and key themes of the New Labour government's approach, read pages 117–22 of Newburn, T. (2003) *Crime and criminal justice policy*. Harlow: Longman Criminology Series/Pearson Education Limited.
- Wilson, D. (2004) 'The Politics and Processes of Criminal Justice'. In J. Muncie and D. Wilson (eds) *Student Handbook of Criminal Justice and Criminology*, London: Cavendish Publishing.

For a more extensive treatment, read Downes, D. and Morgan, R. (2007) 'No turning back: the politics of law and order into the millennium'. In Maguire *et al. Oxford Handbook of Criminology*. (4th edn) Chapter 9.

---

As the debating of this point implies, there are differing perceptions of what the purpose of criminal justice is, not least among its practitioners. If so, the use of the word 'system' may be incongruous. Although the protection of the innocent remains fundamental to the process of justice, and for many the sole purpose, it should not be absolute according to Ashworth (1998: 30). The acquittal of guilty persons can also be seen as a 'miscarriage of justice'.

**Task**

- Read: Ashworth, A. (1998). *The Criminal Process: An Evaluative Study*. Oxford: Oxford University Press, Chapters 1 and 2.

We shall see that the process of justice is one marked by the use of agency and individual discretion, most notably by the police. Both the due process and crime control models allow for that discretion, although the former does seek legislative means for reducing its use and influence (e.g. PACE 1984). There is however a notorious gap between theory and practice, or in this case, between the law on the statute books and the law on the street. Packer (1968) concluded that the American **criminal justice process** accorded strongly with **crime control** values, whilst the **legislation** was much more in accord with **due process**. In England and Wales, the introduction of the Police and Criminal Evidence Act (1984) on one hand saw an extension of due process safeguards, whilst on the other it introduced a significant increase in crime control powers. The fact that certain infamous miscarriages of justice, particularly the 'Cardiff Three' (see <http://www.innocent.org.uk/cases/cardiff3_1>), occurred following the introduction of PACE, is suggestive of crime control values remaining pervasive.

**Task**

Look at one or other of these two official reports/policy documents:

- 'Rebalancing the criminal justice system in favour of the law-abiding majority', <http://www.crimereduction.gov.uk/criminaljusticesystem19.htm>
- 'Doing law differently', <http://www.dca.gov.uk/dept/doinglawdiff_print.pdf>

Note down the key issues/recommendations and assign them either to a due process or crime control heading.

How does the policy document fare along the crime control continuum?

How easy was it to assign components of the document under the two headings? Were there any 'mixed' recommendations?

Do you think Packer's model is too simplistic? Why?

If this type of policy analysis is a major factor in your work, look at an official report/policy document published closest to the time you are writing and using the same method.

As Sanders and Young (2007) argue, Packer's models are of limited value, especially in that Packer does not attempt to 'prescribe what the goals of criminal justice should be'. Other models of criminal justice have therefore been developed.

---

**Task**

You should therefore also read and make notes on:

- The **6 models** of criminal justice developed by King (1981) largely built upon Packer's original continuum and summarised in Davies *et al.* (2010) Chapter 1.
- The **framework of ethical principles** developed by Ashworth (1998) based on the European Convention on Human Rights, in an attempt to define what the criminal justice process goals should be (which links up with Chapter 9 on **suspects' and victims' rights** below).
- Faulkner's (1996) **'social integration or exclusion' model** (which links up with the **retribution, deterrence or restorative justice** debate in Chapter 5).
- Sanders and Young's (2000) **freedom model** in *Criminal Justice*. Oxford: Oxford University Press, Chapter 1 (pp. 11–63) and Chapter 7.
- Sanders, A. and Young, M. (2007). In Maguire *et al.* (eds) *The Oxford Handbook of Criminology* (4th edn). Oxford: Oxford University Press, Chapter 28.

---

The citations and references to all of these models, plus critiques of them, can be found in the early pages of Sanders and Young, 2007, pp. 953–6, and also in Davies *et al.* 2010, Chapter 1.

---

**Task**

You should read the sources referred to above and be clear that you understand the key components of the models and critiques of them. Make notes and try to answer these questions:

Do these newer models take us any further?

Do the newer models represent varying and partial pictures from groups with different relationships or roles within criminal justice?

To what extent are the models useful in explaining the criminal justice process?

---

*Further study*

If you wish to consolidate your learning further, read the following press articles and make notes on which model or models of criminal justice are most useful or explanatory in analysing the content:

- 'Balancing criminal justice?' *Observer*, 10 November 2002, <http://politics.guardian.co.uk/queensspeech2002/story/0,12595, 837252,00.html>
- 'Blair pledge to wage new crime war'. *Observer*, 10 November 2002, <http://society.guardian.co.uk/queensspeech/story/0,837692,00. html>
- 'Professor faces jail in bio terror scare'. *Observer*, 27 February 2005, <http://www.caedefensefund.org/press/ObserverFeb2705.pdf>

For a 'real-life' illustrative example of a crime control/due process argument from within the criminal justice process, read the following pair of articles.

- 'Sir John Stevens calls for criminal justice reform', 6 March 2002, *Guardian*: <http://www.guardian.co.uk/crime/article/0,664344,00. html>
- 'Sir David Bean replies to Sir John Stevens', 8 March 2002, *Guardian*: <http://www.guardian.co.uk/crime/article/0,664348,00. html>

Can any of the other models you have read about be used to better explain the underlying themes of the arguments used here?

Ultimately, as Davies *et al.* (2010) argue, models of criminal justice focus on just one feature of the criminal justice process. Arguments as to their utility will therefore depend on whether your balanced evaluation of the evidence in your assessments suggests that: criminal justice is a single 'system', in which case a single model should be able to explain the purpose of that system; or that criminal justice is a 'process', with different parts of the process and agencies involved having multiple (sometimes apparently conflicting) goals: but that is yet another debate!

**Further study**

If your study requires you to cover the system or process argument in more detail, have a look at:

- Newburn, T. (2007) *Criminology*. Cullompton, Devon: Willan pp. 549–50, for a summary.

Then read the following key sources:

- Feeney (1984) 'Interdependence as a working concept'. In Moxon, D. (ed) *Managing Criminal Justice*. London: Home Office.
- Hahn P.H. (1998) *Emerging Criminal Justice: Tree Pillars for a Proactive Justice System*. London: Sage.
- Padfield, N. (1995) *Text and Material on the Criminal Justice Process*. London: Butterworths.

As you move forward in your study of criminal justice, it becomes more critical to ask 'Does criminal justice work?' Fortunately for you, Garside and McMahon (2006) have published a response to this question, which also includes responses and views from the great and the good. You can find the executive summary at:

- <http://www.crimeandjustice.org.uk/opus297/DCJW_Exec_Summary_Final.pdf>

or if you need more depth, the full report can be found at:

- <http://www.crimeandjustice.org.uk/opus296/DCJW_Final.pdf>

## Further study

Much of this discussion and the sources used in this opening chapter are a good building block from which to consider the rest of the materials and topics below, especially the chapters on prisons and on philosophies of punishment. Before you proceed, try answering the following questions after reading Garside and McMahon *et al.*'s work:

- Is there a 'solution' to crime?
- Is it likely that the criminal justice system (or process) or the agencies within it will be successful on their own in tackling crime?

You might also wish to read here:

- Dixon, David (2005) 'Why Don't the Police Stop Crime?' *Australian and New Zealand Journal of Criminology*, 38(1), 4–24.

Is there any point in studying criminal justice?

*Extended study and seminar/learning materials*

For those who are likely to go on to study this area, there are many directions which can be taken. Here we suggest some possible routes.

*Civil liberties*

The arguments about which justice system is 'best' often require an understanding of civil liberties. This is a huge area in its own right, but a good academic starting point to grasp the key concepts involved is:

---

- Gearty, C. (2007) *Civil Liberties*. Oxford: Oxford University Press.

This is an area in which quality press coverage is very important as the New Labour government made so many rapid changes and amendments to legislation. A good source on developments is:

- www.guardian.co.uk/libertycentral

or from a crime control perspective, have a read of the following:

- 'Liberals who push criminal rights drive me nuts, says Straw', *Daily Mail*, 27 October 2008, <http://www.dailymail.co.uk/news/article-1080803/Liberals-push-criminal-rights-drive-nuts-says-Justice-Secretary-Jack-Straw.html>

Some of the conceptual development in the press is ahead of the academic publishing process and timeframe, but you will still need to search for journal articles and books on the topic as they are published. A good academic source for keeping up to date are the Penal Policy files included in each issue of the *Howard Journal*:

- http://onlinelibrary.wiley.com/journal/10.1111/(ISSN)1468-2311

For a good illustrative case, read:

- 'Meet Sally. Her case should scare us all', *Guardian*, 21 September 2008, <http://www.guardian.co.uk/commentisfree/2008/sep/21/pressandpublishing.police>

---

Some of the more interesting developments in this area, which might be developed as seminar topics, areas for assessment and/or further study are as follows:

*Big Brother: state control of information?*

There is a clear concern about the state becoming too powerful and too pervasive, often enabled by advances in and new uses of technology. Have a look at the following articles and make notes on the extent to which models of criminal justice are able to explain these new developments:

- 'The end of privacy?' *Technology Guardian*, 2 April 2009, <http://www.guardian.co.uk/technology/2009/apr/02/google-privacy-mobile-phone-industry>
- 'Morality of mining for data in a world where nothing is sacred', *Guardian*, 25 February 2009, <http://www.guardian.co.uk/uk/2009/feb/25/database-state-ippr-paper>
- 'ID cards, cameras, border controls – everything is on record', *Guardian*, 25 February 2009, <http://www.guardian.co.uk/uk/2009/feb/25/data-surveillance-identity>
- 'Whitehall departments to share personal data', *Guardian*, 15 January 2009, <http://www.guardian.co.uk/politics/2009/jan/15/sharing-personal-data-whitehall>
- 'New powers for state snoopers on the net', *Guardian*, 16 October 2008, <http://www.guardian.co.uk/technology/2008/oct/16/internet-uksecurity>
- 'No more secrets', *Guardian*, 27 February 2007, <http://www.guardian.co.uk/politics/2007/feb/27/idcards.immigrationpolicy>
- 'This surveillance onslaught is draconian and creepy', *Guardian*, 29 June 2008, <http://www.guardian.co.uk/commentisfree/2008/jun/28/civilliberties.privacy>
- 'Will a change of government reverse the trend? Tories pledge to shrink the "surveillance state" by cutting databases and protecting personal privacy', Guardian 16 September 2009, <http://www.guardian.co.uk/politics/2009/sep/16/conservative-policy-paper-surveillance-privacy>

And for the USA:

- 'FBI and States Vastly Expand DNA Databases', *New York Times*, 18 April 2009, <http://www.nytimes.com/2009/04/19/us/19DNA.html?_r=2&th&emc=th>

*The rise of the 'numerati' and the democracy-surveillance nexus*

Does the state need to stay ahead of big business – or join it? Have a read of the following articles and note what issues they raise for the governance of criminal justice in the future.

- 'Ghosts in the machine', *Guardian* (Work), 11 October 2008, <http://www.guardian.co.uk/money/2008/oct/11/workandcareers-internet>

- 'There are CCTV cameras everywhere', *Guardian*, PODCAST 3 June 2008, <http://www.guardian.co.uk/world/audio/2008/jun/03/dennis.klein>
- 'Under surveillance: Q&A with Naomi Klein', *Rolling Stone*, 29 May 2008, <http://www.rollingstone.com/politics/story/20924284/under_surveillance_qa_with_naomi_klein/print>

## *Little brother: citizens' use of technology to control the state?*

Others have been more optimistic about the potential empowering effect of new technology in combating oppressive crime control tactics and strategies. This would be an interesting and important new area for research. This flurry of articles followed the death of Ian Tomlinson at the hands of a police officer who was filmed committing the assault and made a top media story around the world in April 2009:

- 'The police should take note: little brother's watching you', *Observer*, 12 April 2009, <http://www.guardian.co.uk/media/2009/apr/12/privacy-media-ian-tomlinson>
- 'Put enough cameras on the police and even the serially deferential wake up', *Guardian*, 11 April 2009, <http://www.guardian.co.uk/commentisfree/2009/apr/11/police-surveillance-marina-hyde>
- 'The unstoppable rise of the citizen cameraman', *Guardian*, 11 April 2009, <http://www.guardian.co.uk/commentisfree/2009/apr/11/public-camera-video-technology>
- 'G20 death: 41 seconds of video that raise serious questions for police', *Guardian*, 8 April 2009, <http://www.guardian.co.uk/uk/2009/apr/08/ian-tomlinson-g20-police-assault-footage> [**NB: This article also contains the video footage of the attack which some may find disturbing**]
- 'G20 police officers may face multiple claims over brutality allegations', *Guardian*, 11 April 2009, <http://www.guardian.co.uk/politics/2009/apr/11/g20-ian-tomlinson-death>

## *Criminal justice agencies beyond the law*

Some sources have argued that the police have systematically gone beyond the law. Read the following and assess the extent to which a crime control approach (and/or a bureaucratic efficiency model) inevitably leads to such abuse:

- 'Revealed: police databank on thousands of protesters', *Guardian*, 7 March 2009, <http://www.guardian.co.uk/uk/2009/mar/06/police-surveillance-protesters-journalists-climate-kingsnorth>
- '"Do not touch": the covert database that kept union activists out of work', *Guardian*, 6 March 2009, <http://www.guardian.co.uk/uk/2009/mar/06/ian-kerr-data-protection>

*Incompetence or unrealistic expectations?*

Others still have shown that the state is far from able to establish an effective big brother criminal justice system (perhaps because it is a set of processes with necessarily conflicting aims?). The following examples span almost the full range of the issues covered in this chapter and many others below. See if you can use them to illustrate your arguments from academic sources:

- 'CPS admits disc of suspects' DNA was "mislaid" for a year', *Guardian*, 20 February 2008, <http://www.guardian.co.uk/uk/2008/feb/20/ukcrime. justice>
- 'Consultants pay price after prisoner data loss', *Guardian*, 11 September 2008, <http://www.guardian.co.uk/politics/2008/sep/11/justice.security>
- 'Government faces huge pay outs after court rules detention of sex offender is "unlawful"', *Daily Mail*, 31 July 2007, <http://www.daily-mail.co.uk/news/article-472038/Government-faces-huge-payouts-court-rules-detention-sex-offender-unlawful.html>
- 'Rapist shielded by his "human rights" was free to live where he chose . . . and kill a girl of 14', *Daily Mail*, 9 May 2008, <http://www.dailymail. co.uk/news/article-565189/Rapist-shielded-human-rights-free-live-chose-kill-girl-14.html>
- 'Killer's human rights placed public safety', *Daily Mail*, 10 May 2006, <http://www.dailymail.co.uk/news/article-385683/Killers-human-rights-placed-public-safety.html>
- 'Police vehicles fall foul of resort parking tickets blitz', *Liverpool Daily Post*, <http://www.highbeam.com/doc/1G1-194994010.html>

*Comparative approaches*

We have used a number of sources from other countries in this chapter, especially where we think that they develop the arguments conceptually. This should give you some awareness of a broader perspective and a notion that criminal justice may work differently in other countries. However, true comparative studies are tough to do and are very difficult if they involve more than two countries. If you are interested in a more comparative approach, we suggest the following sources which compare Britain (or is that England and Wales) with the USA.

- Newburn, T. (2006) 'Contrasts in intolerance: cultures of control in the United States and Britain'. In T. Newburn and P. Rock, *The Politics of Crime Control*. Oxford: Oxford University Press/ Clarendon Studies in Criminology, pp. 227–70.

- Newburn, Tim (2002) 'Atlantic crossings: "policy transfer" and crime control in the USA and Britain'. *Punishment and Society*, 4, 165–94.
- Jones, T. and Newburn, T. (2007) *Policy Transfer and Criminal Justice: Exploring US Influence over British Crime Control Policy*. Maidenhead: Open University Press/McGraw-Hill Education.

## References

### An important note on referencing in this book

As noted in the introduction, we have been rather sly in constructing your references and sourcing materials for students. Some sources are cited in the text above and referred to below in the manner you are most likely to have to replicate in your own work, while others only appear in the text in various formats. However, nearly all of the references are incomplete. Why? It seems harsh, and an extra burden as you juggle your various deadlines. However, a key part of academic study is learning the appropriate discipline of citing and referencing, which is a key skill to take forward beyond your academic studies. Here we have made it very easy to find every source referred to and ensured that you will actually have to read that source in order to be able to reference it properly. You may not thank us for this (at least not initially) but we are sure your tutors will!

Some of the next chapters use a more traditional approach, similar to the one you will be required to use in your assessments, others use a mix of final reference sections and referencing in the text, but make sure you always check you have complete references (and if you have accessed the source, this should be no problem!).

### A hierarchy of evidence?

The quality of your evidence in your assessments is of crucial importance, yet students often only find out about the relative value of cited evidence in their feedback. It can seem rather arbitrary, but the following hierarchy of sources, starting with the most important, is generally accepted and you may find it useful to be clear about this in your writing:

- **Peer-reviewed academic studies,** usually articles. 'Can' be up-to-date, but often refer to statistics and other sources that can easily be updated by the student. Showing you have checked is good spadework and is usually rewarded.

- **Academic books/chapters** The peer review process can be less clear and they may be less up-to-date that some journals. Books, or chapters in them, usually offer a wider consideration of an issue than the more focused articles. Again, secondary evidence referred to should always be checked against the most up-to-date sources.
- **Official Reports** Reports from bodies such as the Home Office, Ministry of Justice, Youth Justice Board etc, are a useful source of information, but can be considered partial given the overall gate-keeping processes usually exercised by all governments. Authors might be considered more impartial if they are external 'independent' academics, but it is usually a good idea to look for critiques of these reports and not to cite them at face value.
- **Magazines, periodicals (e.g. CJM) and press, TV, Radio** These have the advantage of being very up-to-date and initially may be the only source of information on relatively new topics. However, they are not peer reviewed and the citing of sources can be very variable.
- **Your subjective experience/your opinion** This is hard to use in essays, but useful for reflective accounts if required.

The following websites are also useful:

- Law Weblog: <http://sixthform.info/lawblog/>
- CrimeLine: <http://www.crimeline.info/>
- Crime and justice students: <http://www.crimestudents.org/>

# 2 Lay justice or professional justice?

*Steve Savage and Diana Bretherick*

## Lay justice

I want to present the case in favour of one of the most deeply ingrained aspects of British criminal justice – **lay justice**. Put simply, 'lay justice' means justice processes in which ordinary members of the public play an active part – and not just as suspects or offenders! At times we can fall into the trap of thinking that decisions about our lives are best left in the hands of qualified 'professionals' who are properly trained and qualified to work on behalf of the public; for example, we tend to trust medical professionals with our health rather than 'quack' medicine. We seem to trust accountants to look after our finances, lawyers to look after the sale and purchase of our properties, and teachers to look after the education of our children. In each case we tend to feel that we are in 'safe hands' when professionals are in charge. My case is that when it comes to **justice** it is dangerous to leave it all to 'professionals' and vital that a key part in the justice process is played by the lay element.

In order to present this case I will deal with three areas. Firstly, I want to outline the scope of lay involvement in British justice. Secondly, I want to look at what might be called the 'problem with professionals' – how in a number ways 'leaving it to the professionals' can work against justice as such. Thirdly, and the main issue for this discussion, I will be outlining the reasons why lay justice is so important to justice overall and the advantages that lay justice carries into the justice system.

### The scope of lay justice

Historically, lay justice has been a prominent feature of the British system of justice and, if anything, the role of lay justice has in recent years expanded rather than contracted. Unfortunately, very recently, the pendulum has swung back in favour of 'professionalised justice', with, as we shall see, changes to the system of jury trial where the scope for trials where judges, rather than juries, decide on verdict has been extended. This makes it even more important to 'stand up' for lay justice in the current climate.

So what is the scope of lay involvement in the British criminal justice system? If we look across the system as a whole it becomes clear that the lay element is really quite extensive and takes a number of forms. These include the following:

- The lay magistracy. The vast bulk of criminal trials in England and Wales, close to 95 per cent (Davies, Croall and Tyrer, 2005: 233ff.), are dealt with by magistrates, and largely by lay magistrates who, sitting in panels of three, decide both on verdict (where the defendant pleads not guilty) and on sentence. A small number of magistrates are professional magistrates (around 100, now called 'district judges') but the rest, over 28,000, are lay magistrates. That is some measure of the huge significance of the lay element to our courts system. Although lay magistrates are not simply 'ordinary members of the public' – in the sense that they are appointed after a selection process, on the basis of their 'integrity' and 'local standing' – they are nevertheless from and of the local community, in a way that district judges need not be.
- Juries. When we think of 'British justice' we often do so in terms of trial by jury, otherwise known as trial by peers. Although trial by jury only relates to a small percentage of criminal trials, it does embrace the most serious cases and often the cases with the highest public profile. Furthermore, members of the jury really are 'ordinary members of the public' in the sense that jurors are pretty much a cross-section of the community as they are chosen at random from the electoral register. If not numerically, at least symbolically, the jury stands at the forefront of lay justice in Britain.

---

**Further study**

There is a substantial body of research on juries, but, for legal reasons, mainly outside the UK. If you are required to research this area further, the following articles will be a good starting point:

- 'Jurors' verdict on their own judgment – we're clueless', *The Times*, 3 January 2007, <http://www.timesonline.co.uk/tol/news/world/article1288775.ece>
- Culhane, Scott E., Harmon M. Hosch and William G. Weaver (2004) 'Crime victims serving as jurors: is there bias present?' *Law and Human Behaviour*, 28(6), 649–59.
- Honess, R.M., R. Levi and E.A. Charman (1998) 'Juror competence in processing information: Implications from a simulation of the Maxwell trial'. *Criminal Law Review* 763–73.

- Horowitz, Irwin A. and Laird C. Kirkpatrick (1998) 'A concept in search of a definition: the effects of reasonable doubt instructions on certainty of guilt standards and jury verdicts'. *Law and Human Behaviour*, 20(6), 655–70.
- Lloyd-Bostock, Sally (2007) 'The Jubilee Line jurors: does their experience strengthen the argument for judge-only trial in long and complex fraud cases?' *Criminal Law Review*, 255–73.
- Young, Warren, Yvette Tinsley and Neil Cameron (2000) 'The effectiveness and efficiency of jury decision-making'. *Criminal Law Journal*, 24, 89–100.

- **Lay visitors to prisons and police stations.** The idea of introducing schemes for lay people to visit police and prison establishments emerged in the 1980s, and arose as a response to concerns that detained people might be suffering poor treatment, either because of their physical environment of because of the behaviour of police or prison staff ('professionals'?). In the case of the police the lay visitors are local volunteers who, once they are given appropriate training, work in pairs to visit police stations, as often as weekly (calling unannounced) in order to look at and listen to the goings-on in custody centres. After their visits they complete reports which are sent on to police management, police authorities and the Home Office. In the case of the prisons, lay visitors (around 2000 of them) are a part of the Independent Monitoring Boards (formerly Boards of Visitors) which perform a 'watchdog' role and oversight of prisons. Board members can visit prisons at any time and can talk to staff and inmates and their visits lead to reports from each Board which are then sent to the Home Office.
- **Community representation in the oversight of the work of criminal justice agencies.** For example, police authorities and probation boards, as central features of the governance arrangements for police forces and probation services, are required to include representatives from local communities in their membership. The purpose of this is to ensure that issues of local concern can be represented through the governance process. Another example would be police–community liaison committees and Independent Advisory Groups, which provide opportunities for local people, including representatives from minority ethnic groups, to have a voice in local police decision-making.
- **Victim engagement in the justice process.** For too long victims of crime were effectively 'sidelined' in the justice process, in the sense that once the prosecution got underway their role was restricted to little more than a witness to the crime. However, in recent decades, partly as a result of the 'victims' movement', victims have become more and more a central

feature of the application of justice. One example of this is the introduction of victim impact statements, whereby victims can offer the court statements on the effect of the crime on them, and which can be taken on board by sentencers before the actual sentence is passed. Another, much more radical example is the restorative justice agenda, in which victims and offenders can be brought together, instead of or as part of the sentence, to explain each other's position and, possibly to seek some form of restitution to the victim (restorative justice is discussed elsewhere in this unit). Victim engagement in the justice process is another way in which non-professionals can play a part in the administration and application of justice.

It is clear, therefore, that in these and other ways lay justice has a key role to play in the British system of justice. Before going on to explain how and why lay justice can make a positive contribution to justice overall, I want to say a few words about the 'problem with professionals'.

## The problem with professionals

I am not trying to argue that professionals make no useful contribution to British justice. They have a role to play because, at various points in the justice process, technical expertise and professional knowledge and experience is required to ensure due process and fairness. I am, however, saying three things. Firstly, that professional decisions and actions need to be monitored and overseen by others outside those professions and that includes members of the public and local communities – hence lay visitors to police stations and prisons. Secondly, that professional decisions and actions themselves should be informed and influenced by outside people and in particular by people from the local community – hence independent advisory boards for the police. Thirdly, that some decisions are best left to lay people and not to professionals – hence lay magistrates and juries. It is this last issue that raises what I have called the 'problem with professionals'.

The British justice system has the virtue that almost all decisions on whether to convict or acquit defendants are made by lay people – lay magistrates or juries. Once someone decides to plead not guilty and be tried, unless the case collapses mid-stream, he or she will almost certainly have their fate decided by lay people. So why should professionals – judges, in other words – not be left with this critical decision? There are a number of reasons:

- 'Justice' is about more than technical rules and procedures. Professionals may be well versed on rule and procedures, but applying *justice* is more complicated – it involves issues of 'fairness' and whether a particular decision is *right* (and not just 'correct'). The concern is that professionals would apply the *law* rather than *justice*, and the two things are not the same.

- If it were left to professionals to decide the verdict, the efficiency and speed of justice might take priority over the quality of justice. It is interesting that one of the arguments put forward in favour of using more district judges instead of lay magistrates is that they try cases more quickly! Justice should not be about the 'throughput' of cases but the quality of each and every trial.

- Linked to this point is the problem of **case-hardening**. This is a term used to describe what happens when people sit in judgement day-in and day-out, and become so used to hearing the same types of 'story' from defendants, explaining why they are not guilty, that they become increasingly sceptical of defence cases. It is rather like a teacher hearing the 'same old stories' about why pupils have not done their homework – they tend to be suspicious, even if some of the excuses might be legitimate! In this sense professional judges can become 'battle weary' and less and less inclined to accept defence cases as time goes on.

- Judges tend to be socially distant from ordinary people and particularly from the people who appear before them in court. Although the situation has improved over time, in the sense that there are now more women and minority ethnic judges than before (26 per cent of judges are female and 7 per cent are from minority ethnic groups; see <http://www.dca.gov.uk/judicial/diversity/makeup.htm>), there is still a tendency for judges, particularly those who sit in the higher courts, to come from socially exclusive backgrounds. They tend to come from middle-class or upper-class families – largely because of the cost of legal training (usually as a barrister) – and, as such, can find it difficult to relate to the lives of the people who come before them. We have all heard stories about the strange, eccentric or downright bizarre things judges have said in their courts in the past, but there is now a view that judges are no longer like that.

However, as recently as 2003 the following headline appeared in the press: 'Juror wearing "FCUK" logo told to clear off by judge'. Apparently, a Judge, Huw Daniel, took offence at a potential juror wearing a T-shirt sporting the French Connection 'fcuk' logo, believing it to be an attempt to ridicule the court. After the man in question had tried to take the oath, the judge rejected him as a juror on the following grounds (*Guardian*, 12 March 2003):

> He didn't take the oath properly. Secondly, the mode of dress was a potential source of distraction. The misspelling of a basic Anglo Saxon word on a garment hardly dignifies the court proceedings. It is beyond me why anyone can think they should wear anything like that in public, particularly in court.

The impact of this judgement was quite limited as in this case it only affected the composition of the jury. However, the concern is that this case acts as an indication of the extent to which members of the judiciary, or some of them at least, might be too distant from the lives of 'ordinary people' to understand what goes on out there in the community – to use a common expression, they don't get out enough! Such an understanding, I would argue, is vital to forming judgements in the context of criminal justice. This is why it is very dangerous to talk about giving professional judges more power and more scope in the justice process by limiting the lay element.

Taken together, these concerns constitute what I would call 'the problem with professionals'.

---

**Further study**

Those wishing to take a comparative look at these issues related to judges will find the following article a good starting point:

- Dhami, Mandeep K. (2005) 'From Discretion to disagreement: explaining disparities in judges' pretrial decisions'. *Behavioural Sciences and the Law*, 23, 367–86.

---

The other side of this coin is the case for lay justice, to which we can now turn.

## *The case for lay justice*

Some of the arguments in favour of lay justice will already be apparent. I will focus on lay justice in terms of the lay magistracy and, above all, of the jury, although many of the points I make will apply to the other areas of lay justice mapped out at the beginning. So what can lay justice do that is so special? This can be dealt with under two main headings: the quality of lay justice on the one hand and the democratic role of lay justice on the other.

## *The quality of lay justice*

When we talk about the 'quality' of justice we mean that judgements and decisions – in the case of whether someone is guilty or not – are 'right'. This is more, however, than whether they are 'correct' in terms of the evidence available, it is also about whether they are *fair* in the circumstances, or *just* in the wider sense. Lay justice scores strongly on both 'correctness' and 'fairness':

- Lay justice is more likely to lead to correct judgements and decisions because lay people can apply common sense to their decision-making. Due to the fact that lay magistrates and jurors experience the lives of ordinary people – they get out more! – they are better placed than professional judges to weigh up evidence, and assess whether witnesses and suspects are likely to be trustworthy or not. The danger with professional judges is that they can be so socially distant from the people who appear in court – suspects, victims and witnesses – that they are not well placed to judge a person's character and hence whether people are 'reliable' or not. Lay magistrates and juries are much better placed to do this and apply common sense when doing it.

  I can illustrate the importance of common sense from my own experience as a member of a jury. We were presented with a case of a young man charged with possession of cannabis with intent to supply. He was seen going around a nightclub talking to people, then found in possession of cannabis when searched by plain-clothed police officers. His defence was that he was not trying to sell the cannabis but rather he was going around asking for a 'Rizla'. When we retired to reach our verdict, we agreed that the best way to find out whether he was to be believed was to find out what the street value of the cannabis in his possession was. On going back into court we were told that the street value was approximately £5! It did not take much time to find him not guilty after that – by using our common sense (and the experiences of some of the younger members of the jury in this area!) we arrived at what seemed to be a sensible and correct verdict.

- Lay justice can apply fairness even when 'technically' someone might appear guilty. The evidence in a trial might point clearly to a person being technically 'guilty', but justice might not be done if they are found guilty. An example might be an older person charged with theft from a supermarket. If such a case made its way to the courts lay magistrates or a jury might decide that, whatever the evidence, a conviction would not be right – technically 'correct' but just not 'right'. In doing this they would be introducing a sense of community justice into legal proceedings, in a way that a professional judge, steeped in procedure and process, might not be inclined, or able to do. This links in with the idea, to be developed later, that justice should not be something owned by the professions who work within it; it should be owned and driven by the people or the community – and lay justice is the best way to achieve that.

- Lay justice can bring a freshness of perspective into the justice process. Nowhere is this better expressed than in the jury system. Jurors come into court in most cases having never heard a trial before, or at most with only a brief exposure to the trial process before. They hear evidence of a sort they will not have heard before and as such they can form judgements without the cynicism that professional judges may have developed through what was referred to earlier as 'case hardening'. Even lay magistrates, who do hear a fair number of cases because their role is a more permanent one than jurors', nevertheless intersperse their court duties with their other roles – in jobs, community service and so on. This keeps them with one foot in the wider community throughout their time as magistrate. This is unlike the professional judge, who sits day-in and day-out in the same role and the same environment. The freshness of perspective that lay members can bring to justice is also evident in the other areas of lay justice outlined earlier. For example, independent advisory groups can bring a fresh set of views and experiences into police decision-making, instead of those decisions being made solely on the basis of professional experience, which can develop a form of 'tunnel vision'. The point here is that life moves on and views change in the wider world – it is important to bring these views into the justice process as much as possible. The best way to ensure this is to have a steady flow of community perspectives through our lay justice machineries.

- Lay justice has the capacity to demystify the law. Legal processes can of course be highly technical and complicated. One advantage of juries in particular, is that their role in weighing evidence and reaching verdicts according to the law ensures that the court proceedings are presented in a way that can be understood by ordinary people. Judges and lawyers are forced to speak in a language that the jury can understand in order to get their messages across. This is a good thing. If there were no juries the professionals in court would be inclined to speak in legalistic and technical terms – that is not very helpful for defendants, who might find themselves bewildered by the proceedings, and that is not very just! The lay element in this way serves to take the mystique out of the law and legal processes, and render them more accessible to ordinary people and the community at large.

### The democratic role of lay justice

Some of the points just made allude to the role of lay justice as involving something much deeper than the actual quality of decisions made in the justice process. Lay justice has a critical *democratic* role to play as part of the justice system and as such a critical role in democracy as a whole. There are four ways in which lay justice supports the democratic process:

- Lay justice enables public participation in the administration of justice and the law. Lay justice acts as a recognition that the law is *our* law, not something to be controlled and possessed exclusively by legal professionals. The lay magistracy and the jury stand as examples of how the community can actively participate in the justice process, so that most of the decisions on guilt and, through the magistracy, on sentence, are made by people who are of the community and for the community. Similarly, lay involvement, such as in the independent advisory boards mentioned earlier, are about public engagement in the workings of the policing system. If democracy is about participation, then lay justice certainly delivers that.

- Linked with the participatory principle is the power of lay justice to act as a check on unpopular laws and prosecutions. Juries in particular can play a role in making it be known that certain laws and certain prosecutions are unacceptable to the community, simply by refusing to find those charged under them guilty. An example of this might be taken from the eighteenth and nineteenth centuries. In eighteenth-century England there were, at one point, over two hundred capital offences – crimes for which the penalty was execution. This included offences such as forgery, certain types of theft (including rustling) and a whole array of quite bizarre offences – such as 'going in disguise' (see Hay *et al.*, 1975). However, by the mid-nineteenth century there were only four capital offences. There are many reasons for this drastic reduction, but one seems to have been that juries were refusing to convict, even in the face of compelling evidence, because they did not agree with the laws in question which were too severe (Hay *et al.*, 1975). The authorities, faced with the difficulties of being unable to secure enough convictions on a whole raft of crimes, decided that the only way to encourage juries to convict was to reduce the penalty – the death penalty – which these crimes carried with them on conviction. Perhaps juries were sending out a message that the law was unfair and that it needed changing. Popular sentiment and public opinion can find their way into the courts through juries and the lay magistracy in this way. As public opinion changes – over such issues as morality for example – this can be directly reflected through the courts in lay decision-making. Left to socially distant professionals, the engine for change in justice might not be there.
- Lay justice can make the criminal process accountable and transparent. As we have seen, in a sense this is what the jury system does – it acts as a check on the activities of law enforcers and the courts. However, other areas of lay justice also fulfil this role. So, lay visitor schemes for police stations and prisons can act as a part of the accountability machinery for the police and prison services, in the sense that they allow the monitoring and periodic review of the workings of parts of those services. They constitute a form of public watchdog of the criminal process, which makes that process more transparent – we now know what goes on behind the once closed doors of the police station and the prison – and accountable, in the sense that the authorities in question are called to account through such schemes.
- Lay justice can act to control the power of the state and in doing so help protect the citizen from abuses of authority by the state. Again,

it is the jury system that is most at issue in this respect. It is no small matter that, at least at present, almost all serious trials where the defendant pleads not guilty must go before a jury. The exception being cases under 544 of the Criminal Justice Act 2003. This therefore includes any trials in which the state, in the form of the government, chooses to take action under the criminal law against a citizen. For this reason it is for the jury to decide whether to convict in cases brought by the state, not the state itself – and this means that the people, not the government, decide in such cases. This is a very powerful weapon in the hands of the community, because it can mean that, through the jury, state power and state activities can be controlled. The prime example of this in the literature on jury trial is the Clive Ponting case. Ponting was a senior civil servant at the Ministry of Defence at the time of the Falklands War in 1982. He had reason to question the rationale for the decision to torpedo an Argentine cruiser, the *General Belgrano*, which caused the loss of over 300 lives. Ponting claimed to have evidence that the authorities knew that the ship was not in an offensive mode when the decision was taken to fire at it. He was so concerned about what he had witnessed that he decided to talk to the press. This led to him being charged under the Official Secrets Act for breaching the confidentiality binding on civil servants. Subsequently, a high-profile trial ensued at which the presiding judge gave a reading of the law that most commentators felt gave the jury little option but to convict – Ponting himself was apparently convinced he would be found guilty (Ponting, 1985). However, the jury returned a not guilty verdict. We do not know the full story behind the jury verdict, but many have taken it to be an example of the jury using its role to defy the wishes of government and state. The Ponting verdict may be taken as the public, through the jury, passing a message to the government that it did not approve either of the decision to prosecute him or, more fundamentally, of the decision to sink the *General Belgrano* itself – we will never know for certain. At the very least, the jury has the capacity to make such judgements given its pivotal role in the justice process, as one standing between the state and its citizens, potentially protecting the latter from the former.

## Conclusion

Taken together it should be clear that lay justice is an indispensable feature of the British system of justice. We are more likely to accept a framework of justice, of law enforcement, prosecution and trial, if it is one in which ordinary people and the community as a whole is engaged actively in the process. The case I have made is that such a framework guarantees better quality justice and justice that is more flexible, more responsive to change and, overall, more respected than one in which professionals rule the roost. Justice is simply too important to be left to professionals.

# Professional justice

Justice is best left to the highly qualified professionals.

## The Magistrates Court

At the moment, both lay magistrates and professional magistrates or district judges can hear cases in the Magistrates Court. I will argue that lay magistrates should be phased out and replaced by professional district judges.

Firstly, we will examine the extent to which participatory democracy and justice involving lay magistrates is superior to the consistency and the rule of law offered by professional justice. One might argue that, as lay justices come from (supposedly) all walks of life, they bring their wide experiences to their decision-making. This in turn ensures that the standards, sense of fairness and interpretation of justice applied is that of the ordinary and reasonable man and woman on the street – a common-sense view (Morgan and Russell, 2000: 7). This is all very well and good. However, I would argue with Morgan and Russell that justice is neither simple nor a matter of common sense. What one requires is the dispassionate application of the law, which is after all designed to achieve fairness. These rules can be complex, as is evidenced by the fact that lay justices often need to be advised on the law by their legally qualified clerk. Lay justices are relatively poorly equipped for such complexities. Lawyers, however, are trained specifically to understand the law and its impartial and practical application. They are less deferential to the system they serve and so less likely to bow to pressure, whether applied by the government or the media. They are also less likely to be swayed by irrelevancies, such as the way a defendant or witness looks or dresses and where they come from. In addition, a professional magistrate is not so willing to believe the professional, particularly the police witness, without question. Lay justices are notoriously difficult to persuade that a police officer might be lying or at the very least embellishing the truth. One should also remember that lay justices are not representative – lay magistrates tend to be white, middle aged and middle class. About 50 per cent are women and just over 7 per cent are from ethnic minorities (MOJ Statistics on Race and the Criminal Justice System and Women and the Criminal Justice System, 2007/8; see <http://www.justice.gov.uk/publications/statistics-and-data/criminal-justice/index.htm>). One might then observe that they are partly, but not completely representative of society as a whole.

How does the concept of local justice shape up in relation to national consistency? One might argue that a lay justice, having been appointed from a local pool of candidates, will have more local knowledge and be therefore more sensitive to local concerns such as the prevalence of certain offences locally and economic factors. Is this really a benefit? If a professional magistrate is cosmopolitan and has fewer local ties, then surely he or she is far more likely to achieve a consistency in sentencing and other decisions. One might also argue that lay magistrates, who are trained locally, are thus inducted into a kind of local judicial culture that leads them away from consistent judicial decisions (Hood 1972 cited in Morgan and Russell, 2000: 8). Lay magistrates may also be tempted to apply what they think they know and believe rather than the evidence that has actually been presented to them. In any event, a professional magistrate is likely to hold his or her post for some time and will be sufficiently sensitive to local issues whilst legally impartial, thus giving the best of both worlds.

To what extent do lay magistrates possess open rather than case-hardened minds? It has been suggested that lay magistrates are less likely to become sceptical while hearing the accounts offered by defendants when giving evidence. Essentially, because they come from a variety of backgrounds and do not sit as often as professional colleagues, they are less case-hardened and more likely to approach cases with an open mind. It is argued that district judges are more likely to accumulate prejudices as to who is credible. I would argue that this is nonsense. A professional magistrate, being legally trained and thus more confident, can challenge a defendant's account or the evidence of a witness far more effectively than a lay justice who may well be somewhat gullible or naïve and deferential to the prosecution (Morgan and Russell, 2000: 8–9).

## Task

What do the following articles indicate in relation to the differences argued for between judges and magistrates?

- 'Magistrates hit back at call to jail fewer people', *Guardian*, 23 February 2008 <http://www.guardian.co.uk/society/2008/feb/23/prisonsandprobation.jackstraw>
- 'Judges fight plans for US-style sentencing', *Guardian*, 23 June 2008 <http://www.guardian.co.uk/uk/2008/jun/23/law.prisonsandprobation>
- 'Too-tough judges out of touch, says Straw', *Guardian*, 27 March 2008 <http://www.guardian.co.uk/politics/2008/mar/27/justice.prisonsandprobation>
- 'Judges admit they get round law designed to protect women in rape trials', *Guardian*, 1 April 2008 <http://www.guardian.co.uk/politics/2008/mar/27/justice.prisonsandprobation>

Does lay participation help to legitimise the criminal justice process or is this merely symbolic? At what cost to effectiveness and efficiency? In order to maintain at least the illusion of democratic legitimacy, lay magistrates do not sit regularly. Their participation is therefore relatively inefficient and ineffective. Most cases are dealt with over a number of hearings and therefore by a different bench each time. Lay magistrates will therefore have to hear the details of the case afresh on each occasion, which is both time consuming and costly. This also may encourage advocates to take advantage with time wasting and other tactics that can improve their case (Morgan and Russell, 2000: 9). A system with professional magistrates would be quicker and more cost effective. Professional magistrates do not have to retire constantly to consider every facet of the case, but are able to make instant decisions. They do not have to pause to receive legal advice. Research has indicated that one district judge can equal the work of anything between 24 and 32 lay magistrates in metropolitan and provincial areas respectively (Seago *et al.*, 2000: 638). In addition, other research shows that district judges can deal with 30 per cent more work than lay justices in a normal case-load, and they deal with 22 per cent more appearances than lay justices (Morgan and Russell, 2000: 34–43).

We should also address the question of cost. One might assume that lay justices are cheaper than professional district judges given that they are unpaid. However, the difference is nominal given the salaries payable to those employed to advise them, the cost of their training and administrative support necessary for recruitment and drawing up rotas, the extra court-rooms necessary because of their slower decision-making, and other costs from other criminal justice agencies due to their relative inefficiency. Lay magistrates are unlikely to be cheaper than professional judges (Morgan and Russell, 2000: 9–10).

### The Crown Court

The current position is that in most cases juries decide on the verdict in a criminal trial in the Crown Court. They base their decision on the evidence and the facts that emerge during the trial. The judge in a Crown Court trial makes decisions on the law and advises the jury as and when necessary, until they retire to consider their verdict. However, the Criminal Justice Act 2003 has now made some provision for trial by a single judge where there is fear of jury intimidation. This came into effect in 2006. Indeed such a trial has already taken place (see R. V. Twomey, Blake, Hibbard and Cameron 2010). The Act also made provision for measures to introduce trial by a single judge in serious and complex fraud cases. Attempts were made to implement this provision in November 2006 with the introduction of the Fraud (Trials without a Jury) Bill. This however was unsuccessful due to parliamentary opposition (Davies *et al.*, 2010: 316).

I propose that the jury should be replaced with trial by judge alone in all cases.

## History and emotive arguments

We are emotionally attached to the concept of jury trials, but we should remember that only a small minority of criminal cases – about 1 per cent in England and Wales – culminate in trial by jury. I refer to the *Criminal Courts Review* (Auld, 2001), which clarifies the status of the jury from a historical perspective. In England and Wales there is no constitutional or indeed any form of general right to trial by judge and jury, only a general obligation to submit to it in indictable cases.

So what are the arguments for trial by judge alone? Who might benefit? Defendants are given the choice of trial by judge alone in a number of jurisdictions, including most states in the US, Canada, New Zealand and Australia. According to the Police Federation in their response to the *Criminal Courts Review*, it is of benefit to the following (see Auld, 2001):

- those who believe themselves to be innocent of the offence charged, often in serious and factually or legally complex cases, and who are anxious that the tribunal will be able to understand their case (for example, fraud);
- defendants with 'technical' defences who wish a verdict to be accompanied by appealable reasoning or who, in any event, want a fully reasoned decision;
- defendants who are charged with offences that attract particular public opprobrium, such as sexual and/or particularly brutal violence, or from minorities or sects who may consider a judge to be a more objective tribunal than a jury (e.g. Ian Huntley and Maxine Carr);
- where there has been much publicity adverse to the defence, as above; and
- defendants in cases turning on alleged confessions or identification, where judges tend to be more rigorous in the exclusion of alleged confession than when trying cases with a jury, and in the rejection of evidence of purported identification than juries tend to be.

Judge-only trials are of particular benefit in long and complex trials:

- The burden on the jury in such a case is too great. They may spend as long as a year sitting on the jury, which inevitably means there are consequences for their personal and professional lives. It may be argued that only those equipped to deal with this would be expected to serve on such a jury. However, this begs the question: who does this leave in the jury panel? It is often said that one must then depend on the unemployed and the unemployable. Who else is free to do this? Are these the people we really want trying complex cases? They are hardly representative of society, and are unlikely to understand the confusing complexities involved in business fraud, money laundering, commercial and banking practice, taxation and VAT as well as legal issues and the inevitable legal language. This brings me to another point.

- Lengthy cases such as fraud are usually complex in nature with issues that require considerable explanation and thought. Are we confident that the jury will understand these matters? Would it not be better for justice and the cost of justice to have such cases tried by a judge alone? It is, after all, the judges' job to understand the issues as well as the law. Their legal training enables them to decide on these matters without having things endlessly explained to them in layman's terms.

- The jury will not have to be sent out every time a point of procedure arises. A judge-only trial would be shorter because things would not require explanation. A judge knows the law and would almost certainly get it right. The judge will have to give reasons for his or her decisions, thus improving transparency in justice and making the appeal process easier and less necessary.

Why not introduce a system of judge-only trials in the Crown Court for all cases? Most of the arguments above apply. It would bring shorter trials, better, more secure, more informed and more transparent decision-making. At the moment jury research is largely forbidden: one cannot conduct re-search about what happens in the jury room. It therefore remains a mystery. Who knows how trial verdicts are reached? Is it truly based on the evidence? They could be drawing lots for all we know; or using a ouija board, as they did in the case of *R. v Young*, a murder case in which the jurors, who had been sent to a hotel overnight, decided to use an ouija board to try and contact the deceased! They were apparently successful, and he told them to 'vote guilty'. This led to an appeal, which was successful; however, a retrial was ordered and a guilty verdict reached (Wurtzel, 2005). To what extent are jurors swayed by their own personal prejudices, or indeed those of their fellow jury members? To what extent might they be swayed by media coverage in more high-profile trials? Notwithstanding the contempt of court regulations, the media can still construct their coverage in certain ways that can portray a defendant or a witness in an unfavourable or favourable light. Even though jurors are told not to take such matters into consideration, how do we know that they do what they are told? They may be swayed even without realising it. Remember the case of O.J. Simpson. Can we be sure that the acquittal was based on the evidence rather than media coverage?

Jurors are also told not to discuss the case outside of the jury room. How do we know that this is complied with? Is it not natural to talk about your day with your nearest and dearest? Might their views sway a juror? We do not know. We are acting on trust. We cannot be too confident that juries base their verdict on evidence. Juries can sometimes be perverse. Of course you may consider it to be a good thing that the jury is free to return a verdict, not necessarily in accordance with the evidence; that is a form of protest against the law. Examples include the case of Clive Ponting who, as we saw earlier, was charged with leaking two documents about the sinking of the Argentine cruiser *General Belgrano* in the 1982 Falklands War to an MP. He did so on the grounds of public interest (a breach of the Official Secrets Act) but was acquitted by a jury. There is also the case of Randle and Pottle. In 1966, George Blake – the most notorious prisoner in Britain – was miraculously sprung from jail. Blake was a British double-agent serving a prison term of 42 years for spying for the Soviet Union. At the time this was the longest jail sentence ever imposed by a British court. He was helped to escape by Randle and Pottle, who wrote a book about it 25 years later and were promptly tried for helping him to escape. The jury refused to convict (Berlins and Dyer, 2001).

A number of recent acquittals in cases of alleged criminal damage by anti-war and environmental campaigners may be modern examples of juries exercising this right. To quote again from the *Criminal Courts Review* (Auld, 2001):

> But not all perverse verdicts have the attractive notion of a 'blow for freedom' that many attach to them. There are other prejudices in the jury room that may lead to perverse acquittals, for example in sexual offences where the issue is consent or in cases of serious violence where a lesser verdict than that clearly merited on the evidence may be returned. There may also be perverse convictions based, for example, on irrelevant factors or irrational argument which, because of their undetectability, are not capable of being corrected on appeal.

Juries do not have a right to return a perverse verdict. On the contrary, they actually contravene the oath they make in court to try the case according to the evidence.

Juries can also be 'nobbled'. That is to say, they are potentially vulnerable to threats and inducements. This is a very real problem particularly in cases involving professional criminals involved in drugs and so on. A judge sitting alone would enjoy much greater security and a higher level of scrutiny and would be unlikely therefore to be swayed by threats or indeed to accept bribes.

To sum up, then, the jury system should be replaced with one in which cases are tried by a judge alone. It would be cheaper, quicker, more transparent, more effective, more just, more secure and less onerous for the general public.

### Victims

Victims currently have a limited role to play in criminal cases. A victim of crime is not a party to any criminal proceedings, has no legal status, and has no right to legal representation in court. Other than as a witness, a victim's rights in court are limited to those relating to compensation orders, acceptance of pleas, mitigation, reparation and the support of the Witness Service.

Victims are permitted to make written victim impact statements if they choose, which the sentencer can take into consideration. Other than that, the sentence is left to those who have heard the case: judge, district judge or lay magistrate. I would suggest that, given the risk of prejudice, this should remain the case and no further part should be played in the sentencing, or indeed in any other part of the criminal justice process, by lay members of the community whether as victims or members of the jury.

Looking at this in more detail, there are a number of ways and stages at which the victim could be involved in the process:

- Making the decision whether to prosecute: involving the victim seems quite attractive initially, but is less so when one considers that the case on reaching court can only be effectively prosecuted if there is sufficient evidence of sufficient quality. Decisions about the availability and quality of evidence can only be taken by a legally qualified professional.
- Bail and remand decisions: victims' evidence here can be relevant in some cases, but only when directly related to the issue of what should happen to the defendant prior to trial. If the victim is frightened, then the court can be informed that there is a danger of interfering with witnesses, and this will be taken into consideration when the decision as to bail is made. Any other lay intervention is unnecessary, as all legitimate concerns can be met by this process.
- Sentencing: victims can make an impact statement describing the extent to which the crime has affected their lives. They cannot give evidence in person about this. Should there be more involvement in this process?

The Practice Direction on Victim Personal Statements (HM Courts Service, 2001) issued by the Lord Chief Justice in October discusses the role of a victim in relation to sentencing. It states:

> The court must pass what it judges to be the appropriate sentence having regard to the circumstances of the offence and of the offender taking into account, so far as the court considers it appropriate, the consequences to the victim. The opinions of the victim or the victim's close relatives as to what the sentence should be are therefore not relevant, unlike the consequence of the offence on them. Victims should be advised of this. If, despite the advice, opinions as to sentence are included in a statement, the court should pay no attention to them. The court should consider whether it is desirable in its sentencing remarks to refer to the evidence provided on behalf of the victim.

The case for disallowing such evidence is as follows. It is important for the administration of justice that there should be, as far as is possible, consistency in sentencing. However, it should be remembered that each victim is affected differently: some victims of burglary may feel unable to leave their house or be left unable to sleep at night; others might be relatively unscathed by the experience. Therefore, victim-led sentencing would inevitably harm consistency in sentencing. It is, in addition, an important principle of justice that it is the crime, not the consequences, that dictates the level of sentence.

Should the jury be involved in sentencing decisions, as they are in the US, or should this remain the sole responsibility of the judge? In my submission, the jury might well be far too influenced by their own prejudices and emotions to reach a just sentencing decision. They, like victims, have differing attitudes towards offenders and this, again, would adversely effect consistency.

Finally, decisions as to whether to prosecute and grant bail or remand in custody should be left to the professional legally qualified and experienced lawyer or judge. These matters are already taken into consideration and further intervention is unnecessary and potentially harmful. Sentencing should not be influenced by the effect on or consequences for the victim. This protects the adversarial system and encourages consistency.

The jury should not be involved in sentencing; this should be done in an objective and fair way according to guidelines. Emotion and prejudice have no part to play in this process. Lay participation may endanger these principles. Sentencing should therefore, like so many other things, be left to the legal professional.

### Conclusion

Justice is best left to the professionals, because to leave it to the amateur – notwithstanding their training, their desire to do the right thing and their supposed experience of life – is to leave it to the uninformed and the unqualified. You would not ask a man at a bus stop to remove your appendix; why, then, do we suppose that it is acceptable to leave a decision as to someone's guilt or innocence, which could result in the loss of reputation, financial security and at worst their liberty, to his equivalent? A legal qualification is not just a piece of paper. It is proof of knowledge, skill and, for those senior enough in their profession to be appointed to a judicial post, their experience. Why leave it to the man on the street when you can go to the experts? They are cheaper, and quicker, and the justice they dispense is more transparent, more effective and more secure. This is the case for the uninformed and the unqualified versus the informed, the qualified and the experienced. In my submission there is simply no contest.

## References

NB These are the references used in the above 'text' only – those inside the exercise boxes are full enough of citations for you to find easily. In all cases, check you are citing all of the correct and full details from the sources themselves.

Auld, Lord Justice (2001) *Review into the Workings of the Criminal Courts in England and Wales* (the Auld Report). London: Home Office.

Berlins, M. and Dyer, C. (2001) 'Perverting the course of justice'. Retrieved on 30 May 2006 from: <http://www.guardian.co.uk/jury/article/0,426241,00.html>

Davies, M., Croall, H. and Tyrer, J. (2005) *Criminal Justice* (3rd edn). Harlow: Pearson/Longman.

—— (2010) *Criminal Justice* (4th edn). Harlow: Pearson/Longman.

Hay, D., Linebaugh, P., Rule, J. and Thompson, E. (1975) *Albion's Fatal Tree: Crime and Society in Eighteenth Century England.* London: Allen Lane.

HM Courts Service (2001) 'Practice direction: victim personal statements'. Retrieved 23 May 2007 from: <http://www.hmcourts-service.gov.uk/cms/933.htm>

Morgan, R. and Russell, N. (2000) *The Judiciary in the Magistrates' Courts.* Home Office Research, Development and Statistics Directorate. Occasional Paper 66. London, HMSO.

Ponting, C. (1985) *The Right to Know: The Inside Story of the Belgrano Affair.* London: Sphere.

Seago, P., Walker, C. and Wall, D. (2000) 'The development of the professional magistracy in England and Wales'. *Criminal Law Review*, August, 631–51.

Wurtzel, D. (2005) 'Jurors: who knows what they're up to? Worrying tales from the retiring room'. Retrieved on 30 May 2006 from: <http://www.timesonline.co.uk/article/0,8163-1532411,00.html>

# 3  Adversarial or inquisitorial justice?

## Jane Creaton and Francis Pakes

The debate over the relative merits of the inquisitorial and adversarial systems is a long-running one, and tends to resurface in the wake of miscarriages of justice. In 1993 the Royal Commission on Criminal Justice, which was set up in response to the Birmingham Six and Guildford Four cases, gave the issue detailed consideration, and the acquittal of the defendants in the Damilola Taylor case prompted discussions on whether the adversarial system dealt with vulnerable witnesses appropriately (BBC, 2003). These debates raise fundamental questions over the nature and purpose of the criminal justice system and the role of the state in the adjudication of disputes. The purpose of this chapter is to outline the key features of the two systems and to identify and discuss some of the key differences.

It is important to note at the outset that no single system of justice is purely adversarial or purely inquisitorial in nature. Most systems of justice are rooted in one or other of the traditions, but have developed or adopted different procedures in response to local problems or pressures. As Tulkens (1995: 8) notes, 'nowhere is the model any longer pure; it is, for better or worse, contorted, attenuated, modified. As a system adds, superimposes or eliminates certain features, one can now only say that it reflects a "dominant model"'. Furthermore, in the European Union, the developing jurisprudence in European law spanning both traditions, have led some commentators to believe that convergence is inevitable, an issue which is explored further below. Nevertheless, legal systems and methods of procedure are still frequently characterised by reference to inquisitorial and adversarial models and remain a useful framework for analysis.

The final point to make is that, although worldwide we can identify three modes of trial that are deeply rooted in history as well as geographically widespread, in this section we will discuss only two – adversarial and inquisitorial justice. The third – the Islamic law tradition based on Sharia law – will not be examined (for that, see Pakes, 2007).

## Two systems: adversarial and inquisitorial

Both the adversarial and inquisitorial models of criminal justice share an overriding, common objective: to convict the guilty and to acquit the innocent. In so doing, both also seek to protect the rights of the accused and the interests of society. Where the two systems differ is in the most effective and efficient way of achieving this result.

The adversarial system is based on the premise that the fairest and most effective way of determining guilt is for both the prosecution and defence case to be argued before impartial observers, who will determine whether the prosecution has proved beyond all reasonable doubt that the defendant is guilty of the offence charged. This gives rise to the distinctive features of adversarialism: the centrality of the trial itself, the reliance on oral evidence from witnesses, rules determining the admissibility of evidence and the roles of the judge, the jury and the parties.

The trial is of central practical and symbolic significance in the adversarial system, because it is only at this point that the jury is presented with the evidence. The jury knows nothing of the pre-trial investigation other than that which is admitted in evidence before it, and must therefore rely on its assessment of the credibility of the evidence, particularly from witnesses, on which to base its verdict. Rules of evidence limit the nature and scope of evidence that is admitted before the jury, to ensure that the jury are not unduly prejudiced. It should, however, be noted that, in England and Wales, some categories of evidence, such as hearsay and evidence of bad character, are now admissible following the implementation of the Criminal Justice Act 2003.

The role of the judge in the adversarial system is characterised as that of a neutral referee who adjudicates impartially between each side. He or she rules on matters of law and sums up to the jury, but the responsibility for a finding of guilty or not guilty rests with the jury. In an adversarial system, therefore, the boundaries of the dispute and the contested areas are determined by the parties themselves and by the advocates representing them. Again, however, recent shifts in law and policy have revised traditional conceptions of the role of the judge. Judges have been taking an increasingly active role in criminal case management and the Criminal Procedure Rules 2005 aim to change the culture of the criminal courts by introducing 'active case management' by judges to ensure that cases are dealt with 'efficiently and expeditiously' (1.1(2)(e)).

Finally, it should be noted that the role of the jury has acquired a significance within adversarial systems that goes beyond its practical fact-finding function. Lord Devlin, in an oft-quoted passage, said that trial by jury is 'more than an instrument of justice and more than one wheel of the constitution: it is the lamp that shows that freedom lives' (Devlin, 1956: 164). The ability of the jury to refuse to return guilty verdicts, even where the evidence appears overwhelming, can be considered an important constitutional safeguard against unfair laws or oppressive prosecutions (see for example, Ponting, 1985; Clive Ponting was acquitted of offences under the Official Secrets Act 1911).

In contrast, the inquisitorial legal tradition is of continental European origin and was exported widely across the continent in the Napoleonic era around 1800 (Vogler, 1996; Van Koppen and Penrod, 2003). The systems differ between European countries, but many of the principal differences apply to most inquisitorial systems (Pakes 2004).

A number of differences to the adversarial way of conducting trials can readily be identified. First, the jury, as a means of deciding cases, is a far less common phenomenon. Some inquisitorial systems operate without a jury or any form of lay participation altogether (such as in the Netherlands; see Tak, 1999), whereas others have very limited provision for juries, and that provision often takes the form of mixed tribunals in which both judges and juries have to come to a joint verdict (Vidmar, 2001).

Whereas in England and Wales (and the US) the jury symbolises honesty, fairness and impartiality (Lloyd-Bostock and Thomas, 2001), it is often associated with error and unpredictability in inquisitorial systems. This was strongly felt in the principality of Luxembourg, in particular, where the jury was abolished in 1987. The reasons given for its abolition there included the fact that jury decisions are usually unexplained, which was seen to be unfair to the defendant, and the fact that appeals against jury verdicts are often difficult, which was also regarded as unfair to the defendant (Spielmann and Spielmann, 1993).

However, the key difference between adversarial and inquisitorial justice is not what happens in the courtroom; it is the role of the pre-trial process. All results of police investigative actions are written up and compiled into a case file or dossier. That case file is ultimately available to both parties and to the judges at trial, and should contain all relevant information. All parties involved will therefore have intimate knowledge of the evidence and all circumstances relating to the case prior to trial. That quite often will make the trial almost unnecessary, so that the trial serves a largely symbolic and confirmatory function. The system has faith in the pre-trial investigative phase because police conduct is tightly regulated and overseen by judges, at least in France (Hodgson 2001, 2002) and in the Netherlands (but not in Germany) (Pakes 2004).

Thus, the evidence gathered during the investigation is, by-and-large, the evidence upon which a conviction (or an acquittal) will be gained. It does not need to be presented afresh during a contested trial in front of a jury that, thus far, has no knowledge of the case. It makes for an expedient, smooth and efficient process during which the chance of error has been effectively minimised.

## What is wrong with adversarial justice?

The key problem with an adversarial, partisan mode of trial is the fact that it is a game – a point frequently acknowledged (Carson and Pakes, 2003). The game metaphor is unsuitable for the job of delivering justice; that is better achieved in a context that promotes consensus and sharing of information rather than one that turns the stage into a battlefield. It is usually acknowledged that an adversarial setting is unsuitable for a wide range of disputes, including those involving children and issues of family law, as well as those that assess whether a mentally ill person can be released into society (Simon, 2003). The traditional criminal trial oddly goes against common sense and unfortunately the results prove that indeed adversarial justice fails to deliver the goods.

Kelly *et al.* (2005) found that rape convictions in 2004 were at an all-time low in England and Wales. Their report showed that the proportion of rape allegations resulting in a conviction had fallen from 24 per cent in 1985 to 5.6 per cent in 2002. In 2002, 11,676 rape cases reached court, but just 655 led to a conviction – and in 258 of those the accused had pleaded guilty. Not all this can be blamed on adversarial justice, of course. Their report also identified a culture of disbelief towards rape victims within the police, but the fact remains that the adversarial courtroom is not a good place to be for a vulnerable, traumatised victim. There is a realistic chance of further traumatisation during cross examination and a very high chance of an acquittal for the defendant at the end of the trial anyway.

Of course it has to be acknowledged that various measures have been put in place to make testimony in court less traumatic for victims and other vulnerable witnesses (Home Office, 1998; 1999; 2001). These include videotaped evidence in chief, live video-link so that a vulnerable witness does not need to appear in the courtroom, and prevention for suspects of certain offences to conduct their own defence and cross-examine their alleged victim themselves. These measures have been put into place widely, particularly in Crown Courts, and have been evaluated positively: victims who made use of such measures were more positive about their experience (Hamlyn *et al.*, 2004). Nevertheless, the point remains that such no doubt well-intended measures tinker with the system, rather than achieve wholesale change.

The persistence in regarding adversariality as the engine for justice inevitably and invariably produces questionable verdicts and traumatised victims as collateral damage. It admittedly offers a truly innocent defendant a fighting chance. However, the persistent failure in bringing the truly guilty to justice is too serious to be offset by that.

The inquisitorial approach to such cases is altogether different. Vulnerable witnesses are interviewed by a judge at the pre-trial stage in a non-adversarial manner. The defence can, either directly or via the judge, put questions to any victim or vulnerable witness as well. It is not uncommon in such situations for the defendant not to be present, but to be represented by the defence lawyer. More often than not, however, the interview will be conducted by the investigative judge. The chance of witness traumatisation is therefore much reduced.

The non-adversarial context is advantageous in other ways. Counsel (prosecution or defence) will be less inclined to utilise courtroom drama or the power of persuasion to impress the decision-makers. As the judge (or panel of judges) tends to be a seasoned professional, such antics are unlikely to work. That increases the chance for the evidence to be judged on merit, nowhere more so than where expert evidence is concerned. The nature, collection and analysis of forensic evidence, for instance, does not need to be explained from scratch in each and every trial, as the judge is assumed to be familiar not only with these forensic techniques and what they can and cannot produce, but also with the evidence in written form because it has invariably been made available beforehand. The system therefore relies on calm scrutiny prior to trial, rather than on courtroom drama, in order to uncover the truth.

On reflection, the oddity of the jury must be emphasised. It is difficult to conceive of any other sphere of life where a small group of complete strangers, without any specific skills or knowledge, are judged to be the best group of people to make far-reaching decisions about people's lives:

> it brings together a small group of lay persons who are assembled on a temporary basis for the purpose of deciding whether an accused person is guilty of a criminal offence . . . The jurors are conscripted and often initially reluctant to serve. They are untutored in the formal discipline of law and its logic. They hear and see confusing and contested evidence and are provided with instruction, most often only in oral form, about arcane legal concepts and sent into a room alone to decide a verdict without further help.
>
> (Vidmar, 2001: 1)

Within the adversarial legal tradition there is great fondness for what is called 'the day in court': the drama, the tension, the twists and turns, the oratory skills and the mystique of the jury room. But it can hardly be denied that the beneficiaries of these ingredients are lawyers on the one hand and the reporting media on the other. Neither are essential stakeholders in the process, which harms and alienates the parties that it really concerns.

The inquisitorial trial cannot compare in relation to such characteristics: in comparison to a full-blown adversarial trial, the typical inquisitorial trial can almost be considered a non-event. But, when considered as a whole, it is a coherent process that treats both suspect and victim with integrity and in which justice is done in the way it is supposed to be done.

---

**Task**

How well do vulnerable people fare in the adversarial system?

Read the following article and make notes:

- Burton, M., Evans, R. and Sanders, A. (2007) 'Vulnerable and intimidated witnesses and the adversarial process in England and Wales'. *International Journal of Evidence and Proof*, 11(1), 1–23.

## What is right with the adversarial system?

Critics of the adversarial system frequently disparage it by reference to the game metaphor; thus Sir John Stevens said:

> The fact is that all too often, the criminal trial is simply an uneven game of tactics . . . The very fact that the Criminal Trial Process is seen as a game is in itself debilitating to the notion of honesty, morality and getting at the truth.
>
> ('Police chief attacks justice system'. *Daily Telegraph*, 6 March 2002)

The game metaphor is not inaccurate insofar as there are opposing parties (the prosecution and the defence), formal rules (the law of evidence) and the neutral referee (the judge). However, the suggestion that the rules are there simply for the amusement of the players or for the purpose of giving a defendant an unfair advantage misses the point. The purpose of the 'game' is to ensure that the prosecution proves the case beyond reasonable doubt. For example, excluding evidence that has been obtained by oppressive or unfair means is not putting a pointless obstacle in the way of the prosecution; instead, it safeguards the reliability and integrity of the investigative process.

There is little doubt that the inquisitorial system is an effective method of resolving some civil disputes, particularly those involving complex family disputes and decisions about the best interests of a child where there are several competing interests. However, in criminal cases, there are only two possible outcomes: either the prosecution has proved beyond all reasonable doubt that the defendant is guilty of the offence charged, or it has not.

To explain the low conviction rate in rape cases by reference to the adversarial system is misleading. Sexual offences often turn on two conflicting accounts of whether intercourse was consensual, and therefore are, by their very nature, difficult to prove beyond reasonable doubt. The fall in the proportion of rape allegations resulting in a conviction between 1985 and 2002 can be explained by the increase in the number of cases being prosecuted, particularly in cases where the two parties have had a prior consensual sexual relationship. Faced with two competing accounts and a need for belief beyond reasonable doubt, many juries have no option but to find the defendant not guilty. The evidence from other jurisdictions demonstrates that some countries with inquisitorial systems, such as Sweden, Finland, Slovenia and France, have similarly low conviction rates (Regan and Kelly, 2003: 13). This suggests that the conviction rate is a product of other cultural and contextual factors beyond the type of criminal justice system.

The concern for the welfare of the victim in the courtroom is of course a valid one and, as has already been noted, several measures have been introduced in England and Wales to ensure that the trauma of testifying at a trial is kept to a minimum. However, the interests of the complainant must be balanced against that of the defendant. A complaint is at this stage still an allegation, and it must be the case that the defendant has an opportunity to test the evidence in court. As we know from many cases of miscarriages of justice, witnesses may be dishonest or genuinely mistaken.

To draw a distinction between the 'truly guilty' and the 'truly innocent' is a dangerous path. This implies that the truth is out there and that someone – presumably not the jury – is able to make that determination outside the courtroom. In most cases, the reality is much less clear-cut than that: witnesses may be mistaken; alternative explanations are possible. Furthermore, even where the evidence appears overwhelming, the burden of proof must still rest with the prosecution to prove its case beyond reasonable doubt. The inquisitorial system may well reduce the risk of the alleged victim being traumatised, but it also runs the risk of a defendant being wrongly convicted.

This suggests a more fundamental problem in the inquisitorial context: the reliance on the state. Being a seasoned professional is certainly an advantage in determining matters of law, but may be less of an advantage in relation to fact-finding. The evidence suggests there is a danger of becoming case-hardened (Jackson and Doran, 1997: 767). Criminal law is ultimately the coercive arm of the state, and enables the state to deprive people of their liberty. It is therefore too important to leave to those who are employed by the state; and in order for there to be public confidence in the fairness of the criminal justice system, the public need to be involved.

## Convergence?

We began with Tulkens' observation that both the adversarial and inquisitorial systems are no longer 'pure'. A series of commissions and reports have resulted in the system in England and Wales becoming less adversarial, whilst in some inquisitorial systems (e.g. Italy) attempts have been made to introduce more adversarial features. Jackson (2005) argues that it is the European Court of Human Rights that has been most influential in developing common processes and procedures across the adversarial and inquisitorial systems across Europe. He suggests that 'the adversarial/inquisitorial dichotomy has obscured the truly transformative nature of the Court's jurisprudence' (Jackson, 2005: 747) but that instead of leading towards a convergence of the two systems, there is likely to be a realignment of existing processes of proof to enable diverse application in different institutional and cultural settings.

## References

Ambos, K. (2003) 'International criminal procedure: "adversarial", "inquisitorial" or mixed?' *International Criminal Law Review*, 3(1), 1–37.

Bankowski, Z. (1988) 'The jury and reality'. In F. Findlay and P. Duff (eds) *The Jury Under Attack*. London: Butterworths.

BBC (2003) 'Old adversaries meet again'. Retrieved on 27 January 2006 from: <http://news.bbc.co.uk/1/hi/uk/3132193.stm>

Carson, D. and Pakes, F. (2003) 'Advocacy: getting the answers you want'. In D. Carson and R. Bull (eds) *Handbook of Psychology in Legal Contexts* (2nd edn). Chichester: Wiley, pp. 348–66.

Devlin, P. (1956) *Trial by Jury*. London: Stevens & Sons.

Hamlyn, B., Phelps, A., Turtle, J. and Sattar, G. (2004) *Are Special Measures Working? Evidence from Surveys of Vulnerable and Intimidated Witnesses*. Home Office Research Study 283. London: HMSO.

Hodgson, J. (2001) 'The police, the prosecutor and the juge d'instruction: judicial supervision in France, theory and practice'. *British Journal of Criminology*, 41, 342–61.

—— (2002) 'Suspects, defendants and victims in the French criminal justice process: the context of recent reform'. *International and Comparative Law Quarterly*, 51, 781–816.

Home Office (1998) *Speaking Up For Justice: Report of the Interdepartmental Working Group on the Treatment of Vulnerable or Intimidated Witnesses in the Criminal Justice System*. London: HMSO.

—— (1999) *Criminal Justice Strategic Plan 1999–2002*. London: Home Office.

—— (2001) *Measures to Assist Vulnerable or Intimidated Witnesses in the Criminal Justice System: Implementing the Speaking Up For Justice Report*. London: Home Office.

Jackson, J. (2002) 'The adversarial trial and trial by judge alone'. In M. McConville and G. Wilson (eds) *The Handbook of Criminal Justice Process*. Oxford: Oxford University Press, pp. 335–51.

—— (2005) 'The effect of human rights on criminal evidentiary processes: towards convergence, divergence or realignment?' *Modern Law Review*, 68(5), 737–64.

Jackson, J. and Doran, S. (1997) 'Judge and jury: towards a new division of labour in criminal trials'. *Modern Law Review*, 60(6), 759–78.

Kelly, L., Lovett, J. and Regan, L. (2005) *A Gap or a Chasm? Attrition in Reported Rape Cases*. Home Office Research, Development and Statistics Directorate. London: HMSO.

Lloyd-Bostock, S. and Thomas, C. (2001) 'The continuing decline of the English jury'. In N. Vidmar (ed.) *World Jury Systems*. Oxford: Oxford University Press, pp. 53–91.

McEwan, J. (1995) 'Adversarial and inquisitorial proceedings'. In R. Bull and D. Carson (eds) *Handbook of Psychology in Legal Contexts*. Chichester: Wiley, pp. 495–508.

Pakes, F. (2004) *Comparative Criminal Justice*. Cullompton, Devon: Willan.

—— (2007) 'The changing nature of adversarial, inquisitorial and Islamic trials'. In D. Carson, B. Milne, F. Pakes, K. Shalev and A. Shawyer (eds) *Applying psychology to criminal justice*. Chichester: Wiley, pp. 250–64.

Ponting, C. (1985) *The Right to Know: The Inside Story of the Belgrano Affair*. London: Sphere.

Regan, L. and Kelly, L. (2003) *Rape: Still a Forgotten Issue*. Briefing document for Strengthening the Linkages – Consolidating the European Network Project. London: London Metropolitan University.

Sanders, A. and Young, R. (2000) *Criminal Justice*. London: Butterworths, Chapter 1.

Simon, L. (2003) 'Proactive judges: solving problems and transforming communities'. In D. Carson and R. Bull (eds) *Handbook of Psychology in Legal Contexts* (2nd edn) Chichester: Wiley, pp. 449–72.

Spielmann, A. and Spielmann, D. (1993) 'Luxembourg'. In C. Van den Wijngaert, C. Gane, H.H. Kühne and F. McAuley (eds) *Criminal Procedure Systems in the European Community*. London: Butterworths, pp. 261–78.

Tak, P.J.P. (1999) *The Dutch Criminal Justice System: Organization and Operation*. The Hague: WODC.

Tulkens, F. (1995) 'Main comparable features of the different European criminal justice systems'. In M. Delmas-Marty (ed.) *The Criminal Process and Human Rights: Toward a European Consciousness*. Dordrecht: Martinus Nijhoff, pp. 5–13.

Van Koppen, P.J. and Penrod, S.D. (2003) 'Adversarial or inquisitorial: comparing systems'. In P.J. Van Koppen and S.D. Penrod (eds) *Adversarial Versus Inquisitorial Justice: Psychological Perspectives on Criminal Justice Systems*. New York: Kluwer, pp. 1–19.

Vidmar, N. (2001) 'A historical and comparative perspective on the common law jury'. In N. Vidmar (ed.) *World Jury Systems*. Oxford: Oxford University Press, pp. 1–52.

Vogler, R. (1996) 'Criminal procedure in France'. In J. Hatchard, B. Huber and R. Vogler (eds) *Comparative Criminal Procedure*. London: British Institute of International and Comparative Law, pp. 14–95.

# 4   Private policing or public policing?

*Mark Button and Les Johnston*

In this debate we consider the case for and against the privatisation of the police. The first section considers the case for privatisation, including an overview of the nature of private sector involvement in the police service. The section then moves on to outline a radical proposal for the privatisation of the police called 'extreme profitshire'. In the second section the case against privatisation is considered and an alternative model of provision is discussed.

## The case for privatising the police

Privatisation, or what constitutes it, is the subject of much academic and political debate. It can vary from very wide definitions of the shrinking of the state to the more precise definition of replacing public sector workers with identical private sector workers (Donahue, 1989). The underlying theme, however, is the reduction in the role of the state and the a priori belief that the private sector is more efficient and effective at providing goods and services (Atkinson, 1990). Butler (1991) has identified a range of privatisation policies, starting with the most complete – the sale of state assets to the private sector. Secondly, there is deregulation, where the regulatory burden on industries is reduced or removed, which may as a consequence lead to greater private sector involvement. Thirdly, there is contracting out, where public authorities contract out to the private sector to undertake functions that previously they provided directly. Finally, Butler distinguishes vouchers, where the government gives recipients of their services vouchers to shop around for the best service. Privatisation could even involve the removal or reduction of subsidies or the provision of tax incentives (Johnston, 1991). Where privatisation has not been possible in the public sector, attempts have been made at introducing the market and private sector practices. This has led to the rise of what has become known as 'New Public Management' or 'Managerialism' (Flynn, 1997). It is also important to note that privatisation does not always mean an increasing role for private companies vis-à-vis the state. There are other organisations that have also benefited (Johnston, 1991). There are also a range of non-state organisations, such as charities, voluntary organisations and consumer groups, that have replaced the public sector as well.

---

Write down a list of functions in the criminal justice system (not the police) which have been privatised.

---

### Privatising the police

In applying the policy of privatisation to the police, a range of different policies has been pursued in different countries (Chaiken and Chaiken, 1987; Johnston, 1992; Forst and Manning 1999). They range from the complete replacement of police departments with private security staff (O'Leary, 1994), to hiring out officers to private organisations, to the charging of fees for services provided (Johnston, 1992). In the UK, the public police have also been subject to these policies. Before this and other international experience is assessed, however, it would be useful to examine the attempts to classify experience of this policy.

In a major study of how public policing could be privately provided in the USA, Chaiken and Chaiken (1987) identified four mechanisms. The first they called **default transfer**, where the public police are unable for various reasons to meet public demands, so the private sector steps in to fill the gap. The second they called **accommodation and cooperation**, where the police informally allow private security personnel to carry out tasks they do not wish to do, in return for which they provide additional services. In an example of this policy they illustrate how the policing of the homeless in bus and train stations in some areas has been handed over to the security staff who police them. In return, if required to deal with an incident at a station, the police will respond immediately. The third type of privatisation they termed **legislation**, where private security personnel have been given specific roles and powers in statute. For instance, in some US states retail security staff have been given special powers of arrest and prosecution, meaning the public police do not have to become as involved. Finally, they distinguished **contracts**, where government have contracted with the police to carry out specific tasks.

The main criticism that can be levelled against Chaiken and Chaiken's classification is that it does not embrace all the policies of privatisation that have been applied to the police. For instance, as Johnston's classification reveals, it does not illustrate how the public police have embraced more commercial practices such as sponsorship and charging fees.

Johnston (1991) has classified the privatisation of policing in three forms. This includes **load shedding**, direct and indirect. This is where the police relinquish roles directly to the private sector, or the private sector usurps the public police because the public police are unable to provide the service the public want. Secondly, there is **contracting out**, where government or police contract with a private organisation to undertake a function for which they remain in ultimate control. Finally, Johnston identifies **charging fees and selling services**, where the public police have begun to increasingly act in a commercial manner by undertaking these functions. Johnston's classification can be strengthened by including, within load shedding, Chaiken and Chaiken's example of **accommodation and co-operation**. Further, by expanding Johnston's final category to embrace private sector practices, the broader range of private sector strategies increasingly used by the public police can also be assessed. This chapter will now use Johnston's amended trichotomy to evaluate the experience of privatisation to the public police in the UK. International examples will also be used where appropriate.

*Load shedding*

This is where the funding mechanism and the delivery of the service is moved from the public to the private sector. It can happen directly, where the police abandon certain functions, or indirectly, where because of constraints on resources they are unable to supply a service that is wanted and the private sector steps in to fill the gap. There are a number of police functions that have been shed by the public police and others where there has been significant speculation. For instance, in 1995 the then Conservative government published the report on *Police Core and Ancillary Tasks* (Posen Review; see Home Office, 1995). This report set out **inner core** tasks, which should remain the responsibility of police constables; **outer core tasks**, which should be managed by the police but could be undertaken by specials, civilians or contracted out; and **ancillary tasks**, which do not require management or delivery by the police service (Home Office, 1995). Initially when the inquiry had been announced there were fears, particularly amongst the Police Federation, that the government was building up towards the significant privatisation of the police. However, the final report made very few radical recommendations for privatisation, and has even been described as a 'damp squib' (Morgan and Newburn, 1997: 57).

Over the last fifty years, the history of the British police has been of incremental load shedding. The police no longer check properties and escort CIT (cash-in-transit) vehicles, which they once did routinely amongst many other functions (Clayton, 1967). There are other areas of policing where load shedding has been prominent in more recent years. Public order policing is a significant area where the police have sought to reduce their role. At football matches up to the late 1980s it was common for many police officers to be deployed within the grounds to undertake safety and public order policing functions. As a consequence of the Hillsborough disaster there were a number of reports into the safety and security strategies at football matches, the most important of which was the Taylor Report (Taylor, 1990). Following the publication of this report, football clubs agreed to undertake a greater role in safety with the police concentrating on crime, public order and emergency management. As a consequence police presence at most routine matches has declined significantly and been replaced by stewards and safety officers. Indeed, there are some Premiership football matches that take place with no police officers within the ground. To illustrate this change, in 1989 Nottingham Forrest would typically have 150 police officers supported by 75 stewards in the ground. In 1995 this had fallen to typically 250 stewards and 22 police officers in the ground (Frosdick and Sidney, 1997).

A further area where the police have effectively shed their role is the investigation of fraud. During the 1950s and 1960s, if an organisation suffered a fraud internally it would be common for the police to undertake the investigation. Such is the extent of fraud in many organisations today that the police will require prima facie evidence before they become involved. They may, indeed, even expect the investigation to be completed. As a consequence of this – and often a reason to keep control of the investiga-tion – many organisations have turned to the private sector to undertake the initial and sometimes the whole fraud investigation (Gill and Hart, 1997). This type of load shedding has exhibited both direct and indirect tendencies. The police have been pleased not to have to investigate some frauds, which could be labour intensive, but pick up the benefits of a suc-cessful investigation by the private sector. Many private organisations, unhappy at the police response to an alleged fraud, have turned to the private sector for help.

Another area of load shedding by the public police in recent years has been the response to intruder alarms. Traditionally, the police would respond to any alarm activation. However, with the huge growth in the use of intruder alarms accompanied by a significant increase in false alarms and consequent drain on police resources, the police have sought to limit their response. In 1995, the Association of Chief Police Officers (ACPO) pub-lished a policy on intruder alarms that set conditions for police response. Those intruder alarms that did not meet set conditions of the policy, or because of repeated failure had been struck off, would not receive an au-tomatic response from the police unless there was some additional factor, such as an eyewitness report (Cahalane, 2001). This policy, and a subse-quent policy published in 2002, have marked a gradual reduction in police response to intruder alarms. Some forces have attempted to go much fur-ther. The West Midlands Police attempted to introduce a policy that would have meant not attending alarm activations on commercial premises between 06.00 and 19.00 hrs Monday to Saturday unless it was a confirmed call. After legal action by the British Security Industry Association (BSIA) they were forced to revert to the national policy (BSIA, 2000). Nevertheless, this is an area where the private security industry has stepped in to offer these services. It is an activity that many private security companies would like to see completely shed or contracted out. Another significant police activity that has effectively been usurped by many private initiatives is the patrol of public streets. There is also a degree of informal load shedding that has taken place in policing in recent years. For instance, many private shopping centres are left to the private sector police unless there is a specific demand for a public police presence.

## Contracting out

In this form of privatisation the public provider retains responsibility for the funding of the activity, but contracts out the service to the private sector. There are a wide range of functions that have been contracted out to the private sector, some of which are not directly related to policing – such as catering, cleaning and maintenance. Contracting out in the field of policing is of more interest in this section. One of the most lucrative examples for the private sector was the contracting out of the escorting of prisoners following the 1991 Criminal Justice Act. This had previously been undertaken by a mix of police and prison officers, but under the scheme was divided into eight areas in England and Wales managed by companies ranging from Group 4 and Securicor to Reliance in business worth nearly £100 million per annum and employing nearly 3,500 staff (George and Button, 2000). The Criminal Justice Act also provided for the contracting out of Magistrates Court security to the private sector and this has also been a considerable growth area for the private sector. In many police forces the security of police premises has also been contracted out to the private sector, the West Midlands police headquarters, for instance, to Burns (Int) Security Services. The Government's Private Finance Initiative (PFI) has also led to the further contracting out of some roles. In Sussex there is an initiative for the private sector to build, finance and manage custody centres in six sites in the force area. These centres are staffed partly by private security personnel.

## Embracing private sector management practices

Throughout the Conservative governments of the 1980s and 1990s, and continuing under New Labour governments, there has been a gradual application of private sector practices and what has been termed 'managerialism' or 'New Public Management' (NPM) to the public police (Loveday, 1999). Most public sector organisations, including the police, were subject to the Financial Management Initiative (FMI), which emphasised the three Es: economy, efficiency and effectiveness. The rudimentary basis of this initiative was the setting of objectives and determining priorities, and ultimately the encouragement of private sector practices (Morgan and Newburn, 1997). The FMI was followed by Home Office circular 114/1983 with the encouragement of what later became known as 'policing by objectives'. By the early 1990s the pace of reform had intensified. The Police and

Magistrates Courts Act (PMCA) 1994 emphasised the 'chief executive' role of the chief constable, who was responsible for managing the police service rather than administering it. The PMCA also introduced chief constables as budget holders and brought in performance targets and greater business interest to the police authorities. Another significant event was the Sheehy Inquiry (Sheehy, 1993), into police rewards and responsibilities, whose recommendations were largely rejected. Some, such as performance-related pay for ACPO ranking officers, were implemented. Some constabularies have appointed accountants to key positions in the hierarchy, and in Merseyside the chief constable's team is called the 'Board of Directors' (Loveday, 1999). In the government plan for the criminal justice system, more secondments in the private sector for senior managers in the criminal justice system (including the police) were advocated and have now began to be implemented through the Workforce Modernisation Agenda (Home Office, 2001).

The application of NPM to the public police has been the subject of much research (Morgan and Newburn, 1997; Newburn and Jones, 1997; Loveday, 1999); however, the focus of this section will be selling policing services, charging fees and pursuing sponsorship. The police have long charged for 'special services', particularly for the officers they provide at football matches and public order events (Gans, 2000). Under the Police Act 1964 (now section 25 of the Police Act 1996):

> The chief officer of police of any police force may provide, at the request of any person, special police services at any premises or in any locality in the police area for which the force is maintained, subject to the payment to the police authority of charges on such scales as may be determined by the authority.
>
> (cited in Gans, 2000: 187)

Under section 18 of the same Act the police authority can also supply goods and services to local authorities. It is not the aim here to explore the debate over what constitutes 'special policing services', but rather to illustrate some of the services the police have provided. As mentioned, it has been a longstanding practice for the police to charge for the services they provide at football matches and other public events on private land. In recent years, however, some constabularies have offered officers for hire in a much wider range of roles. For instance, Liverpool City Council has recently 'rented' an additional 12 officers to patrol its city centre at a cost of £350,000 (Liverpool City Council, 2000). Some constabularies have offered their officers to local businesses for special duties; South Wales Police, for example, has hired out its officers to guard factories and business premises (*Cynon Valley Leader*, 1 September 1994). It was also recently announced that BMW, Mercedes and Lloyds UDT were to fund a complete unit of detectives in the Metropolitan Police to investigate stolen vehicles.

A *Sunday Times* investigation found Essex police would be willing to supply officers to a private party for £35.40 per hour. Many other local authorities, health trusts and businesses have also purchased additional police officers.

Such practices occur on a much larger scale in other countries. In the US, Reiss (1988) found three models of employment of the public police for private purposes. The first was where the officer found secondary employment and charged for his or her services directly. The second was through police unions who coordinated their secondary employment. Finally, a model exists where the police department contracts with the organisation for secondary employment, for which they receive fees and then pay the police officer.

The police are also increasingly charging for a range of services that they used to provide free of charge. If a car is stolen and the police recover it, in some constabularies a fee will be charged for this (the fee is usually shared between the police and the recovery company). In December 2000, when the government introduced the Vehicle (Crimes) Bill to Parliament, it was announced that the police would be able to keep some of the revenues from the fines from speed cameras (Home Office, 2000). Thus the police will actually have a financial incentive to prosecute more offenders.

Through sponsorship, police forces can also raise an additional 1 per cent of their budget. An exposé by the *Sunday Times* illustrated some of the more bizarre sponsorship deals many forces would consider. Posing as executives from a fictional firm called 'Keystone Security' (Keystone Cops!), for the appropriate fee several forces offered to emblazon their name on their vehicles. North Yorkshire police even offered to name an anti-burglary campaign after them, and in Leicestershire it was suggested their name, Keystone Security, could be located on the wall of a new police station shared with the local authority. Many forces have been successful in receiving money for advertising certain companies. Harrods has sponsored a police patrol car for the Metropolitan police, Thresher sponsored a police van for £10,000 and Avon and Somerset Police have received over £500,000 in sponsorship. Some constabularies even established companies to market some of their services. For instance, Thames Valley Police in partnership with Surrey Police and Focus Investigative Analysis established the Innovative Solutions Consortium, which offered a range of training courses to the public and private sector.

Linked to the charging of fees and selling of services, Bryett (1996) has also identified four methods in which privately owned non-police resources have been expended to the public police. At its simplest level, monies and physical resources have been given to the police. Clearly the donation of large sums of money or resources to the police raises concern over the independence of the police should an investigation into the donor ever become necessary. At a second level, another donation is that of space, which can also be a form of physical resource. Bryett provides one example from the USA where the McDonald's food chain gave part of one of its stores as premises for a police station. A third type of private sector aid is giving time. This most frequently takes the form of private individuals offering their time as special constables. At another level it might be helping the police in a search for a missing person or for evidence. The pursuit of cooperative ventures between the public and private sectors is the fourth means of cooperation. For instance, in Montgomery County, USA, the local police department cooperated with IBM to produce a sophisticated computer disaster and security capability. In the UK the Private Finance Initiative (PFI) has also enabled some forces to use the private sector to design, finance, build and manage police facilities. Some of these include police stations and firearms ranges.

---

Consider your local constabulary and, using the Internet, identify the extent to which privatisation has occurred and write it down.

---

### The inefficiency of the public police

The police are inefficient at delivering a range of services. Take one of the most important and symbolic functions of the police: patrol. In a famous experiment in Kansas City the effects of varying the level of mobile patrols in the city were assessed. It was found that increasing the level of mobile patrols by as much as two or three times had no discernible effect on the level of crime (Kelling *et al.*, 1974). Other similar studies in the US in the cities of Newark, NJ, and Flint, MI, have shown similar results (PF/PSI, 1996). Other research has shown that increasing the response time by the police also has little impact on rates of crime. This is because most crimes are not discovered until some time has passed. Loveday (1998) in an overview of research on police patrols has also identified the low status given to police patrols. The inherent bureaucracy in policing is also illustrated by findings from the Audit Commission (1996) which found that out of a typical force of 2,500 officers only 125 would be on the streets. The others would be on leave, sick, in court, on other shifts, management, specialists, support staff and so on. Consider also the example of successful criminal investigation, which is another significant symbolic function of the police. Detection rates are poor, with an overall rate of 23.5 per cent, and variations between forces ranging from 7 per cent to 39 per cent for burglary (Home Office, 2004). These are just two areas of policing that illustrate the inefficiency of the police and the scope for the pursuit of privatisation to improve the effectiveness of policing.

Johnston (1992) has discussed the hypothetical constabulary of 'Profitshire'. In this model he considers how a company could be established by the constabulary to sell security services. This has already occurred in Northumbria. One could take the 'Profitshire' model much further (Button, 2002).

---

Are the police inefficient? Could the private sector perform these functions more effectively?

Search the Internet for the websites of private security companies and write down the functions they undertake. Are there any functions you did not expect to see?

---

### The case for 'Extreme Profitshire'

In 2005, the probation service learned of the government's intention to abolish the 42 local boards and allow the 10 regions to market-test their services. This could include any of the services currently provided, and the government envisages some areas where the public probation service would cease to exist; commercial, charitable and voluntary sectors would provide the services instead. This illustrates the scope and possibility of establishing a similar system for the police service. It could be possible to contract out a whole police service or significant functions within it. Given resources issues, it would need to be a small force to begin with.

A government may decide to ask for expressions of interest to provide policing services in Warwickshire after the passage of the hypothetical 2013 Police Privatisation Act. The Act would set out a regulatory authority that awards, monitors and regulates contracts with the private sector. The authority would set out a detailed specification of standards required and targets to be met. After detailed analysis of the tenders, the contract might be awarded to a consortium of a security company, an employment agency and a merchant bank. The majority of police officers would continue to be employed and paid by the consortium. They would continue to swear the same oath of independence and to possess the same powers. Their numbers would be reduced and they would only undertake what the Posen inquiry described as **inner core** functions. **Outer core** and **ancillary** functions would all be contracted out to private security and investigation firms.

At a senior level the management of the force is replaced by a mix of civilians with extensive management expertise and police officers from other forces recruited for their commitment to innovation and reform. The new chief constable could be the ex-managing director of a very successful and large facilities management company. One of the first decisions of the chief constable might be to withdraw from 'inefficient' services such as responding to intruder alarms and investigating many volume property crimes. He or she might also introduce the charging of fees for a range of services that are currently provided free, such as the investigation of a burglary.

Additionally, the force might more aggressively offer to provide its officers and other staff to businesses at the appropriate rate of payment. The force might also pursue sponsorship more actively, and all the police cars might be repainted bright yellow to advertise a major telecommunications company. The officers' uniforms might also be emblazoned with a major sponsor, as professional footballers' shirts are.

This is an extreme example, hence the phrase 'Extreme Profitshire'. However, all of the privatisation policies identified have occurred in some form in the UK police service or comparable sectors such as prisons and probation. It is therefore not inconceivable that this extreme example could be applied if a government was elected with the will to pursue it. The question should therefore not be whether this type of privatisation is possible but rather whether it should occur, and what the implications for policing and society by going down this road towards 'Extreme Profitshire' are. The case against police privatisation will now be considered.

> Discuss with your fellow students and/or colleagues the implications of 'Extreme Profitshire'.

## The case against private policing

During the last twenty years public services have been subjected to increased privatisation. Advocates of privatisation justify it on a number of grounds:

- services provided through the market deliver greater efficiency ('value for money') and effectiveness than those delivered through the state;
- opening up service delivery to the market makes it more transparent and, therefore, more publicly accountable; and
- privatisation maximises individual choice. The justification here is that privatisation shrinks the public sector and leads to a reduction in taxes. This, in turn, is said to give consumers the freedom to spend their money as they think fit, as a result of which they are able to purchase the particular services they choose, rather than having to rely on uniform products provided by the state.

Though policing has been subject to less privatisation than some other public services, pressure for change is increasing. In what follows, the justification for private policing is rejected on four grounds:

- that injecting commercial elements into policing makes it neither more effective nor more efficient;
- that while it is certainly possible to bring about a comprehensive privatisation of policing there are good ethical reasons for not doing so;

- that introducing commercialism into public service delivery is always problematic because there is an inherent conflict between commercial interests and public interests; and
- that in the case of front-line policing better alternatives already exist, thus making privatisation unnecessary.

### Effectiveness and efficiency

Privatisation has been under way in the criminal justice sector and in policing for a number of years. Some examples of privatisation in policing – such as the contracting out of catering, cleaning, police station security and vehicle maintenance – are relatively well-established and cause only minimal controversy as they have no direct impact on front-line police service. The same could be said for police delivery of **special services** (those for which police have the power but not the legal duty to provide) under the 1964 Police Act and of the provision of new police buildings through the PFI. (PFI enables public sector organisations to purchase capital items from the commercial sector. Typically this involves the private sector designing, building, financing and operating facilities based upon public sector specifications and requirements.) However, it is questionable whether the introduction of private finance into the public sector – and with it a more commercially oriented style of 'New Public Management' (NPM) – has enhanced the effectiveness and efficiency of public services. There are two reasons for saying this:

- while private finance can provide a short-term solution to certain problems (such as lack of available public money to build new schools, hospitals or police stations) it can also generate new and far larger ones (such as education, health or police authorities being locked into thirty-year contracts requiring them to pay for facilities that may have long ceased to be fit for purpose);
- NPM reforms, far from having reduced public sector bureaucracy, have introduced quality assessment regimes – together with accompanying 'targets', 'performance-indicators' and 'league tables' – the effect of which has been to increase duplication and bureaucracy. That is why, in the case of policing, front-line officers spend the majority of their time completing paperwork rather than patrolling the streets. In short, commercial involvement in public services enhances neither their effectiveness nor their efficiency, something which is increasingly acknowledged in evaluative studies (Edwards *et al.*, 2004).

Discuss with your colleagues/friends the benefits and downside of the pursuit of privatisation in policing and note down the key points. To what extent do practitioner/public views match those of academics and government? Why do you think this is?

*The case against 'Extreme Profitshire'*

In the previous section the case for privatisation of the police was put forward via a model ('Extreme Profitshire'). Here it is argued that the model suffers from three serious weaknesses:

- **Limited competition and minimal choice.** The 'Police Privatisation Act 2010' would aim to do two things: to end the state monopoly over policing by subjecting it to competition; and to provide consumers with greater choice in policing services by opening up the police 'market' to commercial providers. In fact, neither aim would be achievable. On the one hand, the structure of the private security industry – an industry dominated by a handful of huge transnational corporations – ensures that little meaningful competition for contracts would take place. On the other hand, by introducing charges for certain police services, the Act would make 'choice' dependent upon people's 'capacity to pay'. Better-off individuals and communities would enjoy the highest quality police services, leaving the rest to live off the crumbs.
- **Commercial versus public interests.** The injection of the profit motive into policing would inevitably threaten the ethos of public service and undermine public interests. There is already abundant evidence from contracting-out in schools and hospitals that commercial providers cut corners. Dirty hospital wards are directly connected to the low wages and low standards of training enjoyed by hospital cleaning staff, and to the fact that insufficient staff are employed to do the job properly. However, public interests are not only undermined by poor quality service. Contracts are a poor mechanism for making services publicly accountable. Consider a hypothetical example. Hampshire Constabulary has contracted out its CID services to a private company, 'Cops 'R' Us' (the name used by the investigation and detection department of a transnational security corporation). Halfway through the four-year contract the Police Authority discovers that the detection rate has fallen substantially. The Authority pledges to hold the company accountable. However, when challenged, the company refuses to accept responsibility. It denies that there is a problem and questions the validity of the detection figures. It argues that, according to the terms of the contract, a 'detection' is defined differently from the way it was defined in pre-contract days. The company claims that, when measured by the new definition, the detection rate is, in fact, 10 per cent higher than it was before. There then follows an eighteen-month argument between legal teams acting for the Authority and for 'Cops 'R' Us' regarding the precise contractual meaning of the term 'detection'. With only six months of the contract left, the argument remains unresolved. When the new tender is put out, 'Cops 'R' Us' is the only viable bidder and the company is awarded the contract for a further four years.

- **Negative impact on police–public relations.** The 'Extreme Profitshire' model aims to contract out so-called ancillary police functions to the commercial sector leaving 'core' functions – in particular, those requiring the exercise of coercive powers – in the hands of sworn police officers. This revised division of labour would alter the police role fundamentally and have a disastrous impact on police–public relations. There is considerable evidence to show that good police–public relations in Britain are underpinned by the police's routine involvement in low-level order-maintenance and 'social service' functions (Reiner 2000). Removing such 'ancillary' functions from the police would alter their manner of engagement with the public. In effect, their sole contact with members of the public would become at best adversarial and at worst confrontational. Inevitably, that would undermine the quality of police–public interaction and drive a wedge between the public and the police.

### Is it right?

We now come to the most important issue. Irrespective of the impact of police privatisation on matters of effectiveness, efficiency, choice and accountability, the policy is unacceptable, first and foremost, because it lacks normative or moral justification. In order to understand this point it is necessary to explain why, in normative terms, policing is a necessary function of the state rather than of the market. In liberal democracies, the state serves to protect public interests. One such interest is personal security. For example, if individuals commit criminal acts against others, thereby depriving them of their right to security, the state exercises its moral authority to intervene on the victim's behalf. Offenders will be arrested, charged, brought before a court of law and, if found guilty, punished. Of course, in order to protect public interests in this way, the state needs to possess some coercive capacity. It is for this reason that the German sociologist, Max Weber, defined the state as 'a human community that (successfully) claims the monopoly of the legitimate use of physical force within a given territory' (Weber, 1994: 310–11). The single most important word in Weber's definition is the word 'legitimate' since, by using it, he is emphasising that the state's claim to coercive power is based on a moral justification (in the above example, the need to protect all of us from the criminal acts of a few). Much the same can be said for the police. The powers that police officers exercise on the street are exercised on behalf of the state and, ultimately, on behalf of the public. In that sense, the police officer represents or personifies the state's legitimate authority on the street. The problem is that once policing is privatised the relationship between police and the state is muddied by the profit element. At present, public police enjoy both moral authority and public legitimacy because we believe that, ultimately, they are meant to act in the interests of all of us. Private police would lack moral authority and legitimacy because, ultimately, we believe they would be motivated to act in the interests of their shareholders.

### Is it necessary?

Finally, it is increasingly clear that privatisation of front-line policing is unnecessary because better alternatives already exist under the previous government's Police Reform programme. One of these is what might be termed 'auxiliarisation' (Johnston, 2005). Some years ago, Sir Ian Blair (now Commissioner, then Deputy Commissioner of the Metropolitan Police), fearing the threat of privatisation, expressed concern that policing in London might become 'Balkanised' due to local boroughs setting up their own police forces or deciding to buy police services from private companies. Blair's solution was to propose the recruitment of uniformed auxiliaries dedicated to the provision of street patrol, a solution that he believed would enable public authority over policing to be consolidated:

> By giving such staff the Met badge of excellence, by ensuring that they work under the direction and control of constables, by offering an auxiliary service with powers, we will be able to persuade local authorities and others to spend their money on this kind of service, rather than on schemes without Met backing, without Met intelligence, without Met standards and without Met-based powers.
>
> (Blair, 2002: 31)

This new auxiliary body, called 'Community Support Officers' (CSOs), was introduced into the service by the Police Reform Act (2002). CSOs are uniformed police staff who possess only limited powers (such as the power to issue fixed-penalty notices for certain offences) and who are paid less than regular sworn officers. At present, there are about 4,000 CSOs operating in England and Wales, 1,200 of whom work for the Metropolitan Police Service. This number was set to increase substantially, with the previous government having pledged, in 2007, support for the recruitment of a further 20,000 CSOs over a three-year period. However, the fiscal crisis has caused the new coalition government to pursue substantial cuts in, amongst other things, police budgets, which may mean a substantial decrease in CSOs. CSOs are tasked to undertake visible street patrols and to contribute to the reduction of low-level crime and disorder, thus enhancing levels of public reassurance. The CSO initiative is effective and efficient, and it places substantial numbers of accountable uniformed police on the streets, CSOs being almost entirely dedicated to patrolling. In short, the initiative delivers all of the benefits that advocates of privatisation demand without any of the negative consequences associated with that policy.

> Consider whether this 'Blair' approach could be used instead of privatisation, and whether it would improve efficiency.

## Conclusion

The debate over the privatisation of policing is not *can* the police be privatised but *should* they be privatised. In theory, there is no limit to the privatisation of policing as the state could be completely abolished. In reality, however, there are political limits to the extent of privatisation in the UK. As Dance (1990: 294) has argued:

> It is not so simple however, to decide how far privatisation should go. The mere fact that it is possible to dismantle some or all of policing and spread it around other operators is not an argument for doing so: we must consider the implications more closely.

The central issues that need to be considered are whether efficiency will be improved, the implications for the public rump that might be left, as well as the consequences of more commercially orientated modes of operation.

## Further reading

Button, M. (2002) *Private Policing*. Cullompton, Devon: Willan.
Crawford, A. (2007) 'Networked governance and the post-regulatory state? steering, rowing and anchoring the provision of policing and security', *Theoretical Criminology*, 10(4).
Dance, O.R. (1990) 'To what extent could or should policing be privatized?' *Australian Police Journal*, 45, 9–13.
Forst, B. and Manning, P.K. (1999) *The Privatisation of Policing*. Washington, DC: George Washington University Press.

## References

Atkinson, R. (1990) 'Government during the Thatcher years'. In S. Savage, R. Atkinson and L. Robins (eds) *Public Policy in Britain*. Chatham: Mackays.
Audit Commission (1996) *Streetwise: Effective Police Patrol*. London: HMSO.
Bayley, D. and Shearing, C.D. (1996) 'The future of policing'. *Law and Society Review*, 30, 585–606.
Blair, I. (2002) 'Patrol partnership'. *Police Review*, 110 (no 5670), 30–31.
Bryett, K. (1996) 'Privatisation: variation on a theme'. *Policing and Society*, 6, 23–35.
BSIA (2000) News release, Worcester, British Security Industry Association, 26 June.
Butler, S. (1991) 'Privatisation for public purposes'. In W.T. Gormley (ed.) *Privatisation and its Alternatives*. Madison, WI: University of Wisconsin Press.

Button, M. (2002) *Private Policing*. Cullompton, Devon: Willan.

Cahalane, M. (2001) 'Reducing false alarms has a price – so does response: is the price worth paying?' *Security Journal*, 14: 31–54.

Chaiken, M. and Chaiken, J. (1987) *Public Policing: Privately Provided*. Washington, DC: National Institute of Justice.

Clayton, T. (1967) *The Protectors*. London: Oldbourne.

Dance, O.R. (1990) 'To what extent could or should policing be privatized?' *Australian Police Journal*, 45, 9–13.

Donahue, J.D. (1989) *The Privatisation Decision*. New York: Basic Books.

Edwards, P., Shaoul, J., Stafford, A. and Arblaster, L. (2004) *Evaluating the Role of PFI in Roads and Hospitals*. London: Certified Accountants Educational Trust.

Flynn, N. (1997) *Public Sector Management*. Hemel Hempstead: Prentice Hall.

Forst, B. and Manning, P.K. (1999) *The Privatisation of Policing*. Washington, DC: George Washington University Press.

Frosdick, S. and Sidney, J. (1997) 'The evolution of safety management and stewarding at football grounds'. In S. Frosdick and L. Walley (eds) *Sport and Safety Management*. Oxford: Butterworth-Heinemann.

Gans, J. (2000) 'Privately paid public policing: law and practice'. *Policing and Society*, 10, 183–206.

George, B. and Button, M. (2000) *Private Security*. Leicester: Perpetuity Press.

Gill, M. and Hart, J. (1997) 'Exploring investigative policing'. *British Journal of Criminology*, 37, 549–67.

Home Office (1995) *Review of Police Core and Ancillary Tasks Final Report*. London: HMSO.

—— (2000) Press release. London: Home Office, 7 December.

—— (2001) *Criminal Justice: The Way Ahead*. Cm 5074. London: HMSO.

—— (2004) 'Investigating volume crime'. London: Home Office. Retrieved on 26 June 2006, from: <http://www.homeoffice.gov.uk/rds/ivcrime1.html>

Johnston, L. (1991) 'Privatisation and the police function: from "new police" to "new policing"'. In R. Reiner and M. Cross (eds) *Beyond Law and Order: Criminal Justice Policy and Politics in the 1990s*. Basingstoke: Macmillan.

—— (1992) *The Rebirth of Private Policing*. London: Routledge.

—— (2005) 'From "community" to "neighbourhood" policing: police community support officers and the "police extended family" in London'. *Journal of Community and Applied Social Psychology*, 15, 241–54.

Kelling, G., Pate, T., Diekman, D. and Brown, C. (1974) *The Kansas City Preventative Experiment*. Washington, DC: Police Foundation.

Liverpool City Council (2000) Media release, Liverpool City Council, 5 October.

Loveday, B. (1998) 'Improving the status of police patrol'. *International Journal of the Sociology of the Law*, 26, 161–96.

—— (1999) 'Managing the police'. In S. Horton and D. Farnham (eds) *Public Management in Britain*. Basingstoke: Macmillan.

Morgan, R. and Newburn, T. (1997) *The Future of Policing*. Oxford: Oxford University Press.

Newburn, T. and Jones, T. (1997) *Policing After the Act*. London: PSI.

Noaks, L. (2000) 'Private cops on the block: a review of the role of private security in residential communities'. *Policing and Society*, 10, 143–61.

O'Leary, D. (1994) 'Reflections on police privatisation'. *FBI Law Enforcement Bulletin*, 21–25 September.

PF/PSI (1996) *The Role and Responsibilities of the Police.* London: Police Foundation and Policy Studies Institute Independent Inquiry.

Reiner, R. (2000) *The Politics of the Police.* Oxford: Oxford University Press.

Reiss, A.J. (1988) *Private Employment of Public Police.* Washington, DC: National Institute of Justice.

Sheehy, P. (1993) *The Report of the Inquiry into Police Responsibilities and Rewards.* London: HMSO.

Taylor, P. (1990) *The Hillsborough Stadium Disaster: Final Report.* London: HMSO.

Weber, Max (1994) 'The Profession and Vocation of Politics'. In Peter Lasssman and Ronald Speiers (eds) *Max Weber: Political Writings.* Cambridge: Cambridge University Press, pp. 310–11.

# 5   Restorative justice or retribution?

*Tom Ellis and Steve Savage*

## Introduction and orientation

This key debate is designed to give you a framework, and the terminology, for analysing the principal concepts within the academic literature on the **philosophies of punishment**.

In the first section below, the major focus will be on **retribution**, but you will find in your reading that, for all but the most abstract theorists and philosophers, it is almost impossible to maintain a 'pure' retributivist position. Retribution-based arguments are nearly always combined with those of **deterrence** and **incapacitation**. Although these three principles may conflict at an essential level, you will most often find they are common bedfellows in 'traditional' or 'tabloid' arguments about the purpose of criminal justice.

The following abridged extract from a Peter Hitchen's *Daily Mail* column is perhaps a paradigmatic example, linking many of the themes in this book:

> There is a way to beat crime – Fewer Human Rights, Tougher prisons and admitting that nothing deters like the death penalty.
>
> There is an amazingly easy way to restore peace and order to this country.
>
> It would also be popular and not specially expensive-And it would be a first step towards the restoration of morals, manners, self-restraint and national pride that we so badly need. So why will nobody do what is necessary?
>
> Very simply, we have to rediscover the basic idea that crime is wrong and must be prevented. Where it cannot be prevented, it must be punished.
>
> We must stop being ashamed to punish people. It is good for them, because it forces them to reconsider lives gone wrong. It is good for their victims, nowadays almost all of us. It makes us less likely to want to take personal revenge on those who have wronged us and it makes us feel as if justice has been done. And it is good for potential law-breakers who, seeing what happens to those who are caught, think hard before embarking on crime.
>
> To make punishment effective we first of all have to restore its gold standard, the death penalty for heinous premeditated murder. I am so

certain that the restoration of hanging would deter armed crime, reduce violence and protect the police from danger that I am prepared to make this offer to its opponents. Reintroduce it for an experimental period of ten years.

Then we have to bring back the idea that prisons are for punishment.

At the moment they are warehouses-where people are kept until they are released. The loss of liberty is seen as punishment enough, and the authorities have little control over the prisoners' lives. The result is a double disaster. The jails are often run by the inmates, are full of illegal drugs, and plagued by violence and intimidation.

These simple changes, implemented firmly, would be popular and effective.

Within a few months, they would change the atmosphere of our country and greatly strengthen the forces of good against the forces of wickedness and disorder.

They would not threaten any innocent person. They would prevent many young people from falling into the fumbling hands of the criminal justice system because they would not risk getting into trouble in the first place.

Our society can only remain free if it rediscovers the concepts of right and wrong, and uses all its might to protect the good and restrain the bad. It is not yet too late, but we do not have long.

(*Daily Mail*, 30 March 2003 <http://www.dailymail.co.uk/debate/ columnists/article-228304/THERE-IS-A-WAY-TO-BEAT-CRIME-FEWER-HUMAN-RIGHTS-TOUGHER-PRISONS-AND-ADMITTING-THAT-NOTHING-DETERS-KILLERS-LIKE-THE-DEATH-PENALTY.html>)

**Task**

Once you have read this chapter in full, return to this extract, or better still, read the full article and note down how many underpinning philosophies of punishment you can identify.

Does the argument hold together, or are there philosophical contra-dictions and/or inconsitencies?

You may also wish to revisit the arguments for and against 'crime control' in Chapter 1, and link the issues raised here about philoso-phies of punishment with the 'prison works!' arguments in Chapter 6 and the debate on capital punishment in Chapter 8.

Much of this (con)fusion is related to the dual function of criminal law. Making the many assumptions required, such as certain detection, knowledge of the law and so on, most criminal law is based on what Hudson (2003) calls a forward-looking approach in which all citizens are 'deterred' from offending by the anticipated future punishment that is written down in the statutes.

---

● **Key Text:** Hudson, B. (2003) *Understanding Justice: An Introduction to Ideas, Perspectives and Controversies in Modern Penal Therory* (2nd edn). Buckingham: Open University Press/McGraw-Hill Educational.

---

**Deterrence** (along with **incapacitation**) therefore comes under the utilitarian political–moral philosophical umbrella, which you will also find referred to as **consequentialism**. It is also referred to as **reductivism** (reducing future crime) as the **justifying** principle for punishing people within criminal justice literature.

However, if the citizen is not deterred and commits a crime, the same criminal law then becomes **distributive** and backward-looking, and attempts to match the weight of the punishment required by sentencing (often also discussed in terms of incapacitation) to the gravity of the offence committed – **retribution**. Pure retributivism is based on the idea of placing moral blame on the offender for the offence committed, but it is against retributivist principles to make any stipulations about future conduct once the price for committing an offence has been paid. In this restricted sense, there is no room for remorse, contrition, etc., beyond the end of the penalty. You may find Figure 5.1 helpful in orientating yourself within the terminology of this area of study.

In this debate, Tom Ellis will first argue that the principles of retribution are the most important and appropriate ones on which to base criminal justice. Steve Savage will then argue *against* retribution, outlining its shortcomings, and *for* restorative justice (RJ) as a better alternative, after which Tom Ellis will provide a short critique of RJ. In the third and final section, the authors broaden out the argument, and develop other 'aims of sentencing' and 'philosophies of punishment' that you will need to ensure you read about and understand.

---

NB Before reading the rest of this chapter, be aware that it reflects the huge and burgeoning level of publication in the area of restorative justice. A number of perspectives and possible avenues of inquiry are therefore covered here. However, it is important for you to be very clear about the assessment task/s you have been set and to ensure that you maintain the appropriate focus. You will not need to complete all of the tasks and do all of the additional reading suggested.

| Future-orientated (prevention) | Past-orientated |
|---|---|
| • Reductivist<br>  (Reduces crime)<br>• Utilitarian<br>  Rational choice<br>• Consequentialist<br>  Future consequences | • Retributivist<br>  Moral blame<br>  Proportionate (just deserts)<br>• Least necessary pain should be inflicted<br>  on offender by the state |
| Deterrence through fear, shame, pain, restriction of liberty, 'rehabilitation/community penalties' (death penalty), torture, (prison), tracking | Denunciation & degradation<br>(death penalty), (prison)<br>Chain gangs |

| Restorative |
|---|
| • Relational<br>Aim of punishment is to address harm<br>to victim and restore balance of relations<br>between offender, victim and society |

*Figure 5.1* Terminology associated with retributive and restorative justice

# Retribution and deterrence are what the law requires!

## Principles of retribution

The argument here is that we should focus on the principles on which criminal law is based. In answer to the question 'Why punish?' a deterrence theorist might typically reply 'to prevent future crime', but a purely retributivist reply would be 'because criminals deserve it because of their past actions'.

The two key elements of retribution are:

- offenders must be punished because they have carried out actions in the past that are illegal (akin to a stimulus–response approach); and
- the severity of the punishment can and must be matched to that of the seriousness of the crime.

Retribution is based on denouncing the crime (again, see King's denunciation and degradation model of criminal justice, which you can find from reading Davies *et al.*, 2010, as outlined in Chapter 1). The severity of the sanction imposed is usually justified by the fact that the offender has not played by society's rules and has seized an unfair advantage. For instance, citizens coexist by denying themselves the opportunities to steal or to act violently by obeying laws. Those that transgress the law therefore have to pay the punitive price to remove the unfair advantage they have grasped.

As Hudson (2003: 47–48) argues, this approach is based on the hugely influential *A Theory of Justice* by John Rawls (1972), which itself owes a huge debt to Rousseau's 'social contract'. The key point to bear in mind is that Rawl's vision of retribution is based on a vision of 'justice as fairness' and is intended to be 'anti-oppressive'. When it comes to the most serious crimes such as murder and rape, Duff (1986) has also argued that this is a simpler case of breaching the boundaries of society's moral code than of gaining an advantage.

## Task

Are there divisions within society that mean there is no simple, overall view of what is morally right and wrong? Can you think of examples? It may be worth looking at criticisms of the denunciation and degradation model (see Chapter 1) as your starting point.

Retribution is also based on the notion of the offender as a rational, decision-making, moral agent who accepts the overall enforcement of rules in order to live within a society, but has transgressed one or more of them. This also means that, once the price for transgression is paid through punitive pain, that offender reverts to being morally indistinguishable from the rest of society and should be given an equal chance to choose a non-transgressive course in their future actions. This makes the retributivist approach the most liberal and least oppressive. It is also the only justice approach that allows the offender the free will to choose to obey the law and therefore be certain of avoiding any pain inflicted by state punishment.

## Reflective task

Are the choices of some members or groups of society more constrained than others?

What implications does this have for the fairness of retribution?

The most common, perhaps overused, example of retribution is the biblical notion of 'an eye for an eye' or *lex talionis*. However, Hudson (2003) has based most of her argument on developments since the 1970s, and the principles presented here are based mainly on her discussion of **modern (liberal) retributivism**.

**Task**

After reading this section of the debate, you should ensure you read Chapter 3 of *Understanding Justice* (Hudson, 2003: 38–55) in order to underpin and consolidate your understanding of retributive justice.

The *lex talionis* label is misleading in that it associates retribution with ancient, perhaps primitive-sounding customs such as stoning to death and the corporeal excesses of punishments that continued and developed through the Dark Ages and medieval societies. However, **retribution** is not coterminous with simple **vengeance** or **revenge**.

**Reflective task**

Consider the different coverage of the distinction between legal retribution and vigilantism in the *Guardian* and the *Daily Mail* when looking at the same case of retaliation by initial victims:

- 'Self defence or malicious revenge? Jail for brothers who beat burglar with cricket bat', *Guardian*, 15 December 2009, <http://www.guardian.co.uk/uk/2009/dec/14/jail-brothers-burglar-cricket-bat>
- 'Homeowner jailed while the burglar he attacked walks free: Vigilante? No, a victim of an immoral justice system'. *Daily Mail*, 16 December 2009, <http://www.dailymail.co.uk/debate/article-1236211/PATRICK-MERCER-Homeowner-jailed-burglar-attacked-walks-free-Vigilante-No-victim-immoral-justice-system.html>

Modern retributivism dates from concerns among 1970s liberals, particularly American liberals, about the then perceived ineffectiveness of rehabilitative approaches (see Martinson, 1974) and about the excessive overuse of **incapacitation** through **indeterminate** sentences.

The advantages of a retributive approach are as follows:

- Firstly, retribution works against excessive punitive sanctions, by establishing punishments that are **proportionate** to the seriousness of the offence. It is often seen as a criticism of such approaches that, while distinctions can be made about relative seriousness (e.g. murder is more serious than assault), the overall severity of the sentencing options (the lowest and highest points of seriousness) is a matter of subjectivity and varies between societies. As such, Hudson (2003: 45–46) notes that, for the same offence, you would be subject to relatively moderate scales of retribution in Sweden and Minnesota, USA, but in New Mexico and Indiana (both also USA) the scales are very harsh and your punishment would be much more severe. Hudson is essentially putting forward a criticism first made by von Hirsch (you may wish to use the references in Hudson to track this source down if it is essential to your argument), but it can also be seen as a way in which retributive approaches can be internally consistent, though flexible and adaptable to different cultural norms within different societies. The retributive approach relies on each society, through the formulation, reform and reformulation of criminal law, to establish presumptive sentencing, based on typical cases. These will vary over time and place.

- Secondly, retribution offers protection from extra or **disproportionate** punishment (especially the seemingly liberal rehabilitative approach) because of potentially faulty or unverifiable predictions about future offending through the type of risk analysis now pervasive throughout the probation service and youth offending teams.

In the USA, the Minnesota sentencing guidelines were introduced precisely in order to control professional judicial discretion, which meant in practice that the severity of sentences was affected by the personal or social characteristics of the offenders, such as race, sex, class, etc. This is why retribution is preferred by the public and by the criminals themselves. The Attica prison riots in the 1970s were about the unfairness of sentencing, with a perception among many being that their sentences were too harsh in relation to their offending. Retribution protects against this unfairness because it is the crime that is sentenced, not the offender.

## Summary

It is self-evident that most citizens wish to live in a rational, rule-following, fair society and therefore agree that rules have to be enforced, even against themselves, if they transgress. Retribution is mostly about the **distribution** of penal pain (setting the appropriate level) rather than about **justifying** why punishment is needed. Under this system, we are only punished according to the seriousness of our past crimes, and we are not prevented from exercising our free will in the future. The only sense in which retribution makes claims on our future conduct is the expectation that we will seek to avoid future pain, and that pain may become more severe as our offending is repeated or escalated.

## Task

Read the following case about John Hirst who 'was jailed for brutally killing his landlady' in 1979:

- 'It's not like I'm killing someone now because there's no lids for my jam jars', *Guardian*, 18 November 2006, <http://www.guardian.co.uk/uk/2006/nov/18/ukcrime.weekend7>

1. Make notes on the extent to which philosophies of punishment are explicitly used in the article and by whom.
2. Think about the extent to which pure retributivism has been effected in this case and the role of remorse. Do victims (and/or their families) and convicted criminals have such different views and needs that they can never be reconciled? Has justice been done?
3. Return and make further notes once you have finished the chapter.

## Restorative justice – the way ahead

This section presents the case for restorative justice as *the* way ahead in developing justice systems in progressive and effective directions. Restorative justice (RJ) offers an approach to justice that can move the justice agenda forward and which is all about a justice system that fits the twenty-first century – although, as we shall see, it draws upon some very traditional ideas and practices. In order to do this, the case for RJ will be presented in three sections:

- The problem with retribution.
- Principles of restorative justice.
- Putting restorative justice into practice.

### *The problem with retribution*

We have already seen what retribution is all about and how advocates of this approach to justice see it working to deliver 'justice' itself. From the perspective of RJ, however, the retributive model is far less impressive than is claimed. In a number of ways the retributive model of justice can be found seriously wanting. The retributive model assumes that the committal of a crime will, in most cases, lead to a certain level of punishment. The outcome of this, according to the principle, is that *the offender will be deterred* from committing crimes in the future, *others will be deterred* from committing crime and the community can see justice delivered.

**Task**

Ensure you are clear on the difference between these two types of deterrence, the terminology used to outline them, and their relationship to retribution. Look at Hudson (2003: 18–21).

However, we know that only a small percentage, certainly below 10 per cent, of offences are identified with specific offenders. A large proportion of crimes go unreported and a large proportion of reported crimes go undetected. In which case 'retribution' only falls on the minority of offenders who are unfortunate enough to get caught. Most offenders go unpunished, so why build a model of justice around the principle of punishment?

Retribution is now typically based on the notion of proportionality between the offences committed and the punishment applied – that the punishment somehow 'balances out' the offence. This is also linked to some notion of 'standardised justice' which is consistent, formulaic and applied in the same way to all. From the RJ perspective, however, this approach fails to appreciate the complexities, the 'richness' and the individualised nature of crime, victimisation and penal measures. The same crime can 'hurt' one victim much more than another, for example shoplifting from a corner shop might cause more harm than from a hypermarket. Also, the same 'punishment' might 'hurt' one offender much more than another, for example a period of imprisonment may damage one person much more than another. If this is the case how can 'proportionality' work? One of the goals of RJ is to respect the *individualised* nature of crime and victimisation and to tailor the response accordingly. The 'broad brush' and inflexible approach of retributive justice can only fail in this context. To achieve any genuine 'balance' each case needs to be tackled on its merits – RJ seeks to do precisely that.

Retributive justice focuses on past behaviour rather than future potential. The choice of punishment is based on what has taken place in the past, rather than on what are the best options for the future. Apart from a limited potential for deterrence (and incapacitation), the retributive model for this reason is essentially backward looking. It is also based on who committed the crime rather than on why it happened and how offending might be tackled. Again the 'richness' of a criminal event, in terms of why an offence was committed, how much hurt it caused and how such offending might be prevented in the future, is largely lost in the retributive approach, which reduces the affair to the simple terms of offence and punishment.

Related to this is the role of the victim in justice processes. The retributive model effectively reduces the victim of crime to a 'bit player' in the justice process. Having reported a crime, victims are largely excluded from the process from that point onwards, apart perhaps from giving evidence to help secure a conviction. 'Justice' becomes a matter of a relationship between the state and the offender. From being the person who has suffered the harm of a crime, the victim is sidelined as a passive observer of 'justice', which becomes something well beyond their comprehension and engagement. From the RJ perspective, as we shall see, the victim occupies centre-stage in the justice process.

The retributive model has a very limited, and rather pessimistic, view of offenders and human behaviour more generally. It assumes that offenders will only learn by being 'taught a lesson' and by suffering the consequences of their behaviour. Rather than appeal to people's 'better nature', perhaps by trying to get offenders to really understand what their behaviour has meant to others, the retributive model targets base motives like pain-avoidance and fear. Punishment under this approach is not that far away from the way we house-train a dog – we 'rub their noses in it'. It focuses on discouraging bad behaviour rather than encouraging good behaviour. Surely human behaviour can be modified in more sensitive ways? Why simply add to the amount of pain in society by adding the pain of punishment to the pain caused by the initial offence? This is one reason why retribution can lead to offenders becoming embittered and anti-authority rather than being reintegrated into the law-abiding community.

For these reasons and others, such as cost, the retributive model is found wanting, despite its dominant role in the history of penal strategies. However, that dominance is now threatened by a very different 'paradigm' on justice: **restorative justice**. What are the essential features of RJ that mark such a shift from the retributive model?

### Principles of restorative justice

RJ is not just an alternative technique of responding to offending behaviour, it is in many ways a different world view, certainly a different view of human behaviour to that offered by retributive justice. Indeed, RJ extends well beyond crime itself, because RJ principles can be applied in a wide range of contexts. In many ways we might be using RJ principles without realising that we are doing so.

An example of this might be a student complaints system. If a student has a concern about how they were treated by a lecturer – say, that they were spoken to rather rudely about their timeliness in a seminar – they can turn to the complaints system, which most institutions will have. Now if that complaints system is well designed, it will have within it a framework for informal resolution, whereby the aggrieved student can agree to some process that would satisfy them, without recourse to any formal disciplinary process should the complaint be upheld. This might take the form of a meeting between the student and the member of staff, with a third party as facilitator, at which the student could explain how they felt in the seminar when the lecturer spoke, and the lecturer could explain why he or she had spoken in that way. This might lead to an apology by the lecturer and, hopefully, an agreement that the relationship between the two would get back onto a better footing in the future. The problem or conflict in this case could have been solved without official or formal measures but, more importantly, it might be an outcome that the aggrieved person was more content with than the disciplining of the 'accused'. Maguire and Corbett (1991) found rather similar results. When looking at complaints against the police, the public were often more interested in an apology than the formal discipline process.

## Task

How convincing is this argument?

Read:

- Waters and Brown (2000) 'Police complaints and the complain-ants' experience'. *British Journal of Criminology* 40 (4): 617–38, <http://bjc.oxfordjournals.org/cgi/reprint/40/4/617>

This example actually contains within it many of the features of a RJ process. It was informal, rather than formal, it involved dialogue between the 'victim' and the 'offender', it involved reparation, in the form of an apology, and it established a framework for a better relationship in the future. Above all, the needs of the victim were kept centre-stage, in the sense that the victim was given the choice of process, was allowed to explain their feelings and to hear an explanation in turn from the 'accused', and the outcome was one that repaired the harm done in a way preferable to the victim. That is restorative justice in a nutshell.

The development of such notions as 'informal resolution' bears some of the marks of the rise of RJ as a way of resolving conflicts. It demonstrates that RJ can be used in a variety of contexts, not just crime-based conflicts. In South Africa, in the wake of Apartheid and as a means of bringing more closely together a clearly divided society, the Truth and Reconciliation programme was established, led above all by Archbishop Desmond Tutu. The goal was to bring victims of Apartheid (e.g. families who had lost relatives) together with those responsible (e.g. senior police officers) to develop a mutual understanding of their relative experiences, emotions and reasoning, and ultimately to reach some form of reconciliation between the parties. Here, RJ principles were being employed to resolve national conflicts and problems, rather than the machinery of the courts and penal systems.

## Key issue

Braithwaite (2003) argued that victims' satisfaction came mostly through the empowerment facilitated through the process and the symbolic meaning of receiving an apology. However, Hoyle, Young and Hill (2002) argued that the key element to this complex process is whether the victim perceives the apology as genuine.

## Task

With the above in mind, and the link with conflict resolution, investigate the case of *gacaca*, the traditional community courts that were utilised for genocide cases in Rwanda as a way of dealing with the enormous number of post-massacre cases.

- <http://www.newyorker.com/reporting/2009/05/04/090504fa_fact_gourevitch#ixzz0kKtDFx4f>
- 'Rwanda gacaca criticized as unfair for genocide trials', <http://www1.voanews.com/english/news/a-13-2009-04-09-voa32-68733712.html?moddate=2009-04-09>

Does this convince you that restorative justice 'works'?

Are there issues about due process (see Chapter 1) and offenders' rights (see Chapter 9) that RJ approaches may not ensure?

See also Ashworth's (2002: 592) comments on the ramifications of RJ's approach for principled sentencing, ie, ensuring that sentencing is proportionate.

Other examples that can be used in considering the genuineness of apology and the potential for RJ are:

- 'Student who urinated on war memorial spared jail'. *Guardian*, 26 November 2009, <http://www.guardian.co.uk/uk/2009/nov/26/student-urinated-war-memorial-sentenced>
- 'Leeds man spared jail after drunkenly urinating beside war memorial'. *Guardian*, 6 April 2010, <http://www.guardian.co.uk/uk/2010/apr/06/leeds-man-urinating-war-memorial>
- 'Cambodia torturer Duch – killer of 12,380 – asks court to set him free'. *Guardian*, 27 November 2009, <http://www.guardian.co.uk/world/2009/nov/27/cambodia-duch-asks-court-freedom>: 'This week Duch asked to be allowed to apologise in person to his victims' families. No family members of victims, or victims' groups, have said they want to meet with Duch.'

- 'Leading Bosnian Serb war criminal released from Swedish prison'. *Guardian*, 27 October 2009, <http://www.guardian.co.uk/world/2009/oct/27/bosnian-serb-war-criminal-freed>: 'She's served her sentence and she's at the end of her life. I think it's OK she's been released', said Nezira Sulejmanovic, from Srebrenica whose two sons and daughter were killed by Serbian forces in the war. 'She's just waiting for the end of her life. Let her be.'

On a different level altogether, RJ is being used as a way of tackling bullying in schools, whereby those responsible for bullying are brought together with their victims to enter into some form of dialogue and, hopefully, to resolve the problem for the future.

## Task

Read the following case of bullying and make notes on whether this case could have been resolved through RJ.

- 'Teenage bullies guilty of killing vicar's daughter who jumped from window'. *Guardian*, 18 November 2009, <http://www.guardian.co.uk/uk/2009/nov/18/rosimeiri-boxall-manslaughter-verdict>

Could RJ be employed still for the victim's family and the offenders? If this seems far fetched, read the following article:

- 'How I forgave my daughter's killer'. *Guardian*, 30 January 2010, <http://www.guardian.co.uk/lifeandstyle/2010/jan/30/mary-foley-forgiveness-daughter-killer>

So what, then, are the core principles of restorative justice? It may be best to begin with a definition of RJ. The following definition by Fattah (2002: 310) is a good start:

> Restorative justice is justice that has redress to the victim as one of its primary goals, whether or not the offender has been arrested or charged. It is justice that stipulates that it is society's obligation, the society that has failed to protect the victim or to find the culprit, to redress the harm done to the victim. It is justice for victims with the active participation of those victims. It is justice that recognises their plight and affirms their rights. It is justice that ensures that their wishes are respected, their needs met and their expectations are fulfilled.

RJ in its Western context emerged out of early attempts in the 1970s and 1980s to develop 'victim–offender mediation' (VOM), whereby, either **instead of punishment** or **alongside punishment**, victims and offenders were brought together to talk about the offence, the harm caused, why the offender had done it, and so on, and to aim, if possible, to reach some common ground, most notably through an apology. VOM developed on the basis of a number of assumptions and beliefs which have become key to the RJ 'movement':

- Victims often wish to be involved in what happens after they have been the victim of a crime – at the very least they want to know what is happening, but more fundamentally they also want to be involved with the process of bringing the offender to account.
- Victims often value the offender realising the harm he or she has caused as a result of what they have done.
- Offenders can find having to face their victim more difficult than serving their punishment – RJ is not a 'soft touch' as some critics believe.
- Offenders are more likely to desist from crime after being confronted with their victims and the harm they have caused, than from serving punishment.
- The harm of crime is more likely to be repaired through dialogue between the victim and offender and an apology than by simply punishing the offender.

Since the early attempts at VOM, restorative justice has grown to become a global phenomenon, with an ever-expanding army of advocates and a multitude of schemes. This has made identifying the core principles of RJ more difficult, because RJ now has many dimensions and characteristics. However, Van Ness (2002) offers us a very clear account of the essential components of RJ systems, which includes the following features.

- **Meeting** of the parties. In RJ the parties usually meet in person, most often with a third party as mediator/facilitator.
- **Communication** between the parties. When they meet the parties talk about what happened, how it affected them and how the harm done might be redressed. The key aim here is mutual understanding.
- **Agreement** by the parties. After the two 'sides' have talked through the personal, emotional and material aspects of the offence, they reach a mutually acceptable 'solution', which is specific to their particular circumstances.
- **Apology** by the offender. An apology is a key means by which the offender can 'make amends' to the victim. It is important to ensure that the apology is genuine and that the offender is not forced to apologise (which would reduce its genuineness). It is an acknowledgement that a wrongdoing has taken place and that the offender was responsible for it. The victim may or may not choose to accept the apology.

- **Restitution** to the victim. This is about making reparation to the victim and in some ways it might relate to an apology (which in itself may be a form of reparation as a means of making amends). Restitution involves offenders 'making good' the damage they have caused, and in that sense seeking to bring the situation back to that which applied before the offence was committed, a form of 'restoring equilibrium' or healing. The most obvious form of restitution is payment to the victim, or the undertaking of tasks which repay 'in kind' – such as repairing the property damages when the offence was committed.

- **Change** in the offender's behaviour. A cornerstone to RJ is that the process of applying RJ can alter behaviour in a positive direction. It is not just about dealing with the offence that has occurred, it is about doing things to make it more likely that attitudes are changed and behaviour bettered. The experience of the RJ process is designed to impress upon the offender the harm they have caused and the need to make amends; this in itself is a positive experience (more so than simply suffering punishment). However, some advocates of RJ, such as Braithwaite (1989), argue that the reintegration of offenders back into the community is a key part of the positive/constructive potential of RJ, what Braithwaite calls 'reintegrative shaming'. Put crudely, reintegrative shaming means that after the offender has admitted doing wrong and then sought to make amends, he or she should be forgiven and given a message that 'you are still one of us'. Whereas retributive justice is all about shaming and expulsion from the community (most notably through imprisonment), RJ seeks to keep the offender as a member of the community by being welcomed back 'into the fold'. This will more likely change the offender's behaviour in a positive way.

More generally, RJ is about building up mutual respect between the parties and creating an environment of mutual support to both victims and offenders. This is where 'supporters' and other third parties might be involved in the RJ process, such as friends and relatives, the police and other justice and social care workers. The process is normally overseen by a facilitator (who might be one of the aforementioned), who can help set up the RJ meeting, clarify what may happen and the rules under which it will happen, and may intervene at various stages in the process where necessary. At this point it will help to show how the principles of RJ are reflected in the practice of RJ.

### Putting restorative justice into practice

In many ways RJ is a new and alternative way to deliver justice and in that sense most RJ initiatives are of relatively recent origin. However, we need to acknowledge that RJ in fact has inherited some traditional features of justice – but not traditional to Western societies. What is interesting is that the lineage for RJ runs back to ways in which indigenous peoples resolved conflicts before the emergence of modern justice systems. Indeed, Braithwaite has argued that 'Restorative justice has been the dominant model of criminal justice throughout human history for all the world's peoples' (quoted in Winfree, 2002: 286).

## Task

Does this sound simplistic and/or unlikely? Have a read of:

- Bottoms (1999) 'Interpersonal violence and social order in prisons'. In *Crime and Justice: A Review of Research*, Vol. 26, Chicago: University of Chicago Press, pp. 205–81. If your university subscribes, you will be able to access this at: <http://www.jstor.org/pss/1147687>

The message here is that before the modern society and the modern state people used to deal locally with conflicts using community-based methods. If a problem arose community elders would call those concerned together in an open, informal way and conflicts could be resolved through dialogue, mutual understanding and agreement. This is one reason why modern RJ initiatives have emerged in countries such as North America, Australia and New Zealand, where elements of indigenous forms of justice – practised by First Nation 'Indians', Aboriginal Australians and Maoris – not only survive but play an active role in guiding 'Western' models of RJ.

I have already mentioned victim–offender mediation schemes, which were perhaps the forerunner of putting RJ into practice. Since their arrival we have seen a variety of schemes, which are fully or partially based on RJ principles, and include:

- **(Family group) conferencing.** Introduced in New Zealand as an alternative to the formal cautioning of young offenders, and since used in many countries (including Britain), family conferencing involves a meeting of offenders and their supporters, the victims and their supporters, and a facilitator. All participants take part on a voluntary basis – although, if the offender refuses, other formal actions might be taken as a consequence. After both sides 'tell their story', the conference will usually end with an agreement between the parties, which sets out a plan to deal with such things as reparation to the victim. Unanimity over the agreement is usually required.
- **Sentencing circles.** In Saskatchewan, Canada, indigenous justice principles have been matched with 'Western' justice to produce 'sentencing circles'.

These are similar in some respects to family group conferencing, with two exceptions. Firstly, they operate *after* a person has been found guilty in a formal court hearing, rather than as an alternative to a court hearing. Secondly, they focus much more on community involvement in the RJ process. Community participation in RJ is for some a key component of a fully restorative programme of justice as it shifts 'ownership' of justice from the courts and justice professionals to the community at large – where it was located originally (as we saw above). The individual must accept responsibility for the offence and agree to take part in the process. The circle involves literally a circle of participants discussing and deciding on sentence. The circle includes the sentencing judge, offenders, victims, community members, community elders, peers and families of the offenders and the victims. Circle members are asked to speak in turn around the circle and anyone can ask questions of the others in the circle at any time. At the end of the process a sentence is agreed, which might involve restitution/compensation, peer counselling, mediation, special programmes (e.g. race awareness programmes), and even a ceremony (based on indigenous traditions).

**Task**

VOM, (family group) conferencing and sentencing circles are three of the five key types of RJ classification. Ensure you read Newburn (2007 pp. 751–8) and are clear on the other two approaches by making notes under the following headings:

- Court-based restituitive and reparative measures
- Citizens' panels and community boards

NB:

- Make sure you understand the current youth justice sentencing options
- Make sure you understand the difference between healing circles and sentencing circles

These are all examples of how RJ values and principles can be put into practice, **alongside or instead of the formal processes of justice**. As we can see, they make justice victim-centred and forward-looking, and seek to appeal to the positive sides of human behaviour and human relations rather than the negative sides.

## Task

Read the section on Assessing restorativeness in Newburn (2007: 758–9).
If you cannot access this, look at McCold and Wachtel's (2003: 3) diagrammatic representation of 'Types and degrees of restorative justice **practice**' that Newburn has reproduced in this section. <http:// fp.enter.net/restorativepractices/paradigm.pdf>. Read their text too.
What are the implications of the following points?

- To what extent 'restorativeness' *should* and *is likely to* involve the active participation of the victim (an encounter between the victim, the offender and the community) in the way that Van Ness and Strong (2006) outline? Newburn has summarised this on pp. 758–9, but you can check out the full text at Van Ness and Strong (2006).
- Sherman and Strang (2007) <http://www.esmeefairbairn.org.uk/docs/ RJ_exec_summary.pdf> found that 'The evidence consistently suggests that victims benefit, on average, from face-to-face RJ conferences. The evidence is less clear about other forms of RJ', and Strang (2002) previously found that victim attendance rates at mediation vary greatly.

So, if McCold and Wachtel's diagram were redrawn so that the size of the text for each of the categories used represented the number of victims involved in each of the categories, what would it look like?

Would there be an imbalance?

What are the ramifications for the type of RJ interventions that should be developed?

You can get a clue by going to the Youth Justice Board's own figures, based on Youth Offending Teams (YOTs') quarterly returns, during 2006–07:

- 'Evidence of victim satisfaction, contact and participation', <http://www.yjb.gov.uk/en-gb/practitioners/WorkingwithVictims/ RestorativeJustice/Targets.htm>:
  - 38,574 victims of youth crime were offered the opportunity to participate in an RJ process;
  - 31 per cent (17,728) chose to participate in indirect/non face-to-face RJ;
  - 15 per cent (5,952) chose to participate in face-to-face RJ.

## Work-related task

If you work in the area of restorative justice, or have contacts who do, try to construct your diagram based on data for your local RJ initiatives on the above basis. If the data either does not exist or is difficult to use, think about the level of commitment there is to evaluation and whether RJ 'works'.

What does this tell you about the balance between restoration, reparation and compensation?

- Make notes on any differences you encounter between what you expected to find and what you actually found.
- Make notes on what you see as the implications for the use of RJ as a 'separate' justice approach, or as one that might be incorporated with other types of punishment approaches.

Then read Dignan's (2005) outline of the three broad policy approaches and make sure you understand the difference between abolitionism, separatism and reformism. Again, Newburn (2007) summarises this on p. 748, but it is worth reading the original text before deciding which of these options is most realistic.

- Dignan, J. (2005) *Understanding Victims and Restorative Justice*. Maidenhead: Open University Press.

### Rounding up

The case presented here is that RJ is the way forward in criminal justice, as in other areas of conflict and conflict resolution. This is not just an academic case. A recent study of public attitudes to criminal justice in the UK and in other countries (Roberts and Hough, 2005) concluded that when the public are made aware of RJ programmes and options they tend to be very supportive, rating RJ options significantly higher than retributive measures (Roberts and Hough, 2005: 128–47). This should not be surprising and certainly not to advocates of RJ – restorative justice is all about **listening** to what people prefer, **involving** them in decision-making and reaching conclusions on which people can **agree**. It is about what justice should be about in a civilised and humane society.

### The problem with restorative justice

RJ, when presented as above, can sound terribly convincing, but, as Newburn (2007: 766) argues, there are many limits to restorative justice and there is a gap between the sometimes evangelical rhetoric of RJ supporters and the evidence in practice. In a nutshell, restorative justice does not work! For instance, if you ask the victims, the cosy notion of community elders deciding on justice issues is a problematic one – just think of the Salem witch hunts for instance. It is the sort of overly romanticised notion of a past golden age that commentators like Nils Christie envisage, but that never truly existed.

---

**Additional study**

Is this a fair comment? Don't take our word for it, read:

- Christie, N. (1977) 'Conflicts as property'. *British Journal of Criminology*, 17, 1–16; and/or
- Christie, N. (2004) *A Suitable Amount of Crime*. London: Routledge.

---

As Hudson (2003: 75–92) has noted, it cannot be assumed that particular groups and particular offences are amenable to the type of agreement required between offender and victim. Are offences of domestic or racial violence (including rape and murder) going to be suitable for the restorative approach, for instance? Certainly, women's groups have campaigned for more penalisation and prosecution of domestic violence offenders. How can you apply restorative approaches to drink-driving?

Hudson (2003) has drawn on Garland's notion that communities and victims within those communities require retribution, through **due process**, in order to relieve the distress and anxiety caused by crimes. The sentencing circles lauded above are fraught with problems, particularly for women. Some have argued that the subordination of women in Canadian First Nations communities ensures that they cannot enter the circle on an equal basis (Goel, 2000; Stewart *et al.*, 2001, Cameron, 2006). Denney and Ellis (2006) have argued that women in this context often felt intimidated by the male 'elders' who wield disproportionate power within the community and whose views might be seen as part of the problem rather than the solution in relation to sexual and domestic violence offences.

---

**Additional study task**

For those who are tasked with looking at the relationship between RJ, gender and race, there is free access to an excellent overview:

- Kathleen Daly and Julie Stubbs, 'Feminist theory, feminist and anti-racist politics, and restorative justice', <http://aegir-4.itc.griffith.edu.au/_data/assets/pdf_file/0012/50331/kdaly_part2_paper11.pdf>

This is an earlier version of Chapter 9 of the Johnstone and Van Ness (2007) *Handbook of Restorative Justice* (see further reading section below) which you should use if you have access to it.

If this does not seem a convincing argument, consider the following two cases. First, one of the most internationally notorious examples of 'restorative justice' is that of Mukhtaran Bibi, whose twelve-year old brother was falsely accused of having an affair with a higher-caste woman in Pakistan (a later formal investigation found that in fact he had been sodomised by two of the higher-caste group). As a result, in 2002, the *panchayat* (tribal council) ruled by male village elders, ordered that Mukhtaran should be gang-raped to restore the damage done. Mukhtaran was duly dragged in front of several hundred people through a field and into a dwelling and gang-raped for more than an hour. Her father and brother had been forced to wait outside. She was left feeling suicidal by this and said, 'In this area there is no law and no justice. A woman is left with one option, and that is to die.' However, she did take the men to court and six men – four rapists and two village elders – were sentenced to death, though eventually only one was found guilty on appeal and received a life sentence. Mukhtaran now lives with a 24-hour police guard 100 metres from the high-caste group and has received death threats.

**Case study task**

Read the source of this story:

- 'She was gang-raped on the orders of village elders. Yesterday, Mukhtaran Bibi's nightmare began again', *Guardian*, 4 March 2005, <http://www.guardian.co.uk/international/story/0,1430203,00.html>; and
- <http://ko.offroadpakistan.com/pakistan/2004_10/mukhtaran_bibi_sentenced_to_be_raped.html>

Make notes on:

- the extent to which this was/was not restorative justice (this is going to be a relative answer, not either/or);
- the extent to which the formal retributive justice process was desired by the victim(s); and
- whether the power imbalance in any community restoration attempt can ever be truly accounted for without recourse to the 'formal' and 'retributive' court processes.

The second case involves consideration of the type of process referred to above in South Africa, but this time in Northern Ireland. As part of the peace process, former illegal 'freedom fighting' organisations are being drawn into the justice system. They may be seen as more representative of their communities and offer, as suggested above, an alternative and re-storative approach to the retributive penal system. However, what happens when power interests are threatened within the community?

In this case, Robert McCartney, a catholic from a republican family, was beaten to death outside a Belfast bar in January 2005 over a minor dis-agreement. The IRA admitted that two of the four men who murdered McCartney were IRA members. As Chrisafis notes (see the next task box for the reference), as a result the IRA came under pressure from its own community 'where there has often been tacit support of punishment beat-ings' (retribution in paradise?). As a result, and in accordance with the restorative approach, the IRA held two meetings with the McCartney fam-ily in the presence of an independent observer. The result of the first 5½-hour meeting? The IRA offered to shoot those directly involved in the murder of Robert McCartney! Consider the response of the victim's family who made it clear that:

> they did not want physical action taken against those involved. They stated that they wanted those individuals to give a full account of their actions *in court* [emphasis added].

**Case study task**

Read the article by Chrisafis on the McCartney case and the other articles about the case you will be able access from there.

- 'IRA offers to shoot McCartney killers', *Guardian*, 9 March 2005, <http://www.guardian.co.uk/Northern_Ireland/Story/0,2763, 1433478,00.html>

Think about the relationship between formal 'retributive' justice and restorative justice.

Why are victims in these types of cases so determined to have their day in court?

What does this say about the viability of restorative justice irrespec-tive of social and cultural conditions?

These issues have essentially occurred within single communities, albeit with an uneven power distribution within them. How much more problematic would the RJ situation be if the offences occurred across community bound-aries, where it is difficult to reconcile cultural differences?

The above examples might be seen as extreme, and perhaps not the type of cases where RJ would be applicable. Yet, this is the crux of the matter: how do you decide where to draw the line if RJ is not appropriate for all offences? Is it the seriousness of the offence alone? Do you consider aggravating and mitigating circumstances in addition? Do you rely on the victim's (or their family's) willingness even in the most serious cases? Is there a reliable way of deciding, and establishing who decides which option to take? RJ does not have consistent answers to these questions. Indeed, it is clear that the original proponents of RJ have had to introduce the notion of a 'punitive ladder' or **'enforcement pyramid'** to deal with offenders who do not comply with RJ ideals (see Hudson, 2003: 87–8).

**Work-based task**

Read Newburn's (2007: 760–63) section on the limits of restorative justice.

How convincingly practical are Ayres and Braithwaite's regulatory pyramid and Braithwaite and Daly's domestic violence enforcement pyramid?

If you are a serving police officer or other criminal justice worker who has dealt with domestic violence cases, you can use your experiences reflectively here, but try to make these entries succinct and relate them to practical issues (e.g. the value of your force's powers and policy in reducing domestic violence, obstacles encountered) rather than simply how you 'feel' about them.

If the offender does not comply with RJ and there is no notion of a punitive ladder (or even if there is), another key criticism of RJ kicks in: **secondary victimisation.** Imagine that you have been assaulted in a public place with witnesses who are prepared to testify that there was no provocation and that you were traumatised and injured. You are given the option of proceeding with the case through the standard 'retributive' court process where, according to the arguments for RJ above, you will be sidelined while the offender and the state fight it out. You are also offered the option of VOM, and decide to go for this. You meet the offender under VOM conditions, who apologises and agrees to write a letter of apology and pay you £200 in compensation. You initially feel that this was a more satisfactory way of dealing with the offending against you, but after three months you have received neither the letter nor the money. You have to complain to the courts that VOM has not worked and they have to have put in place a formal enforcement process to compel the offender to comply or be subject to resentencing through the formal retributive process. You have been victimised once, and then the offender has been able to victimise you again by ignoring the agreement to compensate you. The criminal justice process has left you on the sidelines and you have had to do all of the work to get the case reactivated. Is that an improvement on the retributive process?

Some would also argue that RJ, with its narrow offence-resolution focus, takes us no further than retribution in accounting for social, economic and cultural contexts and that there is often still a power imbalance in favour of the state, especially where mediation or conferencing is police-led, as it is, for instance, in Thames Valley.

We also find that provision of RJ is uneven, and therefore lacks reliability and consistency, and that the actual practice is found to be far removed from the underlying theory.

## Task

Use the index in Hudson (2003) to find these issues and read her expanded arguments.

### Effectiveness

The evidence base for whether RJ is effective is also shaky. Firstly, because so few good-quality evaluations have been carried out, and, secondly, because the focus is often on measuring participants' views, feelings and perspectives on how satisfied they were with the process, but not on whether future offending was reduced. If, for instance, in the case posed above where you had been assaulted, you finally got your letter and your money, but found out that two months later the offender murdered someone in similar circumstances, would you feel justice had been served well?

## Additional study task

If you have been tasked to assess the evidence base on whether RJ 'works', make notes on what you think under the following headings:

How flimsy is the evidence base on whether RJ prevents future offending?

Does evaluation rely too much on views and feelings?

Check for yourself and evaluate the evidence available through Restorative Justice Online: <http://www.restorativejustice.org>

Read Newburn's (2007: 763–6) section on Assessing restorative justice and ensure you make notes under the following headings and are clear about the key ways in which 'outcomes' are measured:

- preventing (re)offending;
- victim satisfaction;
- criminal justice agency/community satisfaction;
- cost effectiveness/benefits.

Which of these might convince you best that RJ 'works' and why?

Are there other ways in which RJ outcomes could/should be measured?

Explain why and how this might be achieved.

Have a look at a selection of RJ case studies provided at: <http://www.restorativejustice.org.uk/?Media:Case_Studies>.

Match these case studies to the typical evaluation outcomes that are listed above and reassess the extent to which you think RJ works.

In addition to the evidence included in Newburn's section, there are a number of other evaluations of the effectiveness of RJ. Some of the key ones are:

- Evidence from meta-analysis suggests that RJ approaches, including mediation appear to significantly reduce reoffending in terms of recidivism (Braithwaite, 2002; Latimer *et al.*, 2005).
- Braithwaite and Liebmann (1997) followed up mediation work in Leeds and found a reconviction rate of 44.6 per cent for participants of mediation compared to 54.2 per cent for the predicted rate.
- Shapland *et al.* (2006) evaluated three Home Office funded mediation schemes and found that, overall, recidivism rates for participants were significantly lower after 2 years than those of control groups (though it was difficult to account for self-selection bias). A 4th report for the Ministry of Justice Research Series (10/08) has been published: <http://www.rethinking.org.nz/images/newsletter%20PDF/Issue%2040/Joanna%20Shapland_Does%20restorative%20justice%20affect%20reconviction_2008.pdf>
- It is also worth reading Robinson and Shapland (2008) 'Reducing recidivism: a task for restorative justice?'. Vol. 48, No. 3, <http://bjc.oxfordjournals.org/cgi/reprint/48/3/337>
- Umbreit (1994) in evaluating mediation schemes reported victims felt higher restitution and reported a reduction in fear of re-victimisation.

Perhaps more significant still are the following key points made by Sherman and Strang (2007) in their main report, <http://www.esmeefairbairn.org.uk/docs/RJ_full_report.pdf>:

- In general, RJ seems to reduce crime more effectively with more, rather than less, serious crimes.
- RJ works better with crimes involving personal victims than for crimes without them.
- RJ works with violent crimes more consistently than with property crimes, the latter having the only evidence of crime increases.

They conclude 'These findings run counter to conventional wisdom, and could become the basis for substantial inroads in demarcating when it is "in the public interest" to seek RJ rather than CJ.'

---

**Work-based task**

If your work involves restorative justice, summarise to what extent do your policies and practices run counter to or in accordance with Sherman and Strang's evidence?

---

The evaluation evidence needs careful reading and fair grasp of statistical techniques, but many of the studies have good summaries which can be understood at a conceptual and logical level. The key issue here is to make a reasoned decision about the relative merits of the different measures of the success or otherwise of RJ initiatives, especially in relation to the issues raised in the next chapter when considering whether prison works.

*Public opinion*

We also need to contextualise public opinion on RJ compared to retributive sentencing. While it is true that Hough and Roberts (2004 in Roberts and Hough, 2005: 135–6) found that the public were supportive of RJ, the scenarios presented to the public in that research were relatively mild, for instance a seventeen-year old committing burglary. Roberts and Hough (1995: 137) also cite the Doble Research Associates' 1994 research in Vermont, which showed overwhelming support for RJ for non-violent offences. However, when asked about offences of armed-robbery and rape 'results changed dramatically: the public were almost unanimous in preferring to imprison these offenders'. Also, consider Strang *et al.*'s (2006) view that although victims felt more satisfied with restorative rather than retributive sentences, it appeared this satisfaction might be more strongly related to their involvement in the sentencing process rather than the mediation process.

*Rounding up*

In concluding this critique of RJ, it is clear that RJ advocates must provide consistent answers to the following questions:

- What are they trying to achieve?
- Who should be targeted and at which criminal justice process points?
- How formalised and/or integrated with traditional criminal justice can RJ be before it becomes something else?
- Is it always culturally appropriate?
- How can the safeguards for victims, offenders and the community be balanced and ensured without being in the 'shadow of the courts'?
- How can secondary victimisation be prevented and if it cannot, then how can enforcement be achieved without recourse to retribution.
- How can evaluation be improved to show the value of RJ?

---

NB These points are taken from Hudson (2003) – you will need to read this source and cite the page numbers from it if you are going to use these points in your assessment (i.e. do not cite this book, *Debates in Criminal Justice*, as your source; use it as a jump-off point).

---

Alternative sources to consolidate your learning on RJ issues are:

- Johnstone (2004), Chapter 18 in the *Student Handbook of Criminal Justice and Criminology*; and
- Hoyle and Young (2002), Chapter 28 in *The Handbook of The Criminal Justice Process*.

You may also wish to link your learning to the issues raised about victims' rights by starting with:

- Zedner (2002), Chapter 13 in *The Oxford Handbook of Criminology* (3rd edn), esp. pp. 428–48.
- Dignan, J. (2005) *Understanding Victims and Restorative Justice*. Maidenhead: Open University Press.

---

### Thinking beyond the debate

Some see the argument in the terms in which we have presented it above, with an easy trade-off as outlined in Zehr's (1985, 2003) presentation of the contrasts between the two philosophies (see Figure 5.2).

| Retribution | Restorative justice |
|---|---|
| • Violation of state | • Violation of victim by offender |
| • Based on guilt/blame for past | • Problem solving for future |
| • Adversarial and process normative | obligations/liabilities |
| • Pain to punish, deter, prevent | • Dialogue and negotiation normative |
| • Right rules, justice by intent | • Reconciliation of victim/offender |
| • Interpersonal obscured by state v | • Justice = right relationship = outcome |
| offender | • Value of interpersonal conflict recognised |
| • Social injury matched by another | • Repair of social injury |
| • State is abstractly representing sidelined | • Community facilitates restoration |
| community | • Encourages mutuality |
| • Encourages competitive individual values | • Victim rights recognised, offender |
| • Victim ignored, offender passive | responsibility |
| • Offender accountability = suffer | • Understanding impact and helping |
| retribution | to put right |
| • Legal *not* moral, social, political, | • Context *is* moral, social, political, |
| economic | economic |
| • Abstract debt to state | • Concrete debt to victim and community |
| • Focus on past behaviour | • Focus on harm caused by offender |
| • Stigma permanent | • Stigma removable |
| • No repentance/forgiveness required | • Facilitates repentance/forgiveness |
| • Depends on proxy professionals | • Direct involvement of participants |

*Figure 5.2* Contrasting aspects of retributive and restorative justice

However, when you have completed your reading, you should begin to feel that while this simple framework may be a good starting point from which to build your understanding of the key philosophies of punishment, it may be a little too simplistic to match the empirical evidence of law- and policy-making in practice.

Indeed, Zehr (2002, 2003) himself has retrenched his views somewhat, arguing that both RJ and retribution have similar goals of vindication, but use different methods to attain it. Daly (2002) has also argued that RJ and retributive measures can have similar goals and, further, that some forms of it, such as mediation, are 'punishing' in their own right (see also Zerona, 2007). She also argues that RJ needs to be applied more realistically and developed alongside retributive and rehabilitative measures (Daly, 2000).

## Task

You should also look at Braithwaite's optimistic and pessimistic accounts of RJ as summarised by Newburn (2007) p. 764.

Do you need to review your evidence for abolitionism, separatism and reformism at this point?

*RJ in prison: the ultimate in reformism?*

---

If your work is prison-related and/or your assessment is focused on this area, the following subsection will be useful to you.

---

While Van Ness and Strong (2006) argue that custodial settings are an obstacle to reparative relationships, others (Edgar and Newell, 2006) argue that RJ principles can be usefully utilised in prison. Indeed, there is already a number of initiatives that combine custody and RJ – see: <http://www.restorativejustice.org/prison>.

One such programme, for example, is the Sycamore Tree Project: <http://www.restorativejustice.org/RJOB/sycamore-tree-victim-awareness-and-restorative-justice/?searchterm=sycamore>. This programme focuses on victim awareness and has been delivered in the UK by the Prison Fellowship since 1998. The programme is underpinned by RJ principles in order to encourage offenders to understand the impact of their crimes on their victims and the wider community. Participants are expected to take responsibility, learn to understand the value of forgiveness and reconciliation, recognise opportunities for change and restoration, participate in a symbolic act of restitution and understand the benefits and responsibilities of RJ. Feasey and Williams (2009) carried out a relatively large pre- and post-programme evaluation which showed significantly positive general attitude changes and a significant increase in victim empathy. However, the study does not extend to subsequent reconvictions and the same issues highlighted above in terms of the evidence base also apply here.

---

### Additional study

For a recent US perspective on RJ in prisons read:

- Swanson, C.G. (2009) *Restorative Justice in a Prison Community: Or Everything I Didn't Learn in Kindergarten I Learned in Prison.* Lanham, MD: Lexington.

---

*Psychological evidence and victim awareness programmes*

If you work with offenders (e.g. in probation or youth offending teams) it is important to consider further an area of evidence that supports the

RJ perspective, but that is rarely included in the RJ literature. This is the body of work by psychologists examining the relationship between empathy and self-reported offending, linking poor perspective taking and moral reasoning to offending (see Kohlberg, 1976). In particular, there are fairly consistent findings that offenders exhibiting low empathy levels tend to score more highly on self-reported offending (Jolliffe and Farrington, 2007; Palmer and Hollin, 1999). While this evidence is not straightforward, it has been used as one of the major influences in setting up victim awareness programmes of the type discussed immediately above, given the congruence with increasing awareness, cognitive understanding of harm, developing accountability and starting to make amends (Putnins, 1997). Victim awareness (VA) approaches are also much cheaper than full mediation processes (Liebmann, 2007).

## Task

Look at the following findings from different studies about the outcomes of VA programmes and consider the strength of this evidence. Are the findings strong enough to conclude that VA works?

- Groenhuijen and Winkle's (1991) evaluation of a victim awareness programme for young offenders found it increased awareness of the seriousness of offending actions and enhanced understanding of the victims' experiences.
- Launay and Murray (1989) concluded that a youth custody centre programme was effective in giving participants a greater understanding of the impact of their crimes on their victims.
- Umbreit (1994) evaluated VA programmes underpinned with RJ principles and included victims of crimes speaking to the groups and found that:

  o  'responsibility' and 'accountability' became more concrete for offenders;
  o  victims reported higher levels of satisfaction and were less fearful of re-victimisation;
  o  self-reported measures showed greater awareness, understanding and victim satisfaction.

May *et al.* (2008) carried out 'recent resettlement surveys re-offending analysis' (RSRA) on three types of prison interventions, one of which included attending a victim awareness course. They found that these interventions were significantly associated with a reduced likelihood of reoffending.

*Other philosophies of punishment*

As noted in the introduction to this debate, it is essentially a vehicle to ensure that you understand all the basic philosophies of punishment and their relationship to each other.

If you are on a Master's or joint/combined honours course and have not studied basic concepts in criminal justice before, or you feel you need a refresher on philosophies of punishment, at this point it is worth revisiting the question 'Why punish?' You can then read some basic reference sources that seek to answer, or at least explain the question.

### Task

- Read: Marsh, Cochrane and Melville (2004) *Criminal Justice: An Introduction to Philosophies, Theories and Practice.* London: Routledge.

Chapter 1 is a good basic introduction. There are some exercises in this chapter that will be helpful to you. It is not envisaged that this book will be used as a major reference source in your assessment, mainly because it is so basic and it does not offer huge amounts of evidence or additional sources. Chapter 2 is also very helpful as background knowledge, but not essential.

Much of the argument presented by Marsh *et al.* (2004), as they acknowledge, is based on the following book:

- Walker, N. (1991) *Why Punish?* Oxford: Oxford University Press.

Further spadework may be required depending on the level and requirements of your assessment and the following will help to broaden and deepen your understanding.

### Additional study task

Read Chapter 12 of Davies, Croall and Tyrer (2010) and try to draw a diagram or a model of the types of (sometimes conflicting) pressures from various penal philosophies that make up the real-life policy process.

Then read (or reread) the section on 'Recent legislation and policy developments' in Chapter 1 of Davies *et al.* (2010: 30–37).

Look at the reasoning behind the Criminal Justice Act 1991. You will find that the framework is based on notions of: just deserts/ proportionality/commensurate seriousness.

With this in mind, note down what you understand from your reading about CJA 1991:

- To what extent is it 'retributive'?
- To what extent is it reparative (RJ-based)?
- What other penal philosophies can you identify?
- What does this mean in terms of the usefulness of penal philosophies in terms of analysing shifts in sentencing policy and practice?

Do not just take the word of Davies *et al.* (2010) for it – you can check the Act itself at:

- <http://www.opsi.gov.uk/ACTS/acts1991/Ukpga_19910053_en_1. htm>

The issue, as with models of criminal justice, is that there are no pure systems or processes – we only study them in this way as 'ideal-typical' constructions in order to explain the underlying principles on which our justice process is built and is continually refashioned. It is perhaps more rewarding to evaluate the overall balance, or imbalance, of philosophies of punishment within a piece of legislation, or in changes in legislation and policy over time, rather than whether these 'principles' or 'tendencies' appear to conflict. Certainly, you will find in the CJA 1991, which was a watershed in criminal justice policy, the notion of bifurcation. The idea here is that the most serious offences are punished in a retributive way, but that for all other offences, other types of punishment, including RJ are possible and even desirable.

This brings us back to Roberts and Hough (2005: 146) who argue that:

> The public appear willing to forego a considerable part of the punishment imposed if there are clear benefits to the victim (for example, in terms of restitution). At the same time, if the crime is relatively serious, the public seem opposed to the use of a restorative solution.

It could be that RJ is a viable option for all but the most serious offences (and these form the bulk of the criminal justice case load each year), while retribution, rehabilitation and other philosophies are required only for the most serious offences. But what of Sherman and Strang's (2007) finding that RJ works better for more serious offences?

Perhaps the key test of which type of justice should be prevalent is asking what the victims think. Interestingly, it was found that:

- victims are no more punitive (retributive) than the general public;
- about one-third of victims are willing to consider RJ only disposal (1984 *British Crime Survey*);
- two-thirds of victims would consider either mediation or reparative compensation, but 47 per cent also wanted prosecution and punishment (1984 *British Crime Survey*).

**Additional study task**

If you would like to read up on this more fully, see:

- Mattinson, J. and Mirrlees-Black, C. (2000). *Attitudes to Crime and Criminal Justice: Findings from the 1998 British Crime Survey.* Home Office Research Study 200. London: Home Office, pp. 35–44. Also available online at: <http://uk.sitestat.com/homeoffice/ homeoffice/s?rds.hors200pdf&ns_type=pdf&ns_url=>    <http:// www.homeoffice.gov.uk/rds/pdfs/hors200.pdf>

If victims are no more retributive than the public, a key question is then 'What do the public think justice is for?' It is also as salient to ask, 'What do those who work in the criminal justice agencies think it is for?'

**Additional study task**

Look at the appendices of the Halliday report online at: <http://www.homeoffice.gov.uk/documents/halliday-report-sppu/>

Are the public retributive?

Do sentencers' views on retribution match those of the public?

Does anyone think justice is about deterrence?

What does this say about whether justice reflects public opinion, or popular newspaper headlines?

**Additional study task**

Read the following article:

- Mascini, P. and Houtman, D. (2006) 'Rehabilitation and repression: Reassessing their ideological embeddedness'. *British Journal of Criminology*, 46, 822–36.

Is this convincing in explaining that the public, or victims, can be for both retribution and rehabilitation at the same time?

Could the same apply to retribution and restoration?

## End note

Consider the following two cases. On 2 December 2005, the *Daily Mail* carried two stories about two appalling murders. The first headline was in relation to Anthony Walker: 'How a mother's forgiveness has reminded us all what it is to be truly human.' The second headline, based on the views of the father of Paul Tanner who was murdered in cold blood during a robbery, ran: 'I want vengeance . . . These days you are not supposed to talk of revenge, but I want revenge and retribution.' Ask yourself which of these reactions you might be most likely to feel and ponder the notion of whether any justice process can ever get the balance right? This begs the question of legal pluralism. In the above cases, given the victims' relatives' views, would it be appropriate, or even workable, to use RJ for the first case and traditional criminal justice for the second?

## References

Ashworth, A. (2002) 'Sentencing'. In M. Maguire, R. Morgan and R. Reiner (eds) *The Oxford Handbook of Criminology* (3rd edn). Oxford: Oxford University Press, Chapter 29, esp. pp. 1077–83.

Braithwaite, J. (1989) *Crime, Shame and Reintegration*. Cambridge: Cambridge University Press.

—— (2002) 'Setting the standards for restorative justice'. *British Journal of criminology*, 42(3), 563–77.

—— (2003) 'Principles of restorative justice'. In A. von Hirsch, A. Roberts and A. Bottoms (eds) *RJ and Criminal Justice*. Oxford: Hart Publishing, pp. 1–20.

Braithwaite, S. and Liebmann, M. (1997) *Restorative Justice: Does it Work?* Bristol: Mediation UK.

Cameron, A. (2006) 'Stopping the violence: Canadian feminist debates on restorative justice and intimate violence', *Theoretical Criminology*, 10(1), 49–66.

Daly, K. (2000) 'Revisiting the relationship between retributive and restorative justice'. In H. Strang and J. Braithwaite (eds) *Restorative Justice: Philosophy to Practice*. Aldershot: Dartmouth/Ashgate, pp. 33–54.

—— (2002) 'Restorative justice: the real story', *Punishment and Society*, 4:1, 55–79.

Davies, M., Croall, H. and Tyrer, J. (2010) *Criminal Justice: An Introduction to the Criminal Justice System in England and Wales* (4th edn). London: Longman.

Denney, D. and Ellis, T. (2006) 'Race, diversity and criminal justice in Canada: a view from the UK'. Retrieved on 1 June 2006, from: <http://www.internet journalofcriminology.com/Denney,%20Ellis%20&%20Barn%20-%20Race,%20 Diversity%20and%20Criminal%20Justice%20in%20Canada.pdf>

Dignan, J. (2005) *Understanding Victims and Restorative Justice*. Maidenhead: Open University Press.

Duff, R.A. (1986), *Trials and Punishments*, Cambridge: Cambridge University Press.

Edgar, K. and Newell, T. (2006) *Restorative Justice in Prisons: A Guide to Making it Happen*. Winchester: Waterside Press.

Fattah, E. (2002) 'From philosophical abstraction to restorative action, from senseless retribution to meaningful restitution: just deserts and restorative justice revisited'. In E. Weitekamp and H.-J. Kerner (eds) *Restorative Justice: Theoretical Foundations*. Cullompton, Devon: Willan.

Faulkner, D. (1996) *Darkness and Light: Justice, Crime, and Management for Today*. London: Howard League.

Feasey, S. and Williams, P. (2009) *An Evaluation of the Sycamore Tree Programme: Based on Crime Pics II data*. Sheffield: Sheffield Hallam University, Hallam Centre for Community Justice.

Goel, R. (2000) 'No women at the centre: the use of Canadian sentencing circles domestic violence cases', *Wisconsin Women's Law Journal*, 15, 293–334.

Goodey, J. (2005) *Victims and Victimology: Research, Policy and Practice*. Harlow: Longman/Pearson, pp. 152–217.

Groenhuijen, M. and Winkle, F.W. (1991) 'The focussing on victims program as a new substitute penal sanction for youthful offenders'. Paper presented at 7th International Symposium on Victimology, Rio di Janeiro, Brazil.

Home Office (1997) *No More Excuses: A New Approach to Youth Crime in England and Wales*. London: Home Office.

Hoyle, C. and Young, R. (2002) 'Restorative justice: assessing the prospects and pitfalls'. In M. McConville and G. Wilson (eds) *The Handbook of The Criminal Justice Process*. Oxford: Oxford University Press, pp. 525–48.

Hoyle, C., Young, R. and Hill, R. (2002) *Proceed with Caution: An evaluation of the Thames Valley Police Initiative in Restorative Cautioning*. London: Joseph Rowntree Foundation.

Hudson, B.A. (2003) *Understanding Justice: An Introduction to Ideas, Perspectives and Controversies in Modern Penal Theory* (2nd edn). Buckingham: Open University Press.

Jackson, J. and Hough, M. (2005) *Understanding Public Attitudes to Criminal Justice*. Maidenhead: Open University Press.

Johnstone, G. (2002) *Restorative Justice: Ideas, Values, Debates*. Cullompton, Devon: Willan.

—— (2004) 'Restorative and informal justice'. In J. Muncie and D. Wilson (eds) *Student Handbook of Criminal Justice and Criminology*. London: Cavendish, Chapter 18, pp. 265–78.

Jolliffe, D. and Farrington, D.P. (2007) 'Examining the relationship between low empathy and self-reported offending'. *Legal and Criminological Psychology*, 12, 265–86.

King, M. (1981) *The Framework of Criminal Justice*. London: Croom Helm.

Kohlberg, L. (1976) 'The development of modes of moral thinking and choice in the years ten to sixteen'. In T. Lickona (ed.) *Moral Development and Behavior: Theory, Research and Social Issues*. New York: Holt, Reinhart and Winston, pp. 31–53.

Latimer, J., Dowden, C. and Muise, D. (2005) 'The effectiveness of restorative justice practices: a meta-analysis'. *The Prison Service Journal*, 85(2), 127–44.

Launay, G. and Murray, P. (1989) 'Victim/offender groups'. In M. Wright and B. Galaway (eds) *Mediation and Criminal Justice*. London: Sage Publications, pp. 200–212.

Liebmann, M. (2007) *Restorative Justice: How it Works*. London: Jessica Kingsley.

McIvor, G. (2004) 'Reparative and restorative approaches'. In A. Bottoms, S. Rex and G. Robinson (eds) *Alternatives to Prison: Options for an Insecure Society*. Cullompton, Devon: Willan, pp. 162–94.

McLaughlin, E., Fergusson, R., Hughes, G. and Westmarland, L. (eds) (2003) *Restorative Justice: Critical Issues*. London: Sage.

Maguire, M. and Corbett, C. (1991) *A Study of the Police Complaints System*. London: HMSO.

Marsh, I., Cochrane, J. and Melville, G. (2004) *Criminal Justice: An Introduction to Philosophies, Theories and Practice*. London: Routledge.

Marshall, T. (1984) *Reparation, Conciliation and Mediation: Current Projects in England and Wales*. Home Office Research and Planning Unit, Paper 27. London: HMSO.

Martinson, R. (1974) 'What works? Questions and answers about prison reform'. *The Public Interest*, 35(Spring), 22.

Mattinson, J. and Mirrlees-Black, C. (2000) *Attitudes to Crime and Criminal Justice: Findings from the 1998 British Crime Survey*. Home Office Research Study 200. London: Home Office, pp. 35–44.

May, C., Sharma, N. and Stewart, D. (2008) *Factors Linked to Reoffending: A One Year Follow Up of Prisoners Who Took Part in the Resettlement Surveys 2001, 2003 and 2004*. London: Ministry of Justice.

Mayhew, P. and van Kesteren, J. (2002) 'Cross-national attitudes to punishment'. In J.V. Roberts and M. Hough (eds) *Changing Attitudes to Punishment*. Cullompton, Devon: Willan.

Newburn, T. (2007) *Criminology*. Cullompton: Willan.

Palmer, E.J. and Hollin, C.R. (1999) 'Social competence and sociomoral reasoning in young offenders'. *Applied Cognitive Psychology*, 13, 79–87.

Putnins, A.L. (1997) 'Victim awareness programs for delinquent youths: effects on moral reasoning maturity'. *Adolescence*, 32, 1–5.

Roberts, J.V. and Hough, M. (2005) *Understanding Public Attitudes to Criminal Justice*. Maidenhead: Open University Press/McGraw-Hill.

Sanders, A. and Young, R. (2000) *Criminal Justice* (2nd edn). London: Butterworths.

Shapland, J., Atkinson, A., Atkinson, H., Colledge, E., Digan, J., Howes, M., Johnstone, J., Robinson, G. and Sorsby, A. (2006) 'Situating restorative justice within criminal justice'. *Theoretical Criminology*, 10(4), 505–32.

Sherman, L. and Strang, H. (2007) *Restorative Justice: The Evidence*. London: The Smith Insitute.

Stewart, W., Huntley, A. and Blaney, F. (2001) 'The implications of restorative justice for aboriginal women and children survivors of violence: a comparative overview of five communities in British Columbia'. Ottawa: Law Commission of Canada, available at <http://www.lcc.gc.ca/en/themes/sr/rj/awan/awan_toc.asp>

Strang, H. (2002) *Repair or Revenge: Victims and Restorative Justice*. Oxford: Oxford University Press.

Strang, H., Sherman, L., Angel, C.M., Woods, D., Bennet, S., Newbury-Birch, D. and Inkpen, N. (2006) 'Victim evaluations of face-to-face restorative justice conferences: a quasi-experimental analysis'. *Journal of Social Issues*, 62(2), 281–306.

Umbreit, M.S. (1994) 'Crime victims confront their offenders: the impact of a Minneapolis mediation program'. *Research on Social Work Practice*, 4, 436–47.

Van Ness, D. (2002) 'The shape of things to come: a framework for thinking about a restorative justice process'. In E. Weitekamp and H.-H. Kerner (eds) *Restorative Justice: Theoretical Foundations*. Cullompton, Devon: Willan.

Van Ness, D. and Strong, K.H. (2006) *Restoring Justice* (3rd edn). Cincinnati, OH: Anderson Publishing.

Walker, N. (1991) *Why Punish?* Oxford: Oxford University Press.

Winfree, L. (2002) 'Peacemaking and community harmony: lessons (and admonitions) from the Navajo peacemaking courts'. In E. Weitekamp and H.-H. Kerner (eds) *Restorative Justice: Theoretical Foundations*. Cullompton, Devon: Willan.

Zedner, L. (2002) 'Victims'. In M. Maguire, R. Morgan and R. Reiner (eds) *The Oxford Handbook of Criminology* (3rd edn). Oxford: Oxford University Press, Chapter 13.

Zehr, H. (1985) 'Retributive justice, restorative justice'. Occasional Paper No.4 of New Perspectives on Crime and Justice series. MCC Canada Victim Offender Ministries Program and MCC US Office on Crime and Justice.

—— (2002) *The Little Book of Restorative Justice*. Intercourse, PA: Good Books.

—— (2003) 'Retributive justice, restorative justice' (reprint of Zehr 1985). In G. Johnstone (ed.) *A Restorative Justice Reader: Texts, Sources, Context*. Cullompton, Devon: Willan, pp. 69–82.

Zerona, M. (2007) 'Aspirations of restorative justice proponents and experiences of participants in family group conferences'. *British Journal of Criminology*, 47, 491–509.

## Further reading and reference sources on restorative perspectives

Crawford, A. (2009) 'Restorative justice and antisocial behavior interventions as contractual governance'. In Knepper, P., Doak, J. and Shapland, J. (eds) *Urban Crime Prevention, Surveillance, and Restorative Justice: Effects of Social Technologies*, Boca Raton, FL: CCRC Press Taylor & Francis.

Hoyle C. (ed.) (2009) *Restorative Justice: Critical Concepts in Criminology* (4 Volumes) London: Routledge, see <http://media.routledgeweb.com/pdf/9780415450010/9780415450010.pdf>

Johnstone, G. and Van Ness, D.W. (2007) *Handbook of Restorative Justice.* Cullompton: Willan.


*For a comparative approach, look at:*

Sullivan , D. and Tifft, L. (2006) *Handbook of Restorative Justice: A Global Perspective.* Abingdon: Routledge International. You can get a good idea of the materials and the approach in this book by looking at the preview provided by Google books at: <http://books.google.com/books?id=u-apPNMIJNEC&pg=PA89&dq=Van+Ness+%26+Strong+(2006)+Restoring+Justice&cd=5#v=onepage&q=Van%20Ness%20%26%20Strong%20(2006)%20Restoring%20Justice&f=false>

UNODC (2006) *Handbook on Restorative Justice Programmes*, available at <http://www.unodc.org/pdf/criminal_justice/06-56290_Ebook.pdf>

# 6  Prison works! Or prison works?

*Tom Ellis and Chris Lewis*

This chapter is divided into five sections. The case for imprisonment is made in the first section. The second section addresses various misapprehensions about prisons. The case against imprisonment is argued in section 3, which outlines how imprisonment fails to achieve any of its main aims and section 4 looks at the reality of imprisonment. Section 5 closes the chapter with suggestions on how to proceed beyond the debate.

NB For Master's or combined/joint honours students with no previous experience of studying prisons, it is best to first read Chapter 28 of Tim Newburn's (2007) *Criminology*, pp. 684–94.

## Prison works!

### Prison works in Europe

There are over 2.5 million prisoners throughout the world and most countries have shown a recent increase (Walmsley, undated). This applies just as much to the USA as it does to small states such as Malta. Nearly all countries in Europe have an increasing prison population and where most countries are following a policy of growing the prison population there is a strong likelihood that they are doing this for a purpose, namely that governments believe that prison works. Why would they believe this if it were not true? After all, prisons are expensive places to build and maintain and the money spent on them could be spent on schools, hospitals or welfare payments.

## Task

Check the figures for prisoners in different countries by visiting the website of the World Prison Brief of the International Centre for Prison Studies at <http://www.kcl.ac.uk/depsta/law/research/icps/worldbrief/>

What patterns come from the Brief: e.g. which countries have highest prison rates? Which have more foreigners in prison? Which have a high proportion of young people among their inmates? Which are increasing the fastest, or even decreasing?

For a US source that provides useful data on imprisonment showing how the trends have developed over the last half century, look at: <http://www.november.org/graphs/>

But first we must ask what is meant by 'Prison works'? Those who believe that prison works rely on common sense which they claim says that:

- **High prison numbers cause crime to fall.** This is an uncomfortable lesson for many so-called liberals but it is only common sense to the vast majority of the population and most of the press.
- **High prison numbers give greater security to the general population.** This is especially true for victims of crime, who do not like to see those who offended against them still at large in the community, possibly to repeat the crime.

If we look in more detail at the most recent police crime and prison figures for Western Europe, we can see what the patterns are in Table 6.1.

In 11 of the 14 countries in this table, including our own, prison numbers increased and in eight of these countries the crime rate fell or remained static. Thus, for those countries at least it can be argued that 'prison worked', at least in the sense of preventing crime.

## Additional study

You can find the latest figures for all EU countries on the website of the European Statistics Office EUROSTAT. Check the figures up to 2007 at <http://epp.eurostat.ec.europa.eu/statistics_explained/index.php/Crime_statistics> or update these figures from the same website in future years.

*Table 6.1* Changes in crime and prison numbers 1999–2007

| Country | Annual change in prison numbers 1999–2007 | Annual change in crime* 1999–2007 |
|---|---|---|
| Austria | +4.0% | No significant change |
| Belgium | +2.0% | No significant change |
| Denmark | +2.0% | −2.0% |
| Finland | +3.0% | −2.0% |
| France | +2.0% | No significant change |
| Germany | −0.4% | No significant change |
| Ireland | +2.0% | −0.5% (02–06) |
| Italy | No significant change | −0.4% |
| Luxembourg | +9.0% | +1.1% |
| Netherlands | +4.0% | No significant change |
| Portugal | −1.0% | +2.0% |
| Spain | +5.0% | No significant change (05–07) |
| Sweden | +4.0% | +1.0% |
| England & Wales | +2.0% | −4.0% |

If we look specifically at England and Wales, we are fortunate in being able to measure crime by a far more precise instrument, the British Crime Survey. Looking at the last ten years, overall crime has continued to fall before stabilising (Home Office, 2009). Since peaking at 19.4 million crimes in 1995, the BCS measure has fallen to 12.6 million in 2002 and further still to around 10.7 million in 2008–9. This was a period when the government pursued a policy on continuing growth in prison numbers from 46,000 in 1991 to 66,000 in 2001 and around 83,900 in mid-2009 (Ministry of Justice, 2009).

Was it just a coincidence that crime fell as the prison population was rising and that it has happened in other countries than our own? After all, no one can dispute that, while in prison, offenders cannot break into your house, whereas if offenders are on a community sentence they still have free time to steal. A common-sense interpretation is that prison has acted as a deterrent and more prison will continue to reduce crime.

## Task

As criminologists we must look further into this than the press is inclined to do. We know that there is a difference between two sets of figures going in opposite directions and one set being the cause of the other. We know that there are likely to be many intervening variables, many of which we do not know about or are able to measure.

Look at the Penal Policy File sections of the *Howard Journal* over this period:

• <http://www.wiley.com/bw/journal.asp?ref=0265-5527&site=1>

Penal policy files are included in each issue and outline the changes that occur in criminal justice police and legislation. Is this a good database for a dissertation project?

We also know that many eminent criminologists and liberal thinkers have criticised the government over the last 15 years of prison growth. Their arguments may seem reasonable to us and many of these key issues are summarised later in this chapter. However, what is also clear is that any arguments to reduce the prison population have not been able to shake the simple statements already made above: that in recent years, throughout Europe and elsewhere, when prison rates have risen, then crime seems to fall. The onus must be on those who wish to prove there is no connection.

**Task**

For a concise summary of the case that prison has worked in this country in the last 15 years read the 2008 *Times* article by the criminologist David Green. This can be accessed at:

• <http://www.timesonline.co.uk/tol/comment/columnists/guest_contributors/article4353433.ece>

Where might the value of this evidence lie in the hierarchy of evidence outlined in Chapter 1?

### *Prison works in the USA as well!*

If we compare the situation as it developed here with that of the USA, we find the same pattern of evidence to show that prison works. Ideally, as social scientists, we would like to conduct an experiment in letting one country reduce its prison population at the same time as another country increased its prison population and see whether crime changed at all. In fact, by sheer accident, the USA and England and Wales did just that during the 1980s and early 1990s. In the USA a vigorous effort was made to incarcerate more criminals. At the same time, crime fell dramatically. In England and Wales, however, the Home Office pursued an anti-prison policy up to 1993, preferring 'community sentences' and 'just deserts' when offenders' past records were not taken into account when sentencing. During this period crime increased dramatically in England and Wales. After 1993 the English policy was reversed and criminals faced an increased risk of imprisonment. Crime subsequently fell. Were the experiences of these two countries again simply a coincidence?

US and UK researchers compared crime and imprisonment rates for murder, rape, robbery, assault, burglary and motor vehicle theft (Langan and Farrington, 1998). An offender's risk of being caught, convicted and sentenced to custody increased in the USA for all six of these crimes, but fell in England and Wales for all but murder. Crime rates increased for all offences in England and Wales but decreased for all offences in the USA (e.g. see Figure 6.1). What is interesting is that the US burglary rate, measured by a victim survey, was double that in England and Wales in 1981, but half by 1995. From 1980 to 2000 there was an 80 per cent decrease in recorded 'burglaries leading to immediate custody' in England and Wales, down from 7.4 per cent to 1.5 per cent.

Why did the risk of punishment fall in England and Wales and increase in the USA? Langan and Farrington (1998) suggest three possible causes in England and Wales:

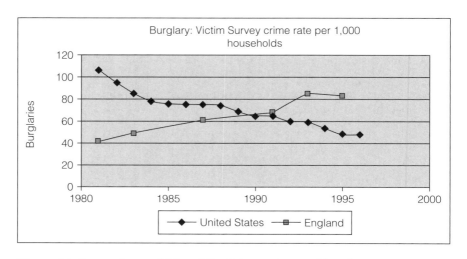

*Figure 6.1* Comparisons of US and English experience of burglary victimisation

- increased use of cautions/unrecorded warnings (a policy that subsequently changed);
- the Police and Criminal Evidence Act 1984 increased safeguards for the accused;
- the Crown Prosecution Service, set up in 1986, led to an increased tendency to drop cases.

Two factors caused the decreasing risk of prison in the period 1987–1991:

- A liberal Home Secretary, Douglas Hurd, encouraged judges and magistrates to make less use of prison.
- Theft of a motor vehicle was downgraded in 1988 to a non-indictable offence, encouraging the use of non-custodial sentences.

In 1993, after the appointment of a new Home Secretary, Michael Howard, much of this changed. This change was announced in Howard's 1993 conference speech claiming that 'prison works' and presented to Home Office officials as a *fait accompli*.

## Task

To understand the policy arguments better, first read the 1999 speech of the Conservative politician Douglas Hurd, which reflects prison policy when he was Home Secretary around 1990 and the prison population was around 40,000. Hurd criticises the overuse of prisons by saying that prisons are 'widely regarded as a wastepaper basket into which we throw offenders because we do not want to think about them again' <http://www.independent.co.uk/arts-entertainment/podium-douglas-hurd-the-government-must-cure-our-sick-nicks-1125255.html>.

In the mid-1990s prison policy changed. The now 'classic' 'Prison Works' statement was made by Michael Howard when Conservative Home Secretary in 1993. Read Howard's statement at <http://www.prnewswire.co.uk/cgi/news/release?id=33411>. Make notes on 'how' Howard says prison is 'working'.

What philosophies of punishment best explain his view?

Has prison been restricted to the most serious offenders as he envisaged?

Comparison of the policies pursued in the USA and in England and Wales suggests that for crimes such as robbery, burglary, car theft and assault, increasing the risk of imprisonment has produced a fall in crime in the

USA. It appears to be less effective for murder and rape, and the psychological motives or emotional drives leading to these offences are less subject to rational calculation. Where the crimes are calculated to acquire material possessions, potential offenders may be more likely to weigh up the risk of being punished.

### Task

A more extensive but still readable summary of the Langan and Farrington (1998) research and other similar work including a longer term study of data from 1950 to 2000 has been produced by the Think Tank Civitas in 'Does prison work: overseas evidence, 2003'. This can be read at <http://www.civitas.org.uk/data/twoCountries.php>.

### Effect of incapacitation

Incapacitation is only one aim of administering a sentence of imprisonment and therefore only one of the benefits. Even if no deterrent effect is assumed, the incapacitation effect of imprisoning on average another 35,000 criminals (as occurred in England and Wales between 1993 and 2007) would have been substantial. The Home Office (2001a) report *Making Punishment Work* estimated that the average offender carried out 140 offences per year. The variation was large, and offenders who admitted having a drug problem were committing an average of 250 offences per year.

If each prisoner carried out the average numbers of offences identified by the Home Office, then nearly five million offences against the public would have been prevented by 12 months in jail. If they were high-rate offenders, the effect would have been around nine million offences. This is the incapacitation effect. This would account for most of the fall in BCS estimates of crime from 19 million to under 11 million.

### Task

Check for yourselves by going to <http://www.crimestatistics.org.uk>. Use this to update your figures for your assessment submissions and/or examinations.

Since 2010 the coalition government has given priority to reducing public expenditure. It is too early to see the impact of this on the criminal justice system as a whole, although plans to reduce prison numbers and close some prisons have been announced.

Prison policy remained remarkably consistent under the Labour governments of 1997–2010. Since 2010 the coalition government has given priority to reducing public expenditure and improving the functioning of prisons as a means of reducing offending. However, apart from the public expenditure cuts, which any alternate government would have had to make in a similar way, there seems little change to criminal justice policy.

Why not evaluate this yourself and see the extent to which the three main political parties have converged in their thinking on prisons policy?

- Read: the plans of the coalition government to improve the way the justice system works, particularly the working of the prisons; see <http://www.justice.gov.uk/docs/breaking-the-cycle.pdf>
- See the way that commentators felt that prison policies were moving closer during the May 2010 election on the BBC comparison website <http://news.bbc.co.uk/1/hi/uk_politics/election_2010/8515961.stm#subject=crime&col1=conservative&col2=labour&col3=libdem>

### Economic arguments for and against prison

It has been argued that prison is 'too expensive' and the usual arguments are that it costs much more to keep someone in prison than it does to punish them with a community sentence. Claims vary, but are usually that the costs of prison are up to four times those of other disposals. However, we need to acknowledge that the proper economic argument is a much more complex one, involving looking at costs of many other things as well. Matrix (Matrix Knowledge group, 2007) has looked into this in detail and come up with a definitive cost–benefits analysis of whether prison sentences are an economical way of reducing offending in those populations which are at risk of further offending.

The first thing they noticed was that the prison population at the time of their study was around 81,500, with a capacity-development programme in place to allow for a further 10,000 inmates by 2012. This plan will, in itself, reduce the unit cost of keeping a prisoner in jail and make any current analyses rapidly out of date. This also confirms the results of the Carter report (Carter, 2007).

Their main analysis looked at the costs based upon what programmes were available and the evidence that such programmes worked. They unpacked which prison programmes and which community programmes worked and came up with a more definitive answer to the question, 'What level of re-offending is likely after such programmes?' Figures 6.2 and 6.3 show that it is not always community sentences that work best. Treatments

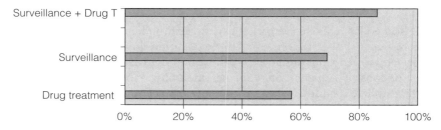

*Figure 6.2* Predicted level of reoffending for community sentences

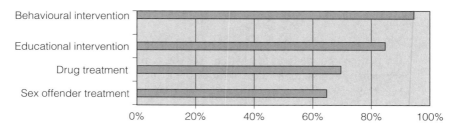

*Figure 6.3* Predicted level of reoffending for enhanced prison sentences

in the community are by no means always more effective than those in prison, and when they are, the difference is by no means great.

Putting all these reoffending rates together with the costs, the Matrix researchers concluded that:

> alternatives to prison are not always a viable option. . . . enhanced prison sentences (incorporating some form of training or treatment) are more effective in reducing reoffending than prison without additional interventions. Such prison sentences result in a saving to the taxpayer, including victim costs, of between £17,000 and £130,000 per adult offender.
>
> (Matrix Knowledge group, 2007)

This implies that investment in such prison programmes, enabling a higher proportion of prisoners to undergo treatment or training, would be very cost-effective indeed.

**Task**

Don't rely on our interpretation. The Matrix report is a very readable document that is worth examination: it can be accessed at:

- <http://www.matrixknowledge.co.uk/wp-content/uploads/economic-case-for-and-against-prison.pdf>

Matrix is not the only group that has concluded that prisons can be more cost-effective. The think tank Civitas has done a similar calculation with similar conclusions. The Home Office estimates (Home Office, 2002) there are about 100,000 persistent offenders responsible for half of all crime, of which about 20,000 are in prison at any one time. Civitas estimated the costs of building prison places for all these offenders and providing for them for 12 months. Even if prison building costs are charged to a single financial year and added to the running costs, they arrive at a total of £144,000 per offender – a saving of over £150,000 for each offender. In fact as Civitas argues:

> When we make more accurate assumptions, based on official crime figures and Home Office estimates of the social and economic costs of crime, incarcerating persistent offenders is not only good value for money, it's a bargain.

**Task**

The think tank Civitas is a strong influence on Conservative Party policy, and their analyses may therefore become very instrumental in prison policy. Go to their website <http://www.civitas.org.uk> to see their report quoted above and judge for yourself whether their arguments are valid.

While you are on their website, look at their thinking and analyses on the subject of the prison population. For example, their 2009 paper, 'Prison policy briefing: serious, violent and persistent offenders', presses for more imprisonment of serious, violent and persistent offenders. Such a policy would be likely to add another several thousand to the prison population, with consequent additional costs but also, as Civitas would argue, potential further falls in crime levels.

## Misconceptions about prison

### 'Too many people are sent to prison'

We are told that England and Wales imprison too many people and that we have the highest level of imprisonment in the EU. That is true as can be seen from a study of the world prison data available in Walmsley (undated).

**Task**

Revisit the figures available in the 'World Prison Brief' produced by Walmsley at King's College London and continually updated. To make sure you know what is available on this Brief visit the website <http://www.kcl.ac.uk/depsta/law/research/icps/worldbrief/> and check the data for this country and at least two others.

1. How will you choose the most appropriate countries to compare with England and Wales?

2. Is the USA the best comparator country?

However, we should not be looking at figures that consider imprisonment per head of population. We should look at imprisonment rates per 100,000 recorded crimes. England and Wales has one of the highest crime rates among industrialised countries and would expect to have to put more people in prison. The International Crime Victim Survey states that people in England and Wales experience more crime per head than virtually any other country in the survey (Van Dijk *et al.*, 2007 ). And this has nothing to do with the police counting more crime than in other countries, which is true, but simply that English people claim, with justification, that they suffer more crime than other countries. A consideration of prison population and volume of crime indicates that we have **lower** imprisonment rates in comparison with some other EU countries – lower than both France and Spain. On this argument, we are not locking away too many people; we are not locking away enough! In fact, not until we reach a prison population of 100,000, most likely by 2012, will we be at 'the correct rate' when compared with France and Spain.

**Task**

To understand further the results from the International Crime Victimisation Survey, it is a good idea to look, at least briefly, at the summary of results *Criminal Victimisation in International Perspective: Key Findings from the 2004–2005 ICVS and EU ICS* which is available through the Dutch WODC web site of crime and justice statistics: see <http://www.nicic.org/Library/022967>. The graphs of victimisation rates are particularly useful as they show that England and Wales is frequently at the top of the chart for suffering more victimisation than other countries.

The Home Office Report *Making Punishment Work* (Home Office, 2001a) found that many offenders with a long track record of previous convictions were not being sent to prison. Only 33 per cent of males over 21 were sentenced to immediate custody when they had ten or more previous convictions. If they had between three and nine previous convictions, only 21 per cent were sent to jail. Even for serious offences like burglary, males over 18 received a custodial sentence in only 70 per cent of cases when they had ten or more previous convictions.

### *'Community sentences show lower reconviction rates than custodial sentences'*

In fact, nothing seems to work particularly well in dealing with offenders. Figures 6.2 and 6.3 have shown that reconviction rates are high for all types of prison and community sentences.

### Task

Those in custody cannot usually reoffend, as we normally understand it, unless it is a very serious offence. But there is a vast amount of bullying, theft and stealing within prison itself, which would probably count as reoffending were it committed outside. The figures released on reconviction rates are therefore quite misleading.

### Read:

- Samantha Banbury (2004) 'Coercive sexual behaviour in British prisons as reported by adult ex-prisoners'. *Howard Journal of Criminal Justice*, 43(2), 113–30.

Can we make a moral judgement that this matters less because victims are offenders themselves?

The following research has highlighted the inadequacies of community sentences:

- Less than half of offenders on Intensive Supervision and Surveillance programmes finished the programme (Youth Justice Board, 2004).
- Offending Behaviour Programmes (costing at least £2,000 per offender) have been found not to work – Home Office figures show that reconviction rates did not fall (Falshaw *et al.*, 2003).
- Drug Treatment and Testing Orders (DTTOs) – 70 per cent of offenders did not complete their order and 80 per cent were reconvicted of a crime within two years (Hough *et al.*, 2003).

## 'Prison does not and cannot rehabilitate'

Nearly half of the juveniles in custody are six years behind the educational standards expected for their age, and a quarter, ten years behind. Adults are similarly disadvantaged. It is a fallacy to say that prisons are not addressing this issue: for example a fundamental aim of a Detention and Training Order (now the main custodial sentence for the under-18s) is to ensure they keep up their education. Half the time is spent in custody, and half in the community continuing the education begun in prison. Rehabilitative programmes are now in place in almost all prisons and Young Offender Institutions. This is an 'unreported penal revolution' (Rose, 2002). In fact, prisons are putting right what has been a failure of educational institutions. The government is worried about public reaction to money being spent on prisoners' rehabilitation. In fact, it should be proud to stand up and inform the public that reduction of crime through the rehabilitation of prisoners is a fundamental aim. In contrast, the National Audit Office (2004) found that only 6 per cent of Youth Offending Teams were providing young offenders with the opportunity to continue the education they had started while in custody.

The effects of rejecting the bleak 'nothing works' philosophy go beyond the courses themselves, to prison culture as a whole. The growth in prisons of offending behaviour programmes, drug treatment programmes and literary programmes, and the increasing involvement of ordinary prison officers in running them, means that the old, militaristic ethos is breaking down in many prisons. Research has long shown that prisoners on these types of programme are less violent, more sociable and easier to work with.

### Task

A good example of a prison programme that can work is shown by the Kainos Community Programme Challenge to Change, which continually produces lower reconviction rates than for prisons as a whole. Research by Portsmouth University confirming this can be found on the Kainos website at <http://www.kainoscommunity.com/portsmouth%20university%20evaluation.html>.

## 'Short prison sentences increase offending'

The Home Office (2002) White Paper *Justice for All* noted that prisoners given short sentences were reconvicted at a higher rate than those who served longer sentences and concluded that short spells in prison 'increase the chances of reoffending'. There is no doubt about this, but Civitas argues that it seems strange to blame an offender's subsequent criminal activity on the very short space of time that that offender was held in prison. They argue that the subsequent offending is much more likely to be due to the attitudes and experiences that were established in the life that the offender had prior to entering the prison. If high reconviction rates are associated with short prison sentences then the rational answer to that problem is longer prison sentences. Home Office research conducted by Taylor (2000) has indicated that reconviction rates can drop by almost 10 per cent by increasing a sentence by 18 months. The benefits of this are that the public are protected from the offender's criminal activity for a longer period of time, the offender can develop key skills whilst within the prison environment, and the financial costs of high reconviction rates are significantly lowered. The Social Exclusion Unit (2002) has estimated that an offender who commits further crime after release costs an additional £65,000, which is almost three times the cost of keeping someone in prison for a year.

## Task

Read Rod Morgan's chapter on Imprisonment in any of the *Oxford Handbook of Criminology* editions – perhaps the older the better in this regard – and consider whether Taylor's argument is a case of 'back to the future?'

Then read: 'Managing offenders on short custodial sentences', (2010) National Audit Office <http://www.nao.org.uk/publications/0910/short_custodial_sentences.aspx>

### *'Prison causes family break-up'*

*Justice for All* (Home Office, 2002) made a further assertion about the effects of imprisonment. It argued that prison can break up families and 'place children at risk of an inter-generational cycle of crime', citing research that stated over 40 per cent of sentenced prisoners claim to have lost contact with their families since entering prison. It also points to the far lower reoffending rates of those who are able to maintain family contact.

The problem with this statement is that family contact is not always positive. There is much evidence that contact with some families can have a detrimental effect on a potential or actual offender. Research by Farrington and Painter (2004) identifies the risk factors in offending behaviour. For example, if a boy has a brother convicted of a criminal offence, his chance of offending and being convicted is about 50 per cent. Likewise, the Social Exclusion Unit (2002) reported that 43 per cent of prisoners had other family members who had been convicted (compared with 16 per cent of the general population) and 35 per cent had a family member who had been in prison. In such cases the family is certainly a bad influence. Thus, to state that any form of family contact will be a positive effect upon the offender is nonsensical.

It is also not true that prison causes the breakdown of positive family contacts. Contact with families is often sporadic anyway, with the Social Exclusion Unit (2002) stating that 47 per cent of male prisoners had run away from home as a child, and 27 per cent had been in care (compared with 2 per cent of the general population). Some 81 per cent were un-married prior to imprisonment, nearly 5 per cent were sleeping rough and 32 per cent were not living in permanent accommodation. If families do separate when an offender is imprisoned, the cause is more likely to be the disapproval of the offending behaviour rather than the custodial sentence itself. The prison service, however, attempts to rebuild the lives of prisoners shattered by criminal activity. The 'Storybook Dads' scheme is now being expanded to more and more prisons across the country (<http://www.storybookdads.co.uk>). Fathers record a story for their child, which is downloaded to a CD, with music and sound effects added. The scheme was awarded the Butler Trust Award 2005. We should ask how likely this sort of father–child contact is to have occurred whilst the offender was involved in crime.

### 'Prison does not act as a deterrent'

This is very difficult to (dis)prove and perhaps a more common-sense approach is needed:

- **Think about Scenario A**: With 100 per cent guarantee nobody would be hurt and 100 per cent guarantee you would never be apprehended, would you steal money from a bank?
- **Think of Scenario B**: With 100 per cent guarantee nobody would get hurt and 50 per cent chance you would be caught, would you steal money from a bank?

It is almost inevitable that the number of people answering 'yes' to Scenario B would be lower than the number answering 'yes' to Scenario A. The reasons are many and varied, but one finding that always emerges when responses are analysed is that few people want to spend time in prison. Felson (1994: 9) provides a useful illustration:

> When you touch a hot stove you receive a quick, certain, but minor pain. After being burned once, you will not touch a hot stove again. Now think of an imaginary stove that burns you only once every 500 times you touch it, with the burn not hurting until five months later. Psychological research and common sense tells us that the imaginary stove will not be as effective in punishing as the real stove.

According to this argument, prison is a deterrent but the problem lies with the certainty of punishment. Increasing the likelihood of punishment would add to the already present deterrent effect of imprisonment.

### Conclusion

*Justice for All* (Home Office, 2002) lists the aims of sentencing as to: protect the public; punish; reduce crime; deter (others as well as the criminal); incapacitate; reform and to rehabilitate; and promote reparation. No current sentencing option fulfils all of those aims but the one option that has the potential to achieve those aims is the prison system. If the government pursues a policy of promoting alternatives to prison then they will weaken two effects of prison:

- **Deterrence**: They will give offenders the impression that there is a smaller chance of them being imprisoned for their offences. If we see crime as essentially a rational choice, offenders' calculations will be more likely to err on the side of committing crime.
- **Incapacitation**: There will be a weakening of the incapacitation effect because more offenders will be within the community rather than in prison. As we have already seen, Intensive Supervision and Surveillance Orders were supposed to combat this problem; but they have been shown to be less intensive than hoped, with less than half of offenders finishing the programme (Youth Justice Board, 2004).

Many offenders lead disordered, chaotic, uncontrolled lives. This is why in many cases they have committed crime in the first place. Control theory tells us that those who have strong bonds of attachment, involvement, commitment and belief are less likely to commit crime (Hirschi, 1969). Prison is ordered, controlled and disciplined. This lifestyle needs emulating in the lives of prisoners. Prison can give them some respite from the chaos, from the temptations and from the struggle to survive. Longer prison sentences are needed to give people the time and opportunity to change their behaviour, to change their habits, to learn new skills, basically to change their lives.

Deprivation of liberty is the legitimate **retribution** democratic nations take against citizens who reject civilised conduct. That is not to say that prison is currently the answer, but prison *could* be 'the answer' if enough resources and time and commitment were put into it. Clearly, causes of crime need to be tackled to reduce the numbers pouring into the prison system. Prison should not be the place for children, for the mentally ill and for many non-violent offenders, particularly women. However, we must be strong in our determination to punish those violent and persistent offenders who have had so many chances to go straight but refused to respond to them.

# Prison works?

## *Prison numbers as a political artefact*

All but the most stalwart of abolitionists would accept that some form of deprivation of liberty is necessary, perhaps to satisfy society's just demands for measured retribution (see Chapter 5), but mainly to ensure effective incapacitation for those dangerous offenders who might offend again. However, the actual level of the prison population in any one country is much more a political artefact than a simple mechanistic response to the level or the mix of crime that comes to the notice of the police. In fact the level of the prison population is to a large extent a choice made by those ruling the country.

---

**Task**

Revisit Table 6.1 above and make notes on the patterns in the relationship between changes in prison populations and crime figures. Make your own table based on the following:

| *Type of change* | *Number of countries* |
| --- | --- |
| Prison population up and crime down | |
| Prison population up and no change in crime | |
| Prison population down and crime down | |
| Prison population up and crime up | |
| No change in prison population and crime down | |

What does this relatively simple table suggest about the relationship between changes in prison populations and in crime levels?

---

When there is public and media pressure for more imprisonment, this can easily be delivered, as long as the money is made available, by passing more punitive laws and issuing more severe sentencing guidelines. The level of imprisonment in England and Wales over the period 1995 to 2010 has more than doubled. When there is political agreement that there is advantage in seeking a low prison population, then this can be achieved, albeit with more difficulty and probably over a longer period. The level of imprisonment in Finland actually halved between 1950 and 1980.

## Task

Look at the two examples of how prison numbers have either increased or decreased, by political action, in England and Wales and in Finland. They are worth examining to see what factors were involved on both occasions.

The Ministry of Justice has produced a short summary of the balance between the different drivers increasing the prison population in England and Wales:

- 'The story of the prison population 1995–2009', Ministry of Justice website <http://www.justice.gov.uk/publications/docs/story-prison-population.pdf>
- See also Jon Silverman's (2010) rather different take in 'Counter-blast: How Tony Blair fed the feral beast of the media and savaged the criminal justice system', *Howard Journal of Criminal Justice*, 49(2), 166–9.

In contrast, political rulers in Finland decided that they wished to reduce the high levels of imprisonment they had suffered up to 1940, when under Russian rule. The story of how they did so and how the principles could be applied in other countries are summarised in a paper by Tapio Lappi-Seppala at: <http://www.unafei.or.jp/english/pdf/PDF_rms/no61/ch06.pdf>.

Given that countries that wish to reduce the prison population can do so, we should ask what drives the thinking that imprisonment should be reduced. Firstly, of course, there is the cost aspect: whatever the economic arguments advanced earlier in this chapter, there is no doubt that, in order to run a justice system which has a large prison population, it has to be paid for up front. In fact, it costs an average of £40,992 to keep a person in prison (House of Commons written answers, 18 April 2006, see <http://www.publications.parliament.uk/pa/pahansard.htm>). The Social Exclusion Unit (2002) found reoffending by ex-prisoners costs society at least £11 billion per year. But savings from lower crime can only be realised at a later stage, if indeed they are cashable at all.

There are two other main reasons that we examine in this section and the next. Firstly, the aims of imprisonment are easy to set out but, in practice, they have proved to be very difficult to deliver. Secondly, delivering a prison system that is decent and humane has proved very difficult to do and most prison systems offend human dignity, both of those imprisoned and of society as a whole. After all it was Winston Churchill himself, when Home Secretary in 1910 who said 'The mood and temper of the public in regard to the treatment of crime and criminals is one of the most unfailing tests of the civilisation of any country.'

### Additional study task

If your assessment (or dissertation) addresses these issues, you may wish to look at the arguments in this section in more detail by reading the book by Thomas Mathiesen (1992) *Prisons on Trial*.

The core question posed by Mathiesen is whether prison can be defended as a major type of punishment and sanction in modern society. It is an international assessment that takes stock of prison as a sanction and fully discusses the evidence and material concerning rehabilitation, general deterrence, incapacitation and individual deterrence and justice. Mathiesen concludes that prison finds no defence in any of them.

### *Prison fails in its main purposes*

It is generally accepted that the main aims of imprisonment can be summarised by looking at prison in the following four different ways and judging whether prison can be said to work against any of these criteria (Mathiesen, 1992):

- prison as rehabilitation;
- prison as retribution;
- prison as deterrent;
- prison as incapacitation.

In fact, those who argue about whether prison works largely talk past each other due to the different measures they use and the different philosophies of punishment that underpin those measures. In short, it depends on what you mean by 'work'.

### Task

See Chapter 5 on the philosophies of punishment. The following materials can be integrated and developed if the focus of your assessment is on custody.

### *Prison as rehabilitation*

A main purpose of sentencing in general and imprisonment in particular is that after the sentence is complete, the offender should be less likely to reoffend. This is traditionally measured in various ways, all of which involve

*Table 6.2* Measures of reoffending for different disposals, based on a 2007 cohort

| Type of disposal | Actual offending rate | No. of offences per 100 offenders | No. of severe offenders per 100 offenders |
|---|---|---|---|
| Community orders | 36.6% | 123.9 | 0.7 |
| Custody | 47.2% | 223.2 | 1.0 |
| Suspended (prison) sentence orders | 35.6% | 115.5 | 0.8 |
| Overall total | 39.0% | 147.3 | 0.8 |

Source: Table A5, Reoffending of adults: results from the 2007 cohort http://www.justice.gov.uk/publications/docs/reoffending-adults-2007.pdf

measuring how likely the offender is to come back in contact with the justice system, either by being arrested, convicted in court, or returned to prison.

The Ministry of Justice regularly monitors reoffending and the most recent results (always check for later updates) are summarised in Table 6.2, with three measures: the actual offending rate within 12 months of end of sentence: the number of offences committed: and the number of severe offences committed.

All measures are worse for those released from prison: 47.2 per cent are reconvicted within 12 months, compared with 36.6 per cent of those who complete community sentences or 35.6 per cent of those who complete suspended sentences. The number of offences for which people are reconvicted is much higher for ex-prisoners: at 2.23 per offender compared with 1.24 for those completing community orders or 1.16 for those completing suspended sentences. There is a similar pattern if the severity of sentences is looked at.

Such results have led to the thinking that to ease overcrowding in prisons, those sentenced to short sentences of six months or so should be given a community order, because of the savings that would be made.

## Task

There are many newspaper articles proposing community orders instead of short jail terms, of which the following is typical:

- 'No jail for short-sentence offenders', *Observer*, 4 November 2007, <http://www.guardian.co.uk/society/2007/nov/04/prisons.prisonsand probation?gusrc=rss&feed=networkfront>

One of the main reasons why prison fares worse in terms of rehabilitation than other sentences is that it is very expensive to offer prisoners any form of programme with a rehabilitative element. Thus, of a prison population of over 84,000, no more than about 10,000 will complete such a programme. Moreover, although it has been shown that some such programmes can be effective in reducing offending, this is only the case when those delivering the programmes are well-trained, experienced and enthusiastic in what they are doing. Falshaw *et al.* (2003) have shown, in their evaluation of cognitive skills programmes in prison, that, although significant reductions can occur in reconviction rates, such success is difficult to replicate and/or maintain over a long period.

The argument has been made that, if there were to be a larger investment in such cognitive programmes, reconviction rates might be reduced considerably. John Halliday (2001) in his report on the future of sentencing claimed that 'if programmes are developed and applied . . . to the maximum extent possible, reconviction rates might be reduced by 5–15 per cent (from 56 per cent after 2 years to around 40 per cent)'. However, this claim, despite being quite a conservative one, has been criticised by respected criminologists with Tony Bottoms claiming that 'Sadly, . . . this appears to be a most unfortunate, and indeed in some ways reckless, claim' (Bottoms, 2005: 62).

Moreover, the likelihood that money will be made available to increase the investment in cognitive programmes is low and reducing considerably because of the public expenditure crisis from 2010 onwards. In early 2010, each prison has been asked to reduce expenditure by 5 per cent and, in many cases, this has resulted in proposals to cut back on programmes at the expense of greater expenditure on security.

*Prison as retribution*

Although retribution ranks highly in the tabloid media and in the minds of sentencers, there is less evidence that the public as a whole is as interested in retribution. The Halliday (2001) report asked the public their views on sentencing and concluded that:

> The general public are very clear about what they want sentencing to achieve: a reduction in crime. When asked unprompted what the purpose of sentencing should be, the most common response is that it should aim to stop re-offending, reduce crime or create a safer community. Next most frequently mentioned are deterrence and rehabilitation. Very few spontaneously refer to punishment or incapacitation.

However, the same report also found a clash between the views of the public and the views of sentencers. Halliday found that all three sentencing groups (Judges, Magistrates and District Judges) placed 'punishment' at the top of their purposes of sentencing. This difference with the general public highlights the question of whether the current freedom allotted to sentencers is too broad, especially as other stakeholders within the justice system, such as Justice's Clerks, the CPS, probation officers, solicitors and barristers, many of whom have much more hands-on experience of offenders and victims, placed rehabilitation at the head of their purposes of sentencing.

Retribution also brings home the question of whether deprivation of liberty as such is sufficient punishment or whether a tough regime within the prison should also be imposed. This is an unresolved question, as can be seen from the discussion in the next section about the way that the current delivery of imprisonment leads to degrading conditions for both prisoners and staff. This is partly due to the rationing of resources and can be seen from the way that the public expenditure cuts starting in 2009 give priority to maintaining security of inmates.

### Prison as deterrent

Deterrence can either be specific in that it applies to the offender in question or more general in that it applies to the way that others are affected. There are differing opinions on deterrence. In the 2004 Civitas report, David Green and colleagues say that:

> Prison works as a method of protecting the public and deterring criminals, but some commentators are reluctant to accept the truth of this conclusion because they feel that punishment and rehabilitation of offenders are mutually exclusive alternatives.
>
> (Civitas website, <http://www.civitas.org.uk/
> crime/articles.phpReport>)

However, imprisonment is only one of many aspects of the justice system that an offender may consider; in particular the police and the courts play a vital part in creating any deterrence and, as claimed by Bottoms (2005: 66), 'Greater certainty of apprehension/conviction is substantially more effective than marginal general deterrent effects of increased severity of punishment.'

### Task

If you are discussing specific deterrence as part of your dissertation, consider how imprisonment is relevant to the four main aspects of specific deterrence from a social psychology perspective (see Sundel and Sundel, 1993):

- The **inevitability** of the offender being punished. Will imprisonment not be relevant if the crime is unlikely to be solved in the first place or if acquittal is possible?
- The **need for** the offender to be dealt with rapidly. How relevant is prison given current court delays of many months?
- High or maximum **severity**. How much of a deterrent are sentences which can be readily and balanced against the likelihood of being caught and the benefits from the crime itself.
- Is imprisonment likely to be **effective** if there is no change in the offender's lifestyle/chances/circumstances on release?

In fact, the debate about making deterrence stronger is really not about changing prisons, or even other forms of punishment. Prisons need to be located within a wider criminal justice and social system. Whereas sentencers work in isolation, for the offender, the current court appearance is simply the latest of a large number of interventions by the current social and justice systems, as well as occasions when the current social system did not intervene when the offender feels it might have done. Offenders can work out the likelihood of being convicted by watching how the local police/sentencers perform. If they 'get away' with 90 per cent of their crimes, then they may think it is 'worth it'. Prisons are less important than earlier stages in the process, especially interventions with young people, policing and sentencing.

---

**Additional study task**

If you need to deepen your study of deterrence, you will find it useful to read through an analysis of research on deterrence by von Hirsch *et al.* (1999) *Criminal deterrence and sentence severity: An analysis a recent research*. This particularly concentrates on the marginal deterrent effect of a) increased likelihood of being caught and b) of more severe sentencing. It concludes that there is little evidence that increased severity of sentencing acts as a deterrent:

- <http://members.multimania.co.uk/lawnet/SENTENCE.PDF>

---

*Prison as incapacitation*

The main argument here is that if offenders are in prison, they cannot commit offences against the general population. This seems to be true but there are perhaps three contrary points to consider:

- A significant number of offences are committed within prisons. These are not included in police crime figures but numbers published by the Ministry of Justice show that at least 100,000 'prison offences' are committed each year (see 'Offender management caseload statistics 2008', Chapter 6, <http://www.justice.gov.uk/publications/docs/offender-management-caseload-statistics-2008-2.pdf>).
- Anecdotal evidence shows that a small number of offenders, especially those who are slightly more sophisticated, continue with their offending while in prison, both by organising criminal activity outside the prison and running drug supply chains within the prisons.
- Even if an offender is stopped from offending while in prison, there is a high probability that the more junior offenders 'learn' from their more experienced co-offenders and leave prison as 'better criminals' than they entered it.

**Task**

How would you find academic sources to support the second and final points above?

Commentators claim that the number of offences against the general population 'saved' by imprisonment is very large. However, research shows that this is more limited: Halliday projected that the prison population would need to increase by 15 per cent to achieve a crime reduction of 1 per cent (Halliday, 2001: para. 1.66). Research from the US shows similar patterns, with a 10 per cent increase in prison numbers yielding a crime reduction of between 1.5 and 3 per cent (Spelman, 2000).

---

**Additional study**

Check out Spelman's later work:

- Spelman, W. (2009) 'Crime, cash, and limited options: explaining the prison boom'. *Criminology & Public Policy*, 8(1), 29–77.

---

Research by the Prime Minister's Strategy Unit highlighted in the Carter report (Carter, 2003) says that a 22 per cent increase in the prison population since 1997 is estimated to have reduced crime by around 5 per cent during a period when overall crime fell by 30 per cent. The report states: 'There is no convincing evidence that further increases in the use of custody would significantly reduce crime.'

Moreover, incapacitation shows diminishing marginal returns. Once the majority of prolific offenders are in prison, and these are the ones with the highest probability of being caught, the incapacitation effect is much lower (Bottoms, 2005). In other words, the incapacitative effect of imprisonment on reducing crime is low, especially when thinking how else crime could be reduced. A US commentator has concluded that:

> If incarceration were the only means available of reducing crime, Texans would very likely be better off releasing inmates and putting up with a higher crime rate. . . . it would be wise to turn our attention from prison construction to good jobs and effective policing.
>
> (Spelman, 2000)

Despite the claims in the early part of the chapter for a strong incapacitative effect, the conclusion of Halliday in his review of sentencing was that 'the available evidence does not support a case for changing sentencing for the sole purpose of increasing an incapacitation effect' (Halliday, 2001: para. 1.68).

## Prisons tend to degrade both prisoners and the society they live in

Even if prisons could be shown to be effective, there is a moral imperative for a civilised society to make the conditions of imprisonment as positive as possible and to ensure that the effects of imprisonment on stakeholders (including prisoners, staff, and prisoners' families) are commensurate with the need for some deprivation of liberty. Also, it is important to ensure that imprisonment does not differentially apply to minority groups, such as the semi-literate, mentally ill, drug addicts or ethnic groups. Undoubtedly, many such groups have specific problems leading to social disadvantage but such problems should be the province of other social agencies and not left for the prisons to cope with.

In fact, those committed to prison are likely to:

- suffer from high levels of drug and alcohol abuse, with around 60 per cent falling into these categories;
- have low educational attainment;
- suffer from higher levels of mental illness (with little or no treatment being available);
- come from ethnic minority communities, which tend to be three times over-represented in prison compared to white groups.

As a result, prisons are forced to provide services such as drug and literacy programmes where they can. In some areas, such as drug and literacy programmes they do this well: in cases such as health treatment for mentally ill people, they are not able to. But the main point is that such people should be dealt with in the community by educational, health and social services, not in prison.

When in prison it is also known that prisoners are:

- more likely to commit or attempt suicide;
- have a higher risk of self-harming in some way, particularly females;
- more at risk of being bullied or attacked (by other inmates or staff);
- likely to suffer poor sanitation leading to higher risk of HIV infection and AIDS and generally poor standards of medical care;
- more likely to respond to imprisonment by becoming institutionalised, making prison addictive.

On release from prison offenders are more likely to be stigmatised as criminals, more likely to be homeless and/or unemployed and to return to previous drug-taking habits. This makes their survival difficult and their return to prison more likely.

Families of prisoners are also affected:

- Home Office research has shown that around two-thirds of women prisoners are mothers, meaning that nearly 18,000 children are separated from their mothers by imprisonment.
- There is a similar experience with fathers: over 50,000 children have a parent in prison during their time at school, with 7 per cent of all children experiencing the trauma of their father's imprisonment.

There have also been adverse consequences of the fast increase in the prison population since 1995: in particular at the end of June 2009, 81 out of 141 prisons were overcrowded (57 per cent).

**Task**

- See Ministry of Justice, 'Prison population statistics monthly bulletin, June 2009': <http://www.justice.gov.uk/publications/docs/population-in-custody-06-2009.pdf>

The effect of overcrowding was summarised by the Prison Reform Trust and National Council of Independent Monitoring Boards Study on overcrowding: 'Overcrowding was threatening prison safety, leading to prisoners being held in inhuman, degrading and unsafe conditions and damaging attempts to maintain family support and reduce re-offending by prisoners' (<http://www.prisonreformtrust.org.uk/subsection.asp?id=333>).

**Task**

Look through the consequences of overcrowding as seen by the Prison Reform Trust and their suggestions as to how overcrowding should be avoided: <http://www.prisonreformtrust.org.uk/subsection.asp?id=349>.

*Case studies of degradation*

Prison staff sometimes treat prisoners in an offhand way and the divergence of opinion on how prisoners should be treated can be found in the *Daily Mail* article responding to the Prison Inspectors' recommendation that prisoners should be treated with more respect: <http://www.dailymail.co.uk/news/article-1041599/Go-easier-inmates-prison-told-try-using-names.html>.

Prisons are also more likely than other institutions to result in extreme examples of inhumane treatment.

**Task**

Look at the case of Zahid Mubarek, who was sentenced to three months in prison for stealing razor blades worth £6, and was murdered by his new cell mate just before he was due to be released from Feltham Young Offender Institute. See:

- <http://www.guardian.co.uk/society/2004/dec/18/prisons>

He was battered to death. Allegations of unacceptable behaviour of prison staff in his cell allocation were been made and were investigated at length. There was further examples suggesting that prison officers were betting on 'gladiator' fights by putting unsuitable inmates together. See:

- 'Inmate killed "in gladiator fight set up for staff bet"', *Guardian*, 4 March 2005, <http://www.guardian.co.uk/news/2005/mar/04/law.uknews>
- 'Inmate died in game of prison gladiators', *London Evening Standard*, 3 March 2005, <http://www.thisislondon.co.uk/news/article-17021518-inmate-died-in-game-of-prison-gladiators.do>

The degradation can also affect senior staff and their approach. In 2009, the 'ghosting' scandal came to light, where difficult prisoners were being transferred in order to be excluded from prison inspections. Read:

- 'How "ghosting" threatens to plunge UK jails into fresh crisis', *Guardian*, 18 October 2009, <http://www.guardian.co.uk/society/2009/oct/18/ghosting-threatens-plunge-uk-jails>

**NB** In using these sources, ask yourself whether these are enough for your argument? Are these press articles strong evidence in themselves or do you need to check the original reports/inquiries etc.? For instance, is there any coverage in HM Inspectorate of Prisons Reports (<http://www.justice.gov.uk/inspectorates/hmi-prisons/>)?

## Thinking beyond the debate

In considering imprisonment, it is important to be clear that much relies on the justification for sentencing. Since we are largely concerned with evidence and definitions of success, the best way to proceed from this debate is to look at Bottoms *et al.* (2005), a book on alternatives to custody. The different chapters give good critiques of the recent prison situation from various viewpoints, with a useful start given by the chapter by Chris Lewis on trends which is particularly important in interpreting the historical claims in the debate.

There are literally dozens of new articles about prisons published every month and the websites of those concerned with the issue are being continually updated. A few suggestions for extra reading are now given.

---

- The Prison Reform Trust stresses the need for lower prison populations but the articles are accurate and informative: www. prisonreformtrust.org.uk. Their Prison Fact Files are particularly instructive: <www.prisonreformtrust.org.uk/temp/FactfilespMaysp2007 spFinal.pdf>
- The Think Tank Civitas, on the other hand, thinks that imprisonment should be used more and its articles are slanted that way, although again accurate and informative: <www.civitas.org.uk>
- Various commentators also produce useful material. Erwin James is an ex-prisoner who writes on prison reform in the *Guardian*: an example of his work can be found at <http://www.guardian.co.uk/society/2001/jan/29/prisonsandprobation.erwinjames>
- Roger Graef is a criminologist and film-maker whose work also follows similar arguments: see <http://www.guardian.co.uk/society/2001/feb/05/penal.comment>
- On the other hand, David Rose is an investigative journalist who is more open to writing about prisons initiatives that have been shown to work: see <http://www.guardian.co.uk/politics/2002/may/05/ukcrime.prisonsandprobation>

---

Most of this debate mirrors much political discussion in the post-modern era, where complex situations tend to be oversimplified for public and media discussion. It is not clear that what people think about prisons is actually related to prison numbers or to what actually happens in prisons but perhaps people are influenced by some wider and vaguer concept of prison being the 'normal' response to those who infringe society's laws.

## Task

If this is the area you have been asked to explore in your assessment, you can deepen your study by using the following sources:

- Chapter 5 of this book
- Roberts and Hough's (2005) book on public confidence (see references section in Chapter 5)
- Steven Van de Walle and John W. Raine (2008) *Explaining attitudes towards the justice system in the UK and Europe*, Ministry of Justice Research Study 4, <http://www.justice.gov.uk/publications/docs/explaining-attitudes-towards-justice-in-ukandeurope.pdf>

## Bibliography

Alvazzi del Frate, A.A. and van Kesteren, J. (2004) *Criminal Victimisation in Europe.* Turin. Available at: www.unicri.it/wwd/analysis/icvs/pdf_files/CriminalVictimisationUrbanEurope.pdf.

Bottoms, A. (2005) 'Empirical research relevant to sentencing frameworks'. In A. Bottoms, S. Rex and G. Robinson (eds) *Alternatives to Prison: Options for an Insecure Society.* Cullompton, Devon: Willan.

Bottoms, A., Rex, S. and Robinson, G. (eds) (2005) *Alternatives to Prison: Options for an Insecure Society.* Cullompton, Devon: Willan.

Carter, P. (2003) *Managing Offenders: Reducing Crime.* Strategy Unit: Cabinet Office. Available at <http://www.thelearningjourney.co.uk/Patrick_Carter_Review.pdf/file_view>

—— (2007) *Securing the Future: Proposals for the Efficient and Sustainable Use of Custody in England and Wales.* Available at: <http://www.justice.gov.uk/publications/securing-the-future.htm>

Department for Education and Skills (2003) *Every Child Matters*, London: The Stationary Office.

Falshaw, L., Friendship, C., Travers, R. and Nugent, F. (2003) *Searching for 'What Works': An Evaluation of Cognitive Skills Programmes.* Research Findings 206. London: Home Office.

Farrington, D. and Painter, K. (2004) *Gender Differences in Risk Factors for Offending.* Home Office Findings 196. Available at <http://webarchive.nationalarchives.gov.uk/20110218135832/http://uk.sitestat.com/homeoffice/rds/s?rds.r196pdf&ns_type=pdf&ns_url=%5Bhttp://www.homeoffice.gov.uk/rds/pdfs2/r196.pdf%5D>

Felson, M. (1994) *Crime and Everyday Life: Insights and Implications for Society.* Thousand Oaks, CA: Pine Forge.

Halliday, J. (2001) *Making Punishments Work: Review of the Sentencing Framework for England and Wales.* London: Home Office. Available at <http://www.home-office.gov.uk/documents/312280/index.html>

Hirschi, T. (1969) *Causes of Delinquency.* Berkeley, CA: University of California Press.

Home Office (2001) *Making Punishment Work: Report of a Review of the Sentencing Framework for England and Wales.* London: HMSO.

—— (2002) *Justice for All.* Cm 5563. London: HMSO.

—— (2009) 'Crime in England and Wales 2008–2009'. Home Office Statistical Bulletin 11/09, available at: <http://www.homeoffice.gov.uk/rds/pdfs09/hosb1109-vol1.pdf>

Hough, M., Clancy, A., McSweeney, T. and Turnbull, P. (2003) *The Impact of Drug Treatment and Testing Orders on Offending: Two Year Reconviction Results.* Home Office Research Findings 184. London: HMSO.

Hough, M. and Roberts, J. (2005) *Understanding Public Attitudes to Criminal Justice*, Milton Keynes: Open University Press/McGraw Hill Education.

Langan, P. and Farrington, D. (1998) *Crime and Justice in the United States and in England and Wales, 1981–1996.* Washington, DC: US Department of Justice.

Mathiesen, T. (1992) *Prisons on Trial*, London: Sage.

Matrix Knowledge group (2007) 'The economic case for and against prison'. Available at: <http://www.matrixknowledge.co.uk/wp-content/uploads/economic-case-for-and-against-prison.pdf>

Ministry of Justice (2009) 'Prison Population, June 2009'. Available at: <http://www.justice.gov.uk/publications/docs/population-in-custody-06-2009.pdf>

National Audit Office (2004) *Youth Offending: The Delivery of Community and Custodial Sentences*. London: HMSO.

Newburn, T. (2007) *Criminology*. Cullompton: Willan.

Rose, D. (2002) 'Crime and punishment'. *Observer*, 5 May, p. 20.

Social Exclusion Unit (2002) *Reducing Re-offending by Ex-prisoners*. London: Office of the Deputy Prime Minister, available at, <http://www.thelearningjourney.co.uk/file.2007-10-01.1714894439/file_view>

Spelman, William (2000) 'The limited importance of prison expansion'. In Alfred Blumstein and Joel Wallman (eds) *The Crime Drop in America*. Boston: Cambridge University Press.

—— (2009) 'Crime, cash, and limited options: explaining the prison boom'. *Criminology & Public Policy*, 8(1), 29–77.

Sundel, S.S. and Sundel, M. (1993) *Behavior Modification in Human Services: A Systematic Introduction to Concepts and Applications*. London: Sage.

Taylor, R. (2000) *A Seven Year Reconviction Study of HMP Grendon Therapeutic Community*. Home Office Research Findings 115. London: HMSO.

Van Dijk, J., van Kesteran, J. and Smit, P. (2007) 'Criminal victimisation in international perspective: key findings from the 2004–2005 ICVS and EU ICS', Ministry of Justice, Netherlands. Available at <http://english.wodc.nl/onderzoeks-database/icvs-2005-survey.aspx?cp=45&cs=6796>

Walmsley, R. (undated) 'World prison brief', International Centre for Prison Studies, King's College, London. Available at <http://www.kcl.ac.uk/depsta/rel/icps/worldbrief/highest_to_lowest_rates.html> (frequently updated).

Youth Justice Board (2004) *ISSP: The Initial Report*. London: Youth Justice Board.

# Part 2
# Issues in criminal justice

# 7  Legalise drugs?

*Tom Ellis and Daniel Silverstone*

This chapter first makes a case for the legalisation of drugs, based on an historical analysis of bad science, racism, class and social exclusion, and drawing on contemporary empirical evidence to support the case. The chapter then moves on to make the case against legalisation, which also draws on empirical evidence and focuses on harm, costs and the enduring problem of regulation. In the final section, there is an outline of a number of sources and issues that need to be addressed between the two extreme positions outlined here.

---

**A note on how to use this chapter**

The topic of drugs in criminology and criminal justice is a vast one and this chapter reflects this. While we focus here on legalisation, the chapter is structured so that it can be used as a learning and teaching resource for many different themes within the drugs field. It is important for you to be clear on the assessment task that you have been set and for you to select the materials and exercises accordingly.

This chapter provides a mix of traditional referencing and sources within the text. As ever, all sources will enable you to easily access these sources. However, you must ensure that you do not 'cut and paste' them into your own text but, rather, use the details from the original sources according to Harvard APA.

---

Before the debate starts, it is important to be aware of the current legal status of the most commonly proscribed drugs in England and Wales, where there is a three-tiered classification system, ranked according to harmfulness:

Class A – opiates (including heroin and morphine), cocaine, crack, LSD, MDMA (ecstasy) and magic mushrooms;
Class B – amphetamines, barbiturates, cannabis (from early 2009); and
Class C – tranquilisers, mild stimulants, cannabis (from 29 January 2004 until early 2009), GHB, ketamine.

Possession of Class A drugs carries a maximum sentence of 7 years in custody, Class B drugs, a maximum of 5 years, and Class C drugs, 2 years. Supplying Class A drugs can lead to life imprisonment, while supplying Class B or Class C drugs carries a maximum custodial sentence of 14 years.

---

You can find out more about the official classification of drugs and drugs legislation at:

- <http://www.homeoffice.gov.uk/drugs/drugs-law/Class-a-b-c/>

---

These classifications are not static. In 2004, cannabis was downgraded from Class B to Class C with huge controversy and publicity coverage.

---

- 'One simple message: law is being relaxed, but drug is still harmful and remains illegal', *Guardian*, 23 January 2004, <http://www.guardian.co.uk/drugs/Story/0,2763,1129584,00.html>

Also, have a look at the lottery of whether you got arrested for possession of cannabis following the reclassification, depending on where you live.

- 'Discrepancies in treatment of offenders', *Guardian*, 23 January 2004, <http://www.guardian.co.uk/uk/2004/jan/23/ukcrime.drugsandalcohol>

---

In 2006, magic mushrooms were changed from being a Class C drug to a Class A drug.

With equal controversy to the downgrading in 2004, in 2009 cannabis was upgraded again to Class B.

---

### History check

For a short background to the changes to the law around cannabis and the Lambeth cannabis experiment, see Tim Newburn (2007) *Criminology*, pp. 496–7.

---

## The case for legalising drugs

> All laws which can be violated without doing anyone any injury are laughed at. . . . He who tries to determine everything by law will foment crime rather than lessen it.
>
> Baruch Spinoza (1632–77)

For most of human history, drugs have been used for self-medication, religious experiences, recreation and other purposes without the need for social control or moral condemnation (see Bennett and Holloway, 2005: 15–24). However, towards the end of the nineteenth century, with the increasing availability of opium-based products, the medicalisation and criminalisation of drugs began (ibid.) in what may eventually be seen as an anomalous blip in the history of drug use. Over the last fifty years, drug taking has become so prevalent that academics are now debating the normalisation of illegal drug use for young people today (Parker *et al.*, 1998, 2001; Blackman, 2004). Indeed, it is now estimated that there are over 11 million cannabis smokers in the UK and 48 per cent of 15-year-olds have tried drugs at some point (Department of Health, 2002). Drugs types are well known by school children, with 94 per cent of pupils having heard of cocaine, 93 per cent of cannabis and 91 per cent of heroin (ibid). Drug use, even class A drug use, is endemic to British life with highly successful and talented public figures such as Kate Moss, Robbie Williams and David Cameron admitting using drugs – prompting the *Guardian* to ask: 'Has any public figure not taken cocaine?' (10 October 2005) <http://www.guardian.co.uk/drugs/Story/0,1588652,00.html>.
Even Graham Norton admits to using cocaine and other drugs:

Graham Norton admits: 'I've taken cocaine', *Daily Mail*, 6 October 2006, <http://www.dailymail.co.uk/tvshowbiz/article-409068/Graham-Norton-admits-Ive-taken-cocaine.html>

This modern rise in both the use of drugs and their social acceptance, is due not to the legality of drugs but to their prohibition. As use has risen, so has the number of those arrested and imprisoned under ever more vindictive laws. It is now time to reconsider the costs and futility of this wretched trajectory. This is not an argument that exhorts the taking of drugs; instead it is a plea to legalise them. Our society is based on the principle of free choice – as long as our actions do not harm others we should be free to pursue them (Mill, 1986). This should include the use of drugs.
The legalisation of drugs would have several significant benefits. Firstly, impure adulterated drugs would disappear along with violent drug markets. Secondly, there would be no need for drug users to commit crime to feed their habit. Finally, drugs could be taxed and controlled in the same way as are other intoxicating or addictive substances, such as cigarettes and alcohol.

(This is the case for **legalisation**, but you will also come across the term **decriminalisation**, which is different in that it normally means that possession will not be prosecuted, but drug dealing will be.)

It is striking to observe how inefficient the current system of drug prohibition is in the UK. The Netherlands has **decriminalised** cannabis and the number of users has gone down. Meanwhile, in EPW, we have raised the penalties for dealing in cannabis, but now have not only the largest proportion, but also the heaviest users of cannabis in Europe.

> See: EMCDDA (2005) 'Annual report 2005: the state of the drugs problem in Europe', <http://ar2005.emcdda.eu.int/en/home-en.html? CFID=1191615&CFTOKEN=de2f32cb6707c2ad-6494FBBA-B766- 05C4-F14CDD224B007B05&jsessionid=2e3076d9035c2d21586c>

Despite our harsh legislation, we still take more ecstasy and cocaine than other European societies. More chillingly, we also experience more drug-related deaths, in stark contrast to countries where the laws are more liberal.

> See: CEPR (1997) 'Dutch drugs policy pragmatism rules OK?', <http://www.cepr.org/PUBS/bulletin/MEETS/1390.htm>

Therefore, we do not need to panic that legal drugs will mean more users, as there does not seem to be a strict correlation between the availability of drugs and their use. It is not true that legal drugs equal cheap drugs and more drug users. Take, for example, ecstasy (MDMA) use. As the price of the drug went down, from £15 per pill to 50p per pill, use actually declined.

> See: Measham (2004) 'Play space: historical and socio-cultural reflections on drugs, licensed leisure locations, commercialisation and control'. *International Journal of Drug Policy*, 15(6), 337–45.

The same could be said of heroin, where the price has halved without the expected doubling of users. Overall, as the the Home Affairs Select Committee (2002) report (p. 6) concluded:

> We could find no link across 15 Member states between the robustness of their policies and the level of prevalence. There are some countries with high prevalence, harsh policies, some countries with low prevalence, harsh policies, other countries with liberal policies and low prevalence. There is no link, there is no conceivable link.

See: Trace (2001) *The Government's Drugs Policy: Is It Working? Third Report, The Home Affairs Committee.* Retrieved on 5 June 2006 from: <http://www.publications.parliament.uk/pa/cm200102/cmselect/cmhaff/318/31803.htm>

If there is no direct link to illegality and the number of users or indeed the prevention of ill health, why are drugs illegal? The answer is complex: it is partly a puritan reaction to the West's monopoly of the opium trade (Davenport-Hines, 2001); provoked by the impact of the First World War in relation to the old sexual roles and class hierarchies (Kohn, 1992); but most glaringly due to the persistent strand of American-led racism, which successfully but erroneously linked the use of drugs with race. This has conclusively been researched and demonstrated in relation to all of the main illicit substances, whether cannabis, opium or cocaine (Davenport-Hines, 2001; Blackman, 2004).

Opium was initially banned in the United States, but only for Chinese people, since the association between these two elements was a convenient response to new competition in the labour market. Meanwhile, comments by a *Literary Digest* article (1914, cited in White, 1979: 3), that 'most of the attacks upon white women of the South are the direct result of a cocaine-crazed Negro brain', were indicative of widespread but completely inaccurate reporting that led to cocaine becoming illegal.

At the heart of this rhetoric was one man: Harry Anslinger, Commissioner of the Federal Bureau of Narcotics from 1930 until 1962. He was an avid racist and his views were close to that of the local press at the time who complained:

> I wish I could show you what a small marijuana cigarette can do to one of our degenerate Spanish-speaking residents. That's why our problem is so great; the greatest percentage of our population is composed of Spanish-speaking persons, most of who are low mentally, because of social and racial condition.
>
> (*Daily Courier*, 1936)

Unfortunately, Anslinger was also well connected and his familial connections were used to help make cannabis illegal. Anslinger was appointed by Andrew Mellon, his wife's uncle. Mellon, the Treasury Secretary, was banker to DuPont, and sales of hemp (cannabis) threatened that firm's efforts to build a market for synthetic fibres (Williamson, 1997). This was due to a crude response to economic competition between black and white workers and not a genuine interest in the health of the public. Yet it is important to realise how much global influence Anslinger had. By 1955, even the World Health Organisation was under the thrall of his rhetoric, reporting that

(WHO, 1955) 'under the influence of cannabis, the danger of committing unpremeditated murder is very great'. (The quotation continues: 'it can happen in cold blood, without any reason or motive, unexpectedly, without any preceding quarrel, often the murderer does not even know the victim, and simply kills for pleasure'.) We now know there is no empirical evidence for this claim at all. Indeed, in the words of Reshard Auladin, Deputy Chair of the Metropolitan Police Authority (MPA): 'most violent crimes in the capital are linked to alcohol. I have never seen an incident where an assault has been linked to cannabis.'

See page 1 of: Metropolitan Police Authority (2004) *MPA debates re-classification of cannabis*, <http://www.mpa.gov.uk/news/press/2004/ 04-086.htm>

Unfortunately, this prejudice masquerading as science was not confined to the beginning of the twentieth century. The prohibition of ecstasy, the dance drug of choice, has been equally misguided. Night-clubs where ecstasy is used are characterised by their tranquillity and mellow ambiance (Parker *et al.*, 2001). In accordance with this, in the US in 1986, Judge Young released his decision on the laws, science, and use surrounding MDMA, declaring that MDMA was safe when used under medical supervision. He declared that it did not have a high potential for addiction, and had legitimate medical use. However, the Drugs Enforcement Agency (DEA) condemned Judge Young as incorrect in his interpretation of the laws. They rejected his non-binding ruling and declared MDMA permanently as a Schedule 1 (most serious) drug. The decision was looked at again by a panel of experts and reversed, but then the DEA intervened again and it remains illegal (Jenkins, 1999). This has had predictable results: the use of ecstasy has rocketed as the penalties for its use have become more severe. Meanwhile, impurities and subsequent drug-induced deaths have also increased. Deterrence will not work with drugs users!

### Research task on bad science, drugs and deterrence

Ben Goldacre is a medic who is also a journalist. As such, he provides a welcome respite from the poor referencing usually in evidence in newspaper coverage. Most of his articles that appear in the *Guardian* also appear on his bad science website <http://www.badscience.net>, although, dissappointingly, often with different titles. Try to use the Bad Science site as a resource, not a source in itself. In the following key example, there are hyperlinks to most of the key research referred to and we are sure that Ben would like us to insist on you reading and citing these sources (access to the sources is sometimes free, but in some cases, it will depend on your university's e-journal subscription policy).

The following example is an extremely useful resource for looking at the **deterrent effect** (or lack thereof) of differing laws, classifications, and levels of enforcement on drug use. There are key links here with philosophies of punishment (Chapter 5) and clear parallels with the prisons debate (Chapter 6), which may be relevant to your assessments.

- 'The Nutt Sack Affair (part 493)' (originally from the *Guardian*, 7 November 2009) <http://www.badscience.net/2009/11/the-nutt-sack-affair-part-493/#more-1396>

The bad science is not confined to the so-called 'recreational drugs', but also to those most maligned by the popular press: heroin, cocaine and crack cocaine. It is medically accepted (Gossop, 2000) that an average person can lead a successful and productive life, yet be a heroin addict. Indeed, when the British heroin population was largely middle aged, educated and white, heroin was legally prescribed by doctors to their patients (South, 2002). The same cannot be said of crack cocaine, which is universally portrayed as the 'most dangerous drug known to man'. However, a close examination of the death records in the United States, shows that deaths attributed to cocaine or crack use are often not classified accurately. For example, in New York City, 935 deaths had been officially labelled as cocaine related. However, upon further investigation, it was found that:

> [about] half these deaths had been due to trauma (caused by accidents, homicides, and suicides) and that less than 12 per cent were even possibly related to the pharmacological effects of cocaine.
>
> (Morgan, J. and Zimmer, 1997: 7)

Indeed, when the addictiveness of crack cocaine is closely monitored, still 'only about one in eight (12.3 per cent) of those who have ever tried crack had used it in the month prior to the survey' (ibid: 10). This indicates that the other 87.7 per cent have managed to resist the drug and its supposed instant addictiveness.

There can also be no argument that the government prohibits the most dangerous of our activities. Ecstasy use, for example, has an estimated mortality rate of one death in 3.7 million, while legitimate activities such as parachuting cause one death in 85,000 jumps and attempting to climb the K2 mountain has a mortality rate of one in every four (Williamson, 1997: 83). Neither can there be any argument that the government only prohibits the most dangerous drugs, when it is widely known that smoking kills about 120,000 people in the UK every year and alcohol around 6,000 to 40,000 per year (Drugscope, 2006). Indeed, the Home Office states that alcohol, now available legally 24 hours a day, is the drug most strongly linked to crime. Their own website declares:

> in nearly half (48 per cent) of all violent incidents, victims believed offenders to be under the influence of alcohol [and] this figure rose to 60 per cent in cases of 'stranger violence'.
>
> (Roe, 2005; Murphy and Roe, 2007)

## Task

Professor David Nutt, who was sacked from the Advisory Council on the Misuse of Drugs (ACMD) in 2009, had already made a striking comparison between alcohol and MDMA in a 2006 article. This is not a technical article and is well worth reading, though access depends on your university's e-journal policy – see:

- Nutt, David (2006) 'A tale of two Es'. *Journal of Psychopharmacology*, 20, 315–17, <http://jop.sagepub.com/cgi/reprint/20/3/315>

This brings us to another classic argument often put forward for keeping drugs illegal: the supposed close relationship between drug use and crime. However, once again the relationship does not stand up to close scrutiny, and the general conclusion from empirical evidence is, 'that whilst there is a clear and significant statistical relationship, casual connections are difficult to establish' (McBride, 2002; cited in Bean, 2005: 30). Indeed, for every drug user who becomes a criminal after starting their drug use there is another person whose criminality precedes their drug use. There are millions of drug users who never become criminals and, similarly, even those who use the most problematic drugs often remain crime free.

To unpick this debate it is useful to refer to Goldstein's tripartite typology for understanding drug crime in which he breaks the links between drugs and crime into three categories, each of which will be dealt with in turn.

## Task

You can use Bean 2005 as your secondary source here, but why not read the original 1985 article?

- Goldstein, P.J. (1985) 'The drugs/violence nexus: a tripartite conceptual framework'. *Journal of Drug Issues*, 39, 143–74.

Firstly, **pharmacological crime**, which is where the drug itself causes a person to behave in a criminal manner due to drug-induced schizophrenia or paranoid symptoms. Though this is a problem in a small minority of cases, the ill effects of drug use are countered by the soporific effects of drugs like cannabis, which actually reduce the chances of crime happening.

---

**Task**

Is this simply a case of majority rule? Read the following article and make notes on what you think would be the implications for the minority if drugs were legalised:

- 'One in four at risk of cannabis psychosis', *The Times*, 12 April 2005, <http://www.timesonline.co.uk/article/0,3561-1565337,00.html>
- 'Skunk users face greater risk of psychosis, researchers warn', *Guardian*, 1 December 2009, <http://www.guardian.co.uk/science/2009/dec/01/skunk-users-psychosis-risk-research>

Or is it a case where deterrence doesn't work?

- 'Reefer madness – December 2009 poll on the risk of psychosis from skunk', *Guardian*, 1 December 2009, <http://www.guardian.co.uk/commentisfree/poll/2009/dec/01/drugs-drugs>

---

Secondly, there is **economic compulsive crime**, where desperate drug users are forced by their addiction to steal and burgle to sustain their habit. This cycle would be broken by legalisation, as users would be able to be pre-scribed their drugs of choice.

Finally, there is **systemic crime**, which is the label given to the internecine violence that is endemic to the operation of illegal drug markets. This was typical of America's ill-fated trial of alcohol prohibition in the 1920s, which provided a massive impetus for organised crime and gangsters. Increasingly, criminologists are aware of the importance of systemic crime. For example, it is argued that violent street robberies or armed robberies are not carried out at random, but are due to the targeting of drug dealers or desperate efforts to reclaim drug debts.

---

See: Hales, G., Lewis, C. and Silverstone, D. (2006) 'Gun crime: the market in and use of illegal firearms'. Home Office Research Report 298/06, <http://www.homeoffice.gov.uk/rds/pdfs06/hors298.pdf>

Indeed it has been estimated that, in America, 90 per cent of drug-related homicides are due to systemic crime (Bean, 2005). Once again, the quickest way to thwart the intimidation and often fatal violence that comes when a market operates outside of the law is to bring it within the law's remit. Then our only fears are from avaricious banks and credit card companies!

This radical step would also free up money from enforcement to help those who become entangled with drug use. It is already estimated that £1 spent on treatment saves £3 on enforcement (Murphy and Roe, 2007). If we survey the evidence on those using the heaviest of drugs, it is clearly more humane to help them rather than punish them. They do not consist of stereotypical Lombrosian throwbacks but, instead, their backgrounds are characterised by social exclusion, poverty and educational failure (Wincup *et al.*, 2003).

In America, Schlosser (2003: 57) estimated that 'the number of drug offenders imprisoned in America today – more than 330,000 – is much larger than the number of people imprisoned for all crimes in 1970'. This huge figure hides a dramatic racial disparity. Since, the Anti-Drug Abuse Act 1968, the possession of five grams of crack carried a mandatory five-year sentence, while it took the possession of five hundred grams of cocaine to get the same sentence. This is essentially the same drug without the mundane ingredient of baking powder. However, 89 per cent of crack cocaine defendants were black, 7 per cent were Hispanic and only 4 per cent were white. Meanwhile, for cocaine powder the figures were reversed with 34 per cent white, 39 per cent Hispanic and 27 per cent black. This has led to black Americans serving, on average, sentences 49 per cent longer than their white counterparts under federal drug laws (Davenport-Hines, 2001: 356).

This discrimination, driven by unjust drug laws, is not confined to America. 'Black people account for 12 per cent of the London population; however, they accounted for 39 per cent of those accused of crack possession and 67 per cent of those accused of crack supply' (GLADA, 2004: 32). Yet this disparity is not present in the numbers who use these drugs; for example, within the 16- to 24-year-old age group, 10 per cent white, 8 per cent mixed race, 2 per cent black people had used a Class A drug in the last year. It is also apparent there are two main ethnic groups 'accused of cannabis possession', in London, accounting for approximately 79 per cent of the total; they are 'White Europeans' (45 per cent) and 'African-Caribbean' (34 per cent).

## Task

- See Table 4 of Metropolitan Police Authority (2004) 'Evaluation report following the re-classification of cannabis', Report 14. <http://www.mpa.gov.uk/committees/mpa/2004/041125/14.htm>

Again, there is no evidence to suggest that the Afro-Caribbean population smoke significantly more cannabis than other ethnicities, only that they are policed more severely.

We also see the results of drug prohibition in other parts of the criminal justice system, pre-eminently in policing and in prisons. The policing of drugs has proven to be an expensive and time-consuming business. May *et al.* (2002) estimated that 770,000 hours per year (equivalent to 500 full-time officers) and £350 million is spent on policing cannabis.

## Task

You can read and/or download a summary of:

* May, T., Warburton, H., Turnbull, P.J. and Hough, M. (2002) *Times they are A-changing: Policing of Cannabis*. York: Joseph Rowntree Foundation, <http://www.jrf.org.uk/publications/policing-cannabis-class-b-drug>

Overall, 80–90 per cent of those arrested for drug offences are arrested for cannabis possession. The numbers sentenced for drug offences has grown from just over 20,000 to over 100,000, yet drug prices have decreased and the numbers using have gone up. It is no wonder that Eddie Ellison, the former head of the Scotland Yard Drug Squad, was moved to state, 'I say legalise drugs because I want to see less drug abuse, not more. And I say legalise drugs because I want to see the criminals put out of business.'

See: 'Statement by Edward Ellison, former head of Scotland Yard's anti-drugs squad, calling for legalization', *Daily Mail*, 10 March 1998, <http://stopthedrugwar.org/cops_against_the_drug_war/edward_ellison_of_scotland_yard_calls_for_legalization>

Those convicted of drug offences now consist of an ever-increasing number of the prison population and again it is telling to see of whom they consist. The answer is: poor foreign men and women who are used as so-called 'drug mules' (Green, 1998). These impoverished people are exploited by drug traffickers to swallow or carry illegal drugs and are easily spotted by customs officers. Sometimes, the so-called 'mules' are deliberately set up as bigger shipments pass through. The proportion of minority ethnic groups in prison for drug offences is significantly higher than for white prisoners. This is often for trafficking offences which attract longer sentences and this helps boost over-representation further and bumps up the wasteful effects of prohibition (see Morgan and Liebling, 2007: 1122).

Globally, in this time of heightened international sensitivities, the UK is also committed to a global war on drugs that is as futile as it is imperialist (Blackman, 2004).

---

### History check: the war *for* drugs

The notion of imperialism is central to the drugs trade. The Opium Wars (1839–42 and 1856–8) were fought between Britain and China, but with Britain successful in forcing the free trade for opium produced in India to the Chinese, with little regard for the social and economic problems caused by it. However, it was only a few years later in the 1870s, that sensational accounts of sinister and stereotypical Chinese opium dens in London began to appear, with no hint of irony or recognition of hypocrisy. Britain and The Netherlands were, in effect, the first Narcotraffickers and were state sanctioned. It seems as though war was a more successful way of enforcing the trade in drugs than it has been in preventing it.

If you wish to pursue this theme, the best place to start is Nigel South's Chapter 24 of the *Oxford Handbook of Criminology* (4th edn), pp. 818–21. You can use the reference sources cited there to further your study.

---

All the contemporary war on drugs succeeds in achieving is the creation of massively lucrative illegal markets run by organised crime and increasingly difficult to disentangle from the licit economy.

---

See for instance:

- 'Spreading fear: how the new cartels deliver chaos to four continents', *Guardian*, 9 March 2009, <http://www.guardian.co.uk/world/2009/mar/09/cocaine-drugs-trade-bolivia>
- 'We let trafficking into our businesses, our houses, our bedrooms. I am very pessimistic we can get it out', *Guardian*, 9 March 2009, <http://www.guardian.co.uk/world/2009/mar/09/mexico-drug-cartels-violence>

---

In the impoverished countries of Afghanistan and Bolivia where, respectively, opium and cocoa are subsistence crops, campaigns of eradication have been tried and failed (Trace, 2005; Farrell and Thorne, 2005). The regulation regime of legalisation could offer farmers legal markets for their crops and would stop the intractable conflict with both Afghan warlords and even elected presidents.

The war on drugs is neither inevitable nor logical. Even in the United States, the credit crunch has shown how drugs can contribute to state economies, rather than drain them, through taxation of medical marijuana.

**Task**

Read the following articles and make notes on whether this would be feasible and acceptable for non-medical consumption, as with alcohol, tobacco and gambling:

- 'California's pot clubs offer to pay more tax in fiscal crisis', *Observer*, 5 July 2009, <http://www.guardian.co.uk/business/2009/jul/05/marijuana-california-clinics-tax>
- 'Smoke dope and save the state of California, dude', *Independent*, 10 July 2009, <http://www.independent.co.uk/news/world/americas/smoke-dope-and-save-the-state-of-california-dude-1740231.html>

Others have decided to develop alternative economies as the licit economy fails:

- 'Americans grow cannabis to beat the recession', *Guardian*, 11 September 2009, <http://www.guardian.co.uk/world/2009/sep/11/cannabis-recession>

The failure of the war on drugs also begs questions about the role of evidence-based drugs policy approaches. It was, arguably, the ignoring of expert advice which ultimately led to the sacking of Professor David Nutt as chair of ACMD and which provoked a *Guardian* editorial on drugs:

> The overall story has long been one of fear-mongering and rank hypocrisy. . . .
>
> The reason respected experts are fleeing has nothing to do with the ACMD's own work. Instead, it is because its most important findings are being routinely ignored in the course of a war on drugs, where reason has long ceased to have any force.
>
> Half the government, as well as the Conservative leader and three US presidents in a row, have used drugs in their own youth, and yet punitive laws continue to threaten others who do the same with prison. The three-year sentence that a teenager can receive for providing friends with a few ecstasy tablets snuffs out his future far more surely than any drug, and does so at great expense to the taxpayer.
>
> ('Drugs: The 40-year failure', *Guardian*, 3 November 2009, <http://www.guardian.co.uk/commentisfree/2009/nov/03/drug-policy-prohibition-nutt-johnson>)

Let us return to those changes in the classification of cannabis outlined at the beginning of the chapter and consider the extent to which government policy on drugs is rational and based on scientific evidence.

The 2009 upgrade of cannabis back to Class B met with predictable relief by the *Daily Mail* whose headline on 29 April 2008 was 'Cannabis: at last a U-turn', <http://www.dailymail.co.uk/news/article-1017122/Cannabis-At-U-turn-Gordon-Brown-concedes-mistake-soft-drug.html>.

In the article, a 'source close to Mr Brown' said: 'He has always believed strongly that it was a mistake to reclassify cannabis to a Class C drug' and that 'It was also a mistake to be guided solely by scientific evidence. He strongly believes that the right thing to do is to reclassify cannabis as a Class B drug.'

So, it seems fairly clear that the governmental approach to drug control, at best, sits uneasily with any kind of rational policy making. Indeed, many commentators at the time argued this. For example, Ben Lynam from the independent UK Drug Policy Commission said that the drugs debate 'needs to be taken out of the political arena by using an independent body like the ACMD but that is listened to and gives recommendations based on scientific evidence rather than political expediency' (see 'Smith upgrades cannabis to class B', *Guardian*, 7 May 2008, <http://www.guardian.co.uk/politics/2008/may/07/drugspolicy.drugsandalcohol>).

In the same *Guardian* article, it was clear that the Home Office was using evidence selectively to regrade cannabis by focusing on the increase in the availability of skunk (81 per cent of cannabis available on the streets compared with just 30 per cent in 2002), which is a stronger type of cannabis, but ignoring that the feared increase in mental health problems had not occurred, with new cases of schizophrenia reported to GPs going down, not up, from 1998 to 2005, 'indicating a weak link between increased potency and use in the past two decades and mental health problems'.

In the same article, it was also stated that

> Since cannabis was downgraded in 2004 the proportion of young people using it has fallen each year from 25.3 per cent in 2003–04 to 20.9 per cent in 2008. Among those aged 16 to 59, the proportion over the same period has fallen from 10.8 per cent to 8.2 per cent, according to the British Crime Survey.

### Task

It is easy to have a look at the British Crime Survey results and decide for yourself rather than rely on this source. You can access all studies and other resources, and download data, at:

• <http://www.homeoffice.gov.uk/rds/bcs1.html>

You can also get a comparative European perspective by looking at the data provided by EMCDDA at:

- <http://www.emcdda.europa.eu/stats09/eyefig1k>

What do you think the groupings of different European countries tell us about the relationship between drug use and other factors?

However you look at it, it is hard to ignore the idea that government policy is not evidence-based, but, rather, based on a misguided moral crusade disguised as public opinion, or in fact, tabloid headlines.

**Task**

- Read Professor David Nutt (2009) *'Estimating drug harms: a risky business?'*, Briefing 10, October 2009, Centre for Crime and Justice Studies, <http://www.crimeandjustice.org.uk/opus1714/Estimating_drug_harms.pdf>

You will find, on p. 10, the comparison between the level of harm by drug type that he researched and the current legal classifications of harmfulness. You can find the original article in *The Lancet*:

- Nutt, King, Saulsbury and Blakemore (2007) 'Development of a rational scale to assess the harm of drugs of potential misuse', *The Lancet*, 369(9566), 1047–53, <http://www.thelancet.com/journals/lancet/article/PIIS0140-6736(07)60464-4/fulltext>
- Also see Nutt (2009) 'Government *vs* science over drug and alcohol policy', *The Lancet*, 374(9703), 1731–3, 21 November 2009, <http://www.thelancet.com/journals/lancet/article/PIIS0140-6736(09)61956-5/fulltext>

Access is free to all, but you do need to register (it is immediate) so put in a small amount of effort and improve your submission by reading the original source.

There is also a useful comparative view from the United States at:

- 'You can't handle the truth', *Boston Globe*, 13 December 2009, <http://www.boston.com/bostonglobe/ideas/articles/2009/12/13/you_cant_handle_the_truth/>

It is hard to avoid the futile hypocrisy of the current attempt to prevent drugs consumption.

## Task

The following are cases of arguments for legalisation from a variety of sources that are to some degree 'official':

- 'Give heroin to addicts, says police chief', *Guardian*, 23 November 2006 (Howard Roberts, deputy Chief Constable of Nottinghamshire), <http://www.guardian.co.uk/drugs/Story/0,1954749,00.html>
- 'Badge of honour', *Guardian*, 12 September 2007 (Jack Cole Former US undercover narcotics officer), <http://www.guardian.co.uk/drugs/Story/0,2166824,00.html>
- 'Prescribe more free heroin: Birt's secret advice to ministers', *Guardian*, 9 February 2006 <http://www.guardian.co.uk/drugs/Story/0,1705587,00.html>

Check out the 'leaked' 2003 'SU Drugs Project Phase 2 Report: Diagnosis and Recommendations' in full yourself:

- <http://image.guardian.co.uk/sys-files/Guardian/documents/2006/02/08/Drugs.pdf>
- 'Britain's fight against drugs "a total failure"', *Observer*, 15 April 2007, <http://observer.guardian.co.uk/uk_news/story/0,2057565,00.html>

Check out the UK Drugs Policy Commission (2007) 'An analysis of UK Drugs Policy' report for yourself:

- <http://www.ukdpc.org.uk/docs%5CUKDPC%20drug%20policy%20review.pdf>

How reliable is the evidence presented in these sources that '**supply reduction**' is unlikely to succeed?

Are these sources convincing in arguing for '**legalisation**', '**decriminalisation**', '**demand reduction**' and/or '**harm reduction**'?

Make sure you understand these terms. For a good basic explanation:

- See Tim Newburn (2007) *Criminology*, pp. 477–80.
- Read: 'The legaliser', *Guardian*, 16 November 2008, <http://www.guardian.co.uk/society/2008/nov/16/drugs-legalisation>

Is Danny Kushlick arguing primarily for legalisation, harm reduction, or something else?

Finally, if we look to the future, such has been the desperate failure of drug prohibition, it seems that the powers of the punitive state have had to be enhanced, threatening the very fabric of our cherished judicial system. The Proceeds of Crime Act 2002, and the Drug Act 2005 are examples of this. The Proceeds of Crime Act 2002 allows the police the powers of forfeiture according to the civil standard of proof, in other words on the balance of probabilities. This can be aimed at anyone who the police suspect of general criminal conduct, regardless of whether a conviction has been obtained. Further, in the Drugs Act 2005, there is an evidential presumption as to the element of intention to supply in an offence of possession with intent to supply a controlled substance, which means it is up to the defendant to prove that they are not guilty (Justice, 2005). This clearly goes against our commitments under the Human Rights Act, where Article 6(2) of the Convention provides that: 'Everyone charged with a criminal offence shall be presumed innocent until proved guilty according to law.'

In conclusion, the prohibition of illicit drugs is unjust, futile and expensive. Prohibition has proved a terrible, inhumane, discriminatory disaster. As the opening quotation suggests, it has been enforced due to a mixture of racial prejudice and fallacious science. As Spinoza wisely suggests, prohibition provokes a wider disgruntlement with the law and foments the problems it was meant to solve. It allows the wealthy to consume illicit substances with impunity, while condemning the disadvantaged to prison, ill health and violence. This is not an argument to take drugs but to consider a more enlightened system of control. In our brave, globalised, post-modern world characterised by consumerism, choice and risk taking, it is futile to prohibit some drugs. It only serves to glamorise them to the young and perpetuate inequities, which the state should be devoted to reducing.

**Task**

What do you think? View

- <http://www.youtube.com/watch?v=bBP-SJqnJGY>

Then take a more academic approach. If your university has free access to the British Medical Association's website, go to:

- 'Legalising illicit drugs: A signposting resource', <http://www.bma. org.uk/ap.nsf/content/legalisingillicitdrugsresource>

A must for those who will tackle this topic. This can be downloaded as a Word file and many of its reference sources/citations can also be accessed electronically through the document.

NO EXCUSE FOR NOT READING THEM
NO EXCUSE FOR NOT REFERENCING THEM CORRECTLY

## The case against legalising drugs

Most of the references in this section can be found in one of the following shorter sources:

- Nigel South's Chapter 25 of the 3rd edition or Chapter 24 of the 4th edition of the Maguire *et al.*, *Oxford Handbook of Criminology*. Oxford: Oxford University Press.
- Chapter 21 'Drugs and alcohol' of Tim Newburn (2007) *Criminology*.

More extensive sources can also be found in:

- Bennett, T. and Holloway, K. (2005) *Understanding Drugs, Alcohol and Crime*. Maidenhead: Open University Press; or
- Bean (2005) *Drugs and Crime*. Cullompton: Willan.

The obvious question to ask is: why are drugs illegal? Rather than focus on the notions discussed above, the answers are manifold:

- First, drugs are illegal because they can harm you. They can even shrink your brain and make teenagers impotent!

**Task**

Read:

- 'Cannabis may shrink brain, scientists report', *Guardian*, 3 June 2008, <http://www.guardian.co.uk/science/2008/jun/03/drugs.drugsandalcohol>
- 'Cannabis "is making teenagers impotent" say doctors', *Daily Mail*, 28 April 2008, <http://www.dailymail.co.uk/news/article-562448/Cannabis-making-teenagers-impotent-say-doctors.html>

Danny Kushlick, director of the Transform Drug Policy Foundation, and hardly a supporter of the war on drugs has already argued:

Lest you think that legal regulation would be a panacea, imagine 12 million heroin addicts instead of tobacco users, a world where crack was aggressively marketed to young people using techniques perfected by the likes of British American Tobacco and alcopops retailers. Haven't we got enough legal drugs on the market to tempt our children?

('The true price of prohibition', *Guardian*, 6 August 2004, <http://www.guardian.co.uk/comment/story/0,1277450,00.html>)

We already have enough addictions to deal with and we simply do not need more legal drugs.

**Task**

Read:

- 'Britons can't imagine a life without booze', *Observer*, 23 March 2008 <http://www.guardian.co.uk/society/2008/mar/23/drugsandalcohol.health>
- 'GPs have got Britain "hooked on painkillers"', *Observer*, 10 February 2008, <http://www.guardian.co.uk/society/2008/feb/10/health.drugsandalcohol>

Drugs cause both physical and mental health problems, which can also lead to death.

**Task**

Have a read of the following 'victim accounts' of the terrible impact of MDMA (Ecstasy), ketamine and heroin/morphine:

- 'First person: A moment of selfish pleasure ruined my life', *Guardian*, 13 March 2009, <http://www.guardian.co.uk/lifeandstyle/2009/mar/13/mark-hennessy-ecstasy-ruined-life>
- 'Enslaved by K', *Guardian*, 21 April 2008, <http://www.guardian.co.uk/lifeandstyle/2008/apr/21/healthandwellbeing.drugsandalcohol>

and the medical case notes on overindulgence in MDMA:

- 'The strange case of the man who took 40,000 ecstasy pills in nine years', *Guardian*, 4 April 2006, <http://www.guardian.co.uk/drugs/Story/0,1746333,00.html>

and of the devastation caused in an entire Scottish generation of young men:

- 'Older generation blamed as drug deaths soar', *The Scotsman*, 13 August 2009, <http://thescotsman.scotsman.com/drugspolicy/Older-generation-blamed-as-drug.5548957.jp>
- 'What happened to the Trainspotting generation?', *Guardian*, 15 August 2009, <http://www.guardian.co.uk/society/2009/aug/15/scotland-trainspotting-generation-dying-fact>

## Public opinion

Is there any need to change the law on drugs when 82 per cent of the public think that current drug laws are either about right (50 per cent) or too liberal (32 per cent). Nearly three-quarters of the public also think that no drugs that are currently illegal should be made legal or decriminalised. The legalisers are in a clear minority.

---

See for yourself:

- 'The Observer Drugs Poll (ICM)', *Observer*, 16 November 2008, <http://www.guardian.co.uk/society/2008/nov/16/uk-drug-use-survey-statistics-poll>

You can find more resources than just the poll results at

- 'Drugs uncovered', *Guardian*, <http://www.guardian.co.uk/society/series/drugs-uncovered>

There are a lot of other useful materials here, but think about how academically sound they are – do you need to trace some original sources (other than the poll)?

---

## The impact of drugs on mental health

The key issue here is that illicit drugs can have a profound effect on **some** users' mental health.

---

**Task**

Read the following and make notes on whether the level of risk identified is un/acceptable to you and whether it would change your attitudes and behaviour toward taking drugs.

- 'One in four at risk of cannabis psychosis', *The Times*, 12 April 2005, <http://www.timesonline.co.uk/tol/news/uk/article1078876.ece>
- 'Off your head? Focus: Cannabis psychosis', *Observer*, 19 February 2006, <http://www.guardian.co.uk/society/2006/feb/19/drugsandalcohol.drugs>

Do you need to find Tom Barnes' research in the *Journal of Psychiatry* or cite the *Guardian* article?

- 'Cannabis use linked to 40 per cent rise in risk of schizophrenia', *Guardian*, 27 July 2007 (and 50–200 per cent in the most frequent users), <http://www.guardian.co.uk/society/2007/jul/27/drugsandalcohol.drugs>

This article provides a link to a summary of the original article in *The Lancet* and you can trace the full study, also in *The Lancet*, from there.

Is cannabis is a 'gateway' drug?

- 'Cannabis "can lead to harder drugs"', *Daily Telegraph*, 6 July 2006, <http://www.telegraph.co.uk/news/uknews/1523174/Cannabis-can-lead-to-harder-drugs.html>

Academically, Professor Robin Murray from King's College (and a critic of Professor Nutt) has been very active is pointing out the dangers of cannabis on mental health.

## Task

Read the following and make notes on the questions posed.

- Professor Robin Murray (and others), King's College, from 7 January 2004, <http://www.guardian.co.uk/society/2004/jan/07/drugsandalcohol.politics>
- 'Cannabis mental health risks "must be taught"', *Guardian*, <http://www.guardian.co.uk/society/2004/jan/07/drugsandalcohol.politics>

and later:

- 'Sacked adviser urges drugs probe', *BBC News*, 19 November 2009 <http://news.bbc.co.uk/1/hi/uk/8366466.stm>

There are links here to iPlayer and a podcast. Look out for Murray's publication referred to here – should you be citing that rather than the BBC source?

1. How balanced are the arguments?
2. Do both sides have a point?
3. Are both sides talking past each other and not engaging?
4. Is Murray against reclassification?

Murray is very clear on the potential harmful effects of drugs on mental health. The following statements are made on the <http://www.shizophrenia.com> website.

- Use of street drugs including LSD, methamphetamine, marijuana/hash/ cannabis have been linked with significantly increased probability of developing schizophrenia. This link has been documented in over 30 different scientific studies.
- Those who were heavy consumers of cannabis at 18 were over 600 per cent more likely to be diagnosed with schizophrenia over the next 15 years than those who were not.
- Experts estimate that between 8 per cent and 13 per cent of all schizophrenia cases are linked to teenage cannabis use.

Have a look at the full evidence at <http://www.schizophrenia.com/prevention/ cannabis.marijuana.schizophrenia.html>.

**Task**

- Make an argument for and against the case for prohibiting drugs for the majority in order to protect the vulnerable, but unaware, minority.
- As you work through this chapter, use a grid to record the contrasting evidence to support each side of the argument. Be very precise here, a statement is not 'evidence' unless it is backed up with research findings.

Is there a clear winner?

Start your trawl of evidence with the following articles:

- 'Skunk cannabis smokers seven times more likely to suffer from psychosis', *Daily Mail*, 1 December 2009, <http://www.dailymail. co.uk/health/article-1232170/Skunk-cannabis-smokers-seven- times-likely-suffer-psychosis.html>
- 'Drug-linked mental illness rises by 100 per cent', *Guardian*, 15 August 2008, <http://www.guardian.co.uk/society/2008/aug/15/ drugsandalcohol.mentalhealth>
- 'Bad Science: Cannabis data comes to the crunch', *Guardian*, 28 July 2007, <http://www.guardian.co.uk/science/2007/jul/28/ drugs.drugsandalcohol>
- 'Panel says link with mental illness is "very small"', *Guardian*, 14 January 2006, <http://www.guardian.co.uk/politics/2006/jan/ 14/drugsandalcohol.immigrationpolicy>

Refer back to the 'hierarchy of evidence' in Chapter 1.

1.  Are these sources good evidence in themselves?
2.  Do you need to find, evaluate and refer to the original sources acknowledged in these press articles?

## Legalising drugs will destroy more families

Think about all those families that have been devastated by drugs and feel that they are ignored because they are in a minority.

### Task

Read the following accounts and make notes on whether you think the risk is justifiable:

*   'The families torn apart by teenage skunk epidemic', *Observer*, 15 March 2009, <http://www.guardian.co.uk/society/2009/mar/15/drugs-skunk-family>
*   'The cannabis diaries: Debra Bell's son William took his first puff at 14. Since then he has lied and thieved to fund a habit that has, five years on, consumed his life – and that of his family', *Guardian* 17 March 2007 <http://www.guardian.co.uk/society/2007/mar/17/drugsandalcohol.familyandrelationships>

If drugs were legalised, parents who are already struggling with their own addictions would be able to purchase the drug of their choice legally, but would their children therefore have much choice about taking it or being harmed by the consequences of others taking it? Is this the sort of society that you want to be a part of?

### Example

The grandmother of five-year-old Ellie Lawrenson, who was killed by a pit bull terrier on New Year's Day 2007, had drunk alcohol, taken anti-depressants and smoked cannabis before the attack.

*   'Dog victim's grandmother had taken drug, court told', *Guardian*, 4 September 2007, <http://www.guardian.co.uk/uk/2007/sep/04/ukcrime.helencarter>

**Task**

Have a read of the following articles, where parents are the pushers, and decide for yourself:

- 'My father gave me my first hit of heroin', *Guardian Weekend*, 9 August 2009, <http://www.guardian.co.uk/lifeandstyle/2008/aug/09/familyandrelationships1>
- 'Learnt Behaviour', *Guardian*, case coverage, 14 January 2009, <http://www.guardian.co.uk/society/2009/jan/14/drug-addiction-children>

1. Are these cases strong enough evidence to make a case for not legalising drugs?
2. Do you need to get a broader picture?
3. Does the following report add further strength to the argument?

- Kroll and Taylor (2009) 'Interventions for children and families where there is parental drug misuse', <http://dmri.lshtm.ac.uk/pdfs/Kroll%20summary.pdf>

## Costs of drug misuse

There are substantial costs to the taxpayer created by drug misuse. Payne-James *et al.*'s (2005) survey of detainees who were seen by a doctor (itself a cost) in police custody in London in 2003 showed that 30 per cent were dependent on heroin or crack cocaine and that of these, 82 per cent had been in prison previously.

- Payne-James, Wall and Bailey (2005) 'Patterns of illicit drug use of prisoners in police custody in London, UK', *Journal of Clinical Forensic Medicine*, 12, 196–8 <http://www.ncbi.nlm.nih.gov/pubmed/15950514>

It has been estimated, in 2002, that the average drug user was costing £30,000 per annum.

## Task

Look up the figures for yourself:

- Godfrey, C., Eaton, G., McDougall, C. and Culyer, A. (2002) 'The economic and social costs of Class A drug use in England and Wales, 2000'. Home Office Research Study 249, <http://www.homeoffice.gov.uk/rds/pdfs2/hors249.pdf>

There is also the misery caused by drug-related acquisitive crime and the legal and criminal justice cost in processing those who are caught.

## Additional study task

Although it is somewhat dated now, you should be aware of the following study which focused on the findings from English-language research about drugs and crime; interventions before sentence; community penalties; and interventions in prison:

- Hough, M. (1996) 'Drug misuse and the criminal justice system: a review of the literature'. Drugs Prevention Initiative Paper 15. London: Home Office, <http://www.scan.uk.net/docstore/HO_-_DPI_Paper_15_-_Drugs_Misuse_and_the_Criminal_Justice_System.pdf>

One of the more controversial elements in this review, that of coerced drug treatment, is also reviewed in a 2007 article:

- Toby Seddon (2007) 'Coerced drug treatment'. *Criminology and Criminal Justice*, 7(3), 269–86, <http://crj.sagepub.com/cgi/content/abstract/7/3/269>

Most universities that teach criminology will subscribe to this journal. You will be able to click on the full article from this link.

### Illegal vs legal drugs

As argued above, many make the case that legal drugs, mainly alcohol and tobacco, account for far more harmful and costly effects than do those drugs that are currently proscribed by law. Alcohol has been our favourite drug of choice, legal or illegal and accounted for 150,000 hospitalisations, 20,000 premature deaths and 1.2 million violent incidents according to the 2003 Strategy Unit's report (see Newburn, 2007, Chapter 21). However, there were only 1,900 drug (legal and illegal) related deaths for the whole UK in 2007 (an increase of 8.4 per cent on 2006).

---

Check the source of the figures yourself and cite it:

- International Centre for Drug Policy (2008) 'Drug-related deaths in the UK – annual report 2008', St George's University of London, <http://www.addictiontoday.org/files/drug-deaths-st-georges-report-2008.pdf>

---

This might seem to prove the point of the opening argument above, but Taylor (1999) has argued that since illegal drugs are far more restricted, this difference could well disappear if the current sanctions were lifted.

---

Taylor, I. (1999) *Crime in Context: A Critical Criminology of Market Societies*. Cambridge: Polity.

---

The question for the policy maker and legislator is simple: do you legalise illegal drugs because they are less harmful, or do you minimise harm from all drugs? However, the answer is anything but clear. Earlier, it was claimed in evidence from elsewhere that there is no causal connection between sanctions and drug use, but this is just another way of saying we do not know. In short, it would be a gamble with public health, and it is too risky.

Just think, if drugs were legalised, you could have teenagers going to cocaine bars. If you think this is far fetched, have a look at the following article:

---

- 'Route 36: the world's first cocaine bar', *Guardian*, 19 August 2009, <http://www.guardian.co.uk/world/2009/aug/19/bolivia-cocaine-bar-route-36>
- see also 'Why can't you buy heroin at Boots', *Guardian*, 23 August 2005, <http://www.guardian.co.uk/comment/story/0,1554564,00.html>

---

Much of the preceding pro-drug evidence and argument rely on the idea that **selective decriminalisation** could reduce harm through disrupting drugs markets and 'outsider cultures' of social exclusion and drug use (Taylor, 1999). But what about the real primary costs of hard drug use? As Currie asks, 'are multiple pathologies of drug use all reducible to prohibitionist regulatory policy?' (Currie, 1993 – see South's Chapter 24 in the *Oxford Handbook*,

4th edn, for this source). There might be a considerable reduction in drug-related feuding and other associated non-pharmacological crimes. However, history shows us that those involved in those drugs markets will not simply give up and become bus drivers, chartered accountants or unemployed. They will be looking for another illegal and lucrative market to exploit, and we do not know the unintended consequences of this. It has to be looked at holistically within criminal justice and wider society, and not just as a drugs issue.

Even if we focus on drugs issues, there is a pernicious combination of likely increases in harmful effects. This harm will disproportionately and negatively affect those with multiple problems of deprivation, and also those with a constitutional or genetic weakness that would not become a problem at all in their lives were they not to have access to illegal drugs.

### Normalisation of drug use?

Much of the pro-legalisation argument also relies on the notion of 'normalisation': that it is now both more prevalent and acceptable to take drugs (Druglink, 2001; Parker *et al.*, 1998; see also http://www.espad.org/, which gives up-to-date information from the European School Survey Project on alcohol and other drugs), and this idea has directly impacted on law making and in-service provision (South, 1999). However, others have argued that the evidence for this growing acceptability has been exaggerated (Shiner and Newburn, 1999). This view has to be balanced against the impact of social exclusion, deprivation and drugs. The 1980s saw high unemployment, and a consequent focus for research on drug use and socio-economic conditions. The north of England in particular had high drug use areas, which also clustered with high unemployment, lone-parent families, poor social mobility, and so on (Pearson, 1987). Faced with this sort of evidence, it is as facile to insist that there is no proven causal relationship between drugs and other criminogenic factors as it is to say there is no proof that there is no connection. Drugs will be in the mix of factors and will certainly hinder, rather than help those already subject to multiple deprivations.

---

Sources used here and additional ones can be found in South's Chapter 24 in the *Oxford Handbook*, 4th edn.

---

### Research task

The normalisation debate has been modified and developed. If this theme is your focus, you should read pp. 482–4 of Newburn (2007) *Criminology*, and the further reading section of his Chapter 21.

The question here is whether legalisation will change the experiences and lives of people in the following examples.

**Task**

- Read 'Cause celebre and effect', *Guardian*, 16 November 2005, <http://politics.guardian.co.uk/farright/story/0,1643670,00.html>

The following are examples of the content:

- 'In Ravensthorpe . . . "J" who runs a drop-in centre for addicts and their parents, is bringing up her grandchildren because her son and daughter are both addicts.'
- 'A white-collar worker tells me her niece buys her two sons a bag [of heroine] each a day, rather than have them stealing to get it.'

Is this the type of future we want to see?

It seems that the logical conclusion of the argument for legalisation is a utilitarian one: that it may be for the greater good, though we cannot be sure. The downside of this argument is that those who would benefit represent a 'tyranny of the majority' in the sense that the sizeable minority with predispositions to mental illness or addiction would be regarded as less important.

As Marjory Wallace from the mental health charity Sane put it to the BBC:

> Cannabis, especially in its more toxic varieties, can double the chance of developing severe mental illness in a significant minority of people, particularly the young, whose brains are still developing. While we do not yet know the cause of psychotic illness, or the ways in which drugs such as cannabis may trigger breakdown, relapse, and worsen outcomes, we need to maintain a clear message that it is dangerous to the 10–20 per cent of people who may be at risk but do not know it.
>
> ('Debate over cannabis classification',
> *BBC News*, 31 October 2009,
> <http://news.bbc.co.uk/1/hi/7845023.stm>)

It is also questionable whether it would really be a majority of overall drug users who would benefit, or, more likely, a majority of those in relatively privileged positions whose personal circumstances are not dire. Even these people may delude themselves about how problematic their drug taking is, but they can afford to buy support.

**Examples:**

- 'So, what's it really like in the Priory?', *Observer*, 15 April 2007, <http://www.guardian.co.uk/lifeandstyle/2007/apr/15/healthandwellbeing.features3>
- 'Cannabis keeps me sane and happy, says George Michael', *G*, 21 October 2006, <http://www.guardian.co.uk/uk/2006/oct/21/arts.drugsandalcohol>

In short, it would be fine to legalise drugs for the middle classes and professional high earners, but not for those who are marginalised with few personal or community resources to fall back on.

**Task**

- Read: 'Britain tops EU league for cocaine abuse', *Guardian*, 25 November 2005, <http://www.guardian.co.uk/drugs/Story/0,1650388,00.html>; and
- 'Cocaine anyone?', *Guardian*, 3 February 2005, <http://www.guardian.co.uk/drugs/Story/0,2763,1404510,00.html>

Make notes on the possible implications of legalisation in terms of social inequalities.

The drugs market is never static and constantly presents new problems and it is unlikely that blanket legalisation would help us to deal with these. You will always need **regulation**. Legalisation (or decriminalisation) is not the same as de-regulation.

Danny Kushlick of Transform, another drug law reform lobby group, said: 'This argument over drug classification is distracting attention away from where the real and substantive debate on whether drugs should *be illegal or regulated*' [our emphasis] ('Smith upgrades cannabis to class B', *Guardian*, 7 May 2008, <http://www.guardian.co.uk/politics/2008/may/07/drugspolicy.drugsandalcohol>).

There is a crucial weakness in the legalisation argument. It is often applied to some drugs and not others, or to some groups of people and not others. This is known as **selective legalisation**. For instance, there is a more recent concern about crystal meth 'invading' the UK from the USA, just as there was with crack cocaine in the 1990s. There are no defenders of this drug, or its effects. Do we just simply allow it to flourish and allow the state to start manufacturing and licensing it? This may seem a ridiculous question, but if your answer is no, then you are already talking about regulating, legislating and attempting enforcement against it. Legalisation has not solved the problem, and you may well have set up new or displaced illegal markets for organised crime.

---

- Read: 'Creeping menace of crystal meth, the drug more dangerous than crack', *Guardian*, 15 November 2005, <http://www.guardian. co.uk/drugs/Story/0,2763,1642885,00.html>

Is anyone seriously arguing for legalisation of these effects?

- <http://www.youtube.com/watch?v=af3RjDntlhs>
- <http://www.drugfree.org/Portal/DrugIssue/MethResources/faces/ photo_12.html>
- <http://www.dtsc.ca.gov/SiteCleanup/ERP/Clan_Labs.cfm>
- <http://www.popcenter.org/Problems/problem-druglabs.html>

Make notes on the impact that blanket de-regulation might have and whether this is ever going to be a viable option.

---

It follows that even if heroin were legalised there would have to be the same regulations and legislation governing which type of people can have the drug, just as we have with the legal drugs of alcohol and tobacco. For instance, what age limit is appropriate? Are pregnant women eligible? Are those with psychiatric disorders (actual or potential) excluded? Given these issues, are we seriously suggesting that we have no existing problems of underage drinking and smoking? Legalisation, will not take us forward, but rather, constitute a new set of problems (and costs) for law enforcement in addition to the existing ones. It would be better to solve our existing problems than think up new ones. Legalisation can only get rid of the problems belonging to the criminal markets associated with existing prohibitions, but it does not address underlying causes of misuse such as: poverty; unemployment; boredom; lack of opportunity; mental health problems; and histories of abuse/being in care.

### Selective legalisation, legal drugs and new drugs

---

Pot versus Crystal Meth? Consider this humorous example, but with a key point to make:

- <http://current.com/items/91503842_master-debaters-pot-vs-meth. html>

---

If we accept that blanket legalisation is neither desirable nor practicable, is there a case for **selective decriminalisation or legalisation**? How will this work as new drugs are developed, perhaps specifically to avoid new sanctions?

Even well known drugs have been modified over time. Coca leaves have been used for centuries, but in the 1800s, cocaine was first extracted, changing the nature and use of what was now a much more powerful drug. In the late 1970s, crack cocaine was developed, changing the method of adminstration for users, and changing the nature of its effects.

This evolution will not desist and we may have seen the evolution of the 'Drig' – the deliberately combined effects of drink and drugs. Cocaine and alcohol together produce **cocaethylene**, a third drug which has a powerful effect of increased euphoria, but is also toxic in the liver and has been blamed for heart attacks in the under 40s, along with social problems.

**Task**

- Read: 'Warning of extra heart dangers from mixing cocaine and alcohol', *Guardian*, 8 November 2009, <http://www.guardian.co.uk/society/2009/nov/08/cocaine-alcohol-mixture-health-risks>

1. How convincing is the evidence?
2. Are you prepared to take a chance?
3. Are drug consumption patterns changing to include more combined cocaine and alcohol taking?

- Read: 'More young cocaine addicts being treated', *Guardian*, 3 December 2009, <http://www.guardian.co.uk/society/2009/dec/03/more-young-cocaine-addicts>

1. Is this strong evidence?
2. Are the numbers too small to tell?
3. Do you need to look at the full NTA Annual report 2008–09, 'Effective Treatment Changing Lives' (<http://www.nta.nhs.uk/publications/documents/nta_annual_report_08-09_(2).pdf>)?

- See: EMCDDA News release from 5 November 2009 (No 9) – 'New Drugs: Difficulties of "Hitting a Moving Target" – Market innovation and sophistication challenge drug policies', <http://www.emcdda.europa.eu/about/press/news-releases#93171>

This news release carries several figures and tables.

Will legalisation or decriminalisation take us any further ahead, or will we simply replace one set of regulatory headaches with another?

There is already a big market in legal highs, with Britain playing a leading role in their development. Once you have new drugs, you either have to ban or regulate them.

**Task**

Read the following articles and make notes on the implications for legalisation and decriminalisation:

- 'Britain is European capital for legal highs', *Daily Telegraph*, 5 November 2009, <http://www.telegraph.co.uk/news/newstopics/politics/lawandorder/6509052/Britain-is-European-capital-for-legal-highs.html>

1. Can you find the original report referred to from this source?
2. Should you cite that instead of this newspaper article?
3. Should you find different or additional points to convince the marker that you read the report and that you understand what is important?

- 'There are many drugs that help people get out of their minds yet stay within the law – they're called "legal highs"', *Observer*, 26 April 2009, <http://www.guardian.co.uk/politics/2009/apr/26/drugs-legal-substances-highs>
- 'Legal drug craze is new killer', *Observer*, 10 February 2008, <http://www.guardian.co.uk/world/2008/feb/10/usa>

Even academics may be tempted!:

- 'Performance enhancing academic drugs', <http://media.www.sacredheartspectrum.com/media/storage/paper747/news/2005/10/06/News/Academic.Performance.Enhancing.Drugs.On.The.Rise.With.College.Students-1010298.shtml>

There are already differing approaches on how to deal with 'legal highs':

- 'Government "to ban legal highs"', *BBC News*, 9 June 2009, <http://news.bbc.co.uk/newsbeat/hi/health/newsid_8090000/8090025.stm>
- Government "to ban legal high" drugs', *Guardian*, 25 August 2009, <http://www.guardian.co.uk/politics/2009/aug/25/government-to-outlaw-legal-high-drugs>

- 'Government to ban harmful "legal highs"', Home Office, 'Tackling Drugs Changing Lives', 25 August 2009, <http://drugs.homeoffice.gov.uk/news-events/latest-news/legal-high-ban>
- 'Legally High', *Guardian* video clip, 14 November 2008 (covers legal drugs but also has very useful section by Professor Colin Blakemore – one of the authors of the 2007 *Lancet* article – on how the new ranking of harm system was compiled <http://www.guardian.co.uk/society/video/2008/nov/14/drugs-legal-highs-salvia-youtube>
- 'Police will target dealers when mephedrone is outlawed', *Guardian*, 29 March 2010, <http://www.guardian.co.uk/politics/2010/mar/29/mephedrone-ban-m-cat-miaow>

It is worth noting that in contrast to the approach to cannabis and other illegal drugs, the Home Office has explicitly followed advice on these drugs from ACMD.

To complicate matters further, there is also abuse of existing prescription drugs, mixed with illegal drugs.

- 'Robbie: I was 24hrs from drugs death', *Sun*, 15 December 2009, <http://www.thesun.co.uk/sol/homepage/showbiz/bizarre/2672976/Robbie-Williams-I-was-24-hours-from-drugs-death.html>

Apart from a classic *Sun* headline, it is important to note that there is a mix of legal but prescribed (i.e. regulated) drugs and illegal drugs. What does this tell us about legalisation arguments? If enforcement is successful in one area, for instance, against heroin, there is going to be displacement to another drug. In the case of the article referred to below, it is the illegal use of the legal drug Valium:

- 'Mother's little helper is back: heroin shortage makes Valium the street drug of choice', *Guardian*, 3 September 2008, <http://www.guardian.co.uk/society/2008/sep/03/drugsandalcohol.drugstrade>

But this is an unpredictable process, and in one example, the clampdown on the heroin trade has even led to 'toad abuse':

Experts say addicts have begun breeding toads for the purpose of rolling their dried skins inside cigarettes. Smoking them releases potentially addictive hallucinogens, which are produced by a poisonous chemical normally used by the amphibians as a weapon against prey and predators.

> ('Toads the latest enemy in Iran's war on drugs: Addicts rolling and smoking skins, says doctor', *Guardian*, 17 February 2009, <http://www.guardian.co.uk/world/2009/feb/16/iran-frog-drugs>)

One result is an ecological disaster for the toads, but drug users in general are bad for the environment in a much more global sense. Do cocaine users ever stop to consider that, apart from all of the other misery and organised crime they help create, they are also helping to destroy the environment?

## Task

- Read: 'Cocaine users are destroying the rainforest – at 4 square metres a gram', <http://www.guardian.co.uk/world/2008/nov/19/cocaine-rainforests-columbia-santos-calderon>

Is this a moral case for legalising drugs or enforcing against them?

## Regulation: who should be drug-tested in a legalised world?

Again, legalising drugs will just create more problems than it is supposed to solve.

## Task

- Read: 'Drunken airline pilot jailed for four months', *Guardian*, 9 December 2006, <http://www.guardian.co.uk/business/2006/dec/09/theairlineindustry.uknews>; and
- 'Amsterdam's drug police demand right to keep on smoking cannabis', *The Times*, 27 September 2007, <http://www.timesonline.co.uk/tol/news/world/europe/article3098016.ece>

If you think drugs should be legalised, make notes on which of the following should be excluded from taking drugs and why.

| Airline pilots | Train drivers |
| Politicians | Surgeons |
| GPs | Students |
| Lecturers | Benefits claimants |
| Police officers | Any employee |

1. How do your views compare with the general public's?

- See: Observer/ICM Poll, 16 November 2008, <http://www.guardian.co.uk/society/2008/nov/16/uk-drug-use-survey-statistics-poll>

2. Should they be barred from taking any drugs at all?
3. Should they be allowed to take drugs when they are not working, but if so, would you need a set of complex regulations for each drug because they stay in the system for differing periods of time?
4. Do you still think legalisation is realistic?

The issue of benefits claimants being drug tested has already sparked a row, with the government proposing, in the Welfare Reform Bill, that those who are addicted and claiming benefits should also be in treatment in order to keep their benefits.

---

**See**

- 'Drugs test for claimants sparks row over unemployment benefits', *Observer*, 27 September 2009, <http://www.guardian.co.uk/politics/2009/sep/27/drugs-test-benefit-unemployed-rehab>

This would allow Jobcentre staff to assess claimants' drug use, and, crucially, share information with police and probation staff.

1. Does this have implications for joined up government, state surveillance, crime control models? (See Chapter 1)
2. Or is it an attempt at ensuring better treatment and rehabilitation?

---

Those Jobcentre staff could, or course, find themselves on the wrong end of drug testing, with no redundancy payment.

> • See: 'Rise in use of drug tests to sack staff without redundancy pay', *Guardian*, 18 May 2009, <http://www.guardian.co.uk/society/2009/may/18/drugs-testing-workplace-redundancy>

It shows how those with little personal discipline and respect for the law can end up in deep trouble through their selfish pursuit of pleasure without responsibility.

### Rounding up

That is the end of the debate which should have helped you to grasp the key themes involved in examining drugs issues. As ever, real life is much messier than the extremes presented in a debate and the move to discuss regulation has already hinted at this.

To summarise (see South's Chapter 24 in the 4th edition of the *Oxford Handbook*), **legalisation** proponents argue that:

- law enforcement is costly, counterproductive and unsuccessful;
- wider availability would not mean an unacceptable rise in use;
- legal taxation would provide education, health and counselling funds;
- regulation over purity and adulteration would reduce harm;
- legality would destroy criminal markets' profitability.

**Anti-legalisation** proponents argue that:

- legalisation would increase use;
- legalisation would increase the social costs to society;
- increasing restrictions have been placed by the Dutch government on perceived abuses of the café system.

The next section is provided as a resource for those who wish to add to, or use the debate format along different lines. After that, there is a section on thinking beyond the debate, which raises issues of balancing the evidence still further and perhaps reframing questions about drugs and their relationship to crime.

## The debates of others

You will find the debate format is used a lot in considering the drugs issue and the following are examples of the types of polarised arguments used in the media. This section can be used as teaching and seminar discussion materials, or to strengthen/undermine some of the points raised in our debate above.

## Debate 1

- Tom Lloyd, former Chief Constable and now of International Drug Policy Consortium (<http://www.idpc.net>): 'The war on drugs is a waste of time', *Guardian*, 20 September 2009, <http://www.guardian.co.uk/commentisfree/2009/sep/20/drugs-british-police>

vs

- Antonio Maria Costa, then Executive Director of the United Nations Office on Drugs and Crime (UNODC): 'How many lives would have been lost if we didn't have controls on drugs?', *Guardian*, 20 September 2009, <http://www.guardian.co.uk/commentisfree/2009/sep/20/drugs-decriminalisation>
- (accompanying article to the above debate) 'The Observer drugs debate', *Observer*, 20 September 2009, Round table (non-experts): Ann Widdecombe, Camila Batmanghelidjh, A.C. Grayling, Erwin James, Philip Pullman, Kenneth Roth and Karol Sikora debate the UK's approach to drugs, <http://www.guardian.co.uk/commentisfree/2009/sep/20/drugs-britain-opinion-debate>

The views of lay people are important, but think about who has been selected and who they might represent.

How much weight should be given to their views compared to Professor Nutt's?

## Debate 2

- 'The war on drugs is immoral idiocy. We need the courage of Argentina', *Guardian*, Comment is free, 3 September 2009, <http://www.guardian.co.uk/commentisfree/2009/sep/03/drugs-prohibition-latin-america>

vs

- 'Drug legalisation is no solution – it's a disaster waiting to happen. Neil McKeganey', *Guardian*, Comment is free, 17 September 2009, <http://www.guardian.co.uk/commentisfree/2009/sep/17/response-drug-legalisation-problemsl>

1. Are they really talking past each other?
2. Does it come down to being more precise?
3. Is Simon Jenkins thinking about crystal meth or new legal highs?

---

**Debate 3**

- Danny Kushlick (then spokesperson for the Drugs and Health Alliance) 'Increment of harm', *Guardian*, 16 May 2007, <http://www.guardian. co.uk/commentisfree/2007/may/16/comment.politics1>

vs

- Vernon Coaker (then Home Office minister) 'It's not a moral panic. Drugs really do destroy communities', *Guardian*, 25 May 2007, <http://www.guardian.co.uk/commentisfree/2007/may/25/comment. homeaffairs>

---

The question for you to decide is whether we need to move beyond the level and type of discussion that we find most often on this topic: the debate.

## Thinking beyond the debate

Raistrick *et al.* (1999) argue that there is no answer to why some become dependent on a single substance, and most avoid or grow out of dependence, or grow into relatively stable and patterned drug use as adults. Since we also have imperfect knowledge on the successes and failures of prevention, treatment and criminal justice intervention, are we in a position to legalise more drugs than we already have?

In broadening and deepening your understanding of this issue, we have put together this final section in order to help you structure your reading. Remember, any solution in the real world always creates a new set of dilemmas and issues to deal with.

**Task**

Read Chapters 7, 8, 9 and 11 in Volume 1 of:

- EMCDDA (2008), *A Cannabis Reader: Global Issues and Local Experiences*, Monograph series 8, Volume 1, European Monitoring Centre for Drugs and Drug Addiction, Lisbon, <http://www. emcdda.europa.eu/attachements.cfm/att_53353_EN_Cannabis %20Vol%201%20FINAL.pdf>

Using the case of cannabis, make notes on:

- the complexity of implementing and managing legalisation;
- the key differences and implications in introducing decriminalisation compared to legalisation and selective approaches;

- the similarities and differences between managing the use of established legal drugs: alcohol and tobacco;
- any evidence of what makes drugs policy effective and how this depends on the aims of the policies.

### *Drugs and crime*

The link between drugs and crime is always hotly debated, and not just by us. It is a little more involved than there was space for in the main debate, so be clear on the extent to which you are being asked to develop the relationship between crime and drugs. If it is a major theme of your assessment, then you should be aware of all of the following models of explanation.

---

**Important note**

The summary below is, like most of this book, not designed to be cut and pasted, but as a way to quickly grasp the key issues and then as a 'jump off point' for your in-depth reading. Most of the summary is based on the two key sources of:

- Chapter 5, Bennett, T. and Holloway, K. (2005) *Understanding Drugs, Alcohol and Crime*. Maidenhead: Open University Press.
- Chapter 21 (pp. 484–7) 'Drugs and alcohol' in Tim Newburn's (2007) *Criminology*. Cullompton: Willan.

All citations for the key points on the models below can be found in the above sources, or in Nigel South's Chapter 25 of the 3rd edition or Chapter 24 of the 4th edition of Maguire *et al.*'s *Oxford Handbook of Criminology*.

  If 'drugs and crime' is your major theme, you do really need to read the Bennett and Holloway (2005) book and also their later (and shorter) treatment of drugs, crime and causality:

- Bennett, T. and Holloway, K. (2009) 'The causal connection between drug misuse and crime'. *British Journal of Criminology* 49(4), 513–31.

---

The first two models are the commonest and simplest.

*Model 1: Drug dependence leads to criminal activity*
*to pay for more drugs*

In which case, legalisation would be expected to have an impact. This recapitulates the model that focused on using Goldstein's typology in the early part of the chapter. This position is characterised by three distinct strands of explanation:

- **Psychopharmacological explanations**: either **direct causation** in that changes in behaviour brought about by taking the drug lead to offending, eg, becoming irritable and excitable leading to a greater propensity to offend, or **indirect causation**, mediated by social context and environmental factors, which also includes the role of the drug in victim precipitation.
- **Economic explanations**: addicts become 'enslaved' to their drug/s and it dominates their lives to such an extent that most legitimate ways of earning cash to pay for their increasingly expensive habit will not yield enough money and so they must engage in acquisitive crime.
- **Drug lifestyle or systemic explanations**: in this model, 'drug lifestyles' are seen to cause crime and are often related to the need to be involved at some level in an illegal trading market where disputes and competition often result in violence.

There is, however, a number of competing models to explain the drugs–crime relationship, or indeed, the lack of one.

*Model 2: Criminal lifestyles facilitate drug involvement*

This position is characterised by the same three strands as in Model 1, but the direction of causality is reversed:

- **Psychopharmacological explanations**: the primary driver is a need to obtain money by illegal means and drugs are used either: as a pleasurable 'chemical recreation' method to celebrate successfully gaining money through crime; or as a way of steadying the nerves or achieving the level of disinhibition required to commit the pre-planned crime.
- **Economic explanations**: rather than enslavement, drugs are just one of the desirable consumer products that can be bought using the surplus generated by involvement in crime.
- **Criminal lifestyle or systemic explanations**: rather than being motivated by addiction, drugs form part of the criminal lifestyle along with other factors such as boom-bust cash availability linked to criminal events, conspicuous consumption between such events, the need to maintain more than one abode, etc. This may be relatively chaotic, or dynamic and entrepreneurial.

These positions have both been criticised and three further key theoretical models have been postulated and are summarised below.

## *Model 3: Reciprocal model*

A perhaps inevitable development from the first two models above, and perhaps a microcosm of how debates between extreme positions help to synthesise more sophisticated models, the reciprocal model is really saying that real life is messy and that both explanations are valid, depending on the context. This is known as a bi-directional theory, and the causation depends on 'opportunity' and 'need'. It implies that at times, individuals may commit crime to fulfil a need created by drug use, but at other times, drugs can bought with the proceeds of opportunistic crime in the same way as other goods. The appeal of this model is that it can explain both onset and persistence of drug taking and criminality. If drug use is casual to start with, then it is not causally connected to criminality, but if drug use intensifies, income from crime will increasingly be used to fund drug use, and if this progresses to addition, then drugs become a cause of crime.

## *Model 4: Common cause model*

Put simply, the common cause model focuses on the fact that many of the risk factors linked to general criminality are also linked to problematic drug use, such that it is not possible to disentangle these causations meaningfully. Therefore, both problematic drug use and crime are 'caused' by other common factors. There is often a strong sub-cultural element which passes these **personal/psychological**, **environmental** and **social/structural** risk factors from generation to generation.

## *Model 5: Coincidence model*

The coincidence model moves away from any causal connection between drugs and crime (in either direction) and from any other common causal factor (ie, in contrast to the common cause model). This model maintains that drugs, crime and other problem behaviours are coincidental and simultaneous, but non-causal and non-reciprocal (so also challenging the reciprocal model).

Addicts and users are not an homogenous group (Nurco *et al.*, 1985 <http://onlinelibrary.wiley.com/doi/10.1111/j.1745-9125.1988.tb00848.x/ abstract>; see also Nurco *et al.* (1991)) and real life explanations are inevitably not as neat as these ideal-typical constructions, so it is important to read some of the fieldwork studies that have incorporated, generated and/or developed these models.

## Task

### Desperate partying?

To examine the drugs-crime nexus, selectively read:

- Neal Shover (1996) *The Great Pretenders*. Westview Press; and/or
- the book (which spawned the cult HBO series *The Wire*) referred to in the following review: 'To deal is to live on the corner', *Observer Book Review* (Wire) 26 April 2009, <http://www.guardian.co.uk/books/2009/apr/26/the-corner-wire-david-simon>. (If you are pursuing this theme for your studies/assessment, it is well worth viewing series 3 of *The Wire* too.)
- In the UK context, you should also read the work of Howard Parker. Newburn's (2007) *Criminology* book provides you with most of the relevent key works in the Bibliography.
- In the US context, the work of Wright and Decker is also important, see their 1997 book *Armed Robbers in Action: Stickups and Street Culture*. Boston, MA: Northeastern University Press.
- Also see: Uggen and Thompson (2003) 'The socio-economic determinants of ill-gotten gains: within person changes in drug use and illegal earnings'. *American Journal of Sociology*, 109, 146–85.

To what extent would legalisation/decriminalisation of drugs reduce the associated crime?

### Do we care about drugs?

Consider whether we really care about drugs in terms of the personal harm they cause (or do not cause) to the users and those with whom they are in contact, or whether we care more about public order/fear of crime. Are problematic users who obtain their drugs in and around the streets going to be complained about and enforced against more than non-problematic users who are relatively well-off?

## Task

- Read: Bennett, T. and Holloway, K. (2005) *Understanding Drugs, Alcohol and Crime*. Maidenhead: Open University Press, Chapter 2, esp. pp. 27–9.
- 'Whatever happened to . . . the middle-class cocaine use clampdown', *Guardian*, 11 March 2006, <http://www.guardian.co.uk/drugs/Story/0,1728639,00.html>
- '14-year-olds selling drugs, report claims', *Guardian*, 28 November 2005, <http://www.guardian.co.uk/crime/article/0,1652550,00.html>

*War on drugs*

If your focus is on the war on drugs, there are some important developments that you should be aware of. The following materials should allow you to update yourself and know where to look for key additional sources.

In 2009, there was a perceptible shift in official views on the war against drugs and it may be the beginning of a recognition that it facilitates organised crime. There was also a recognition that legalised drugs markets may represent a lucrative source of official taxation and revenue. Indeed, Antonio Maria Costa, head of UNODC went so far as to say he had seen evidence that drug money 'saved the banks' in the global credit crunch.

---

'Drug money saved banks in global crisis, claims UN advisor', *Observer*, 13 December 2009, <http://www.guardian.co.uk/global/2009/dec/13/drug-money-banks-saved-un-chief-claims>

---

Danny Kushlick, again, was at the forefront in commenting on the futility of enforcement.

---

Our position is – if cannabis can be dangerous to a few, yet two million people regularly smoke it – we should have a regulated and supervised market for it, rather than putting its distribution in the hands of criminals.
(Danny Kushlick from Transform (Drugs Policy Think Tank),
'Debate over cannabis classification', *BBC News*,
31 October 2009, <http://news.bbc.co.uk/1/hi/7845023.stm>)

---

It has also been noted that the police were not wholeheartedly behind the upgrading of cannabis to Class B once more.

---

'Police reject tougher action on cannabis', *Guardian*, 1 May 2008, <http://www.guardian.co.uk/society/2008/may/01/drugsandalcohol.drugspolicy>

---

The following sources are important in considering the war on drugs:

- <http://www.drogasedemocracia.org/English/>

Think about the hierarchy of sources outlined in Chapter 1 of this book.

1. How impartial are these sources?
2. Who has compiled the collection?
3. Do you need to look at some original sources instead of relying on press articles?

- Read: 'The Final Report of the Latin American Commission on Drugs and Democracy', <http://www.drogasedemocracia.org/Arquivos/livro_ ingles_02.pdf>, which, itself, cites the latest *World Drug Report* from UNODC (United Nations Office on Drugs and Crime) <http://www. unodc.org/documents/wdr/WDR_2008/WDR_2008_eng_web.pdf>

In the report, UNODC recognises that implementation of United Nations Conventions on illicit drugs has produced various unexpected negative consequences:

- The creation of a black market controlled by organised crime.
- The fight against crime, linked to drug trafficking, demands ever increasing resources, often to the detriment of investments in public health, which was the rationale of prohibitionist politics.
- Repression of production in one locale resulted in its transfer to other regions, keeping global production levels stable.
- Displacement of the types of drugs used as a result of relative price changes associated with repression.

Finally, prohibitionist policies have generated the stigmatization of drug addicts who are socially marginalized and struggle to find adequate treatment. The main objective turned out to be unattainable, and the United Nations' own organising bodies recognise that they have moved from the original objective to eliminate drugs to a policy of containment in regard to levels of production and commerce.

4. Is there a growing official and political recognition that the war on drugs cannot be won, that it is counter-productive and that legalisation of drugs is inevitable?

See the following press comments:

- 'Is America ready to admit defeat in its 40-year war on drugs?', *Observer*, 6 September 2009, <http://www.guardian.co.uk/theobserver/ 2009/sep/06/war-on-drugs-latin-america>

5. Is legalisation proposed, or is it decriminalisation?

*Regulation: a more radical rethink?*

Where 'campaigners originally went wrong was in leaping straight from the failure of prohibition to call for an end to any legal sanction' ('Cannabis is bad for you, but it's also impossible to ban', *Guardian*, 30 July 2007, <http://www.guardian.co.uk/commentisfree/2007/jul/30/comment.politics1>).

If the war on drugs is recognised as a failure, could regulated legalisation save billions and raise tax revenue at a time when the world economy is under severe stress?

---

Drugs charity Transform Drug Policy Foundation produced a report in April 2009:

- 'A comparison of the cost-effectiveness of the prohibition and regulation of drugs', <http://www.tdpf.org.uk/Transform%20 CBA%20paper%20final.pdf>

This is based partly on an analysis of Home Office and No. 10 strategy unit reports, but argues:

> The government specifically claims the benefits of any move away from prohibition towards legal regulation would be outweighed by the costs. No such cost-benefit analysis, or even a proper impact assessment of existing enforcement policy and legislation has ever been carried out here or anywhere else in the world.
>
> The conclusion is that regulating the drugs market is a dramatically more cost-effective policy than prohibition and that moving from prohibition to regulated drugs markets in England and Wales would provide a net saving to taxpayers, victims of crime, communities, the criminal justice system and drug users of somewhere within the range of, for the four scenarios, £13.9bn, £10.8bn, £7.7bn, £4.6bn.

---

An Independent Drug Monitoring Unit estimate, quoted in the report, also suggests up to £1.3bn could be generated by a £1 per gram tax on cannabis resin and £2 per gram on skunk.

---

Transform have since published the book, which is fully available online at:

- Transform (2009) *After the War on Drugs: Blueprint for Regulation*, <http://www.tdpf.org.uk/Transform_Drugs_Blueprint.pdf>

The book is dedicated to Mo Mowlam (1949–2005) who was the minister responsible for UK Drug Policy from 1999 to 2001, and who stated:

> From my experience of being responsible for drugs policy ... I came to the conclusion that legalisation and regulation of all drugs was the only way to reduce the harmful effects of this unstoppable activity.
>
> (*Guardian*, 19 September 2002)

---

**Task**

Think about the hierarchy of evidence outlined in Chapter 1.
  Transform has an abolitionist agenda.

1. Has this affected the value and/or quality of its evidence?
2. Is it any more biased that academic accounts?
3. How do you decide on the value of the evidence?

Look at the sources cited. Many of them are hyperlinked, but the ease of access does not make these sources superior, so make sure you check the balance of the evidence systematically.
  Once you are clear on this, have a look at Transform's resources:

- 'After the war on drugs: Tools for the debate' <http://tdpf.org.uk/Tools_For_The%20Debate.pdf>

This also includes many further resources and references.
  Don't forget to read the section entitled: 'You can be "anti-drug" and "pro-reform"'.

---

The following sources are also key resources on this topic.

---

- 'How to stop the drug wars: prohibition has failed; legalisation is the least bad solution' *The Economist*, 5 March 2009 <http://www.scribd.com/doc/21615831/prohibition-has-failed-legalisation-is-the-least-bad-solution>
- Global Cannabis Commission Report (2008) <http://www.beckleyfoundation.org/pdf/BF_Cannabis_Commission_Report.pdf>, commissioned by the Beckley Foundation which was a UN accredited NGO for the 2009 UN strategic policy review.

*Evidence-based drugs policy and political decisions*

As noted, towards the end of 2009, there was a convulsion in the relationship between the Home Office, responsible for regulation and enforcement against drugs, and the ACMD that advises in a statutory capacity under the 1971 Misuse of Drugs Act. Professor David Nutt, the chair of ACMD was sacked. You will by now already be familiar with the issues surrounding the sacking of Professor David Nutt, but if you have been set an assessment task around the extent to which government policy is or should be based on evidence, the following further materials will be of help.

The sacking of Professor Nutt led to fundamental questions being asked, in England and Wales, about the role of scientific evidence and the balance with other considerations that politicians make when deciding on drug policy. It is therefore important that you are aware of the key issues. Much of it relates back to the simmering tensions caused by the downgrading of cannabis to Class C and its subsequent regrading back to Class B, which has been covered above.

---

**Task 1**

1.  Was the 2009 cannabis upgrading based on evidence? Consider these quotations from:

*   'Smith upgrades cannabis to class B', *Guardian*, 7 May 2008, <http://www.guardian.co.uk/politics/2008/may/07/drugspolicy. drugsandalcohol>

The [then] ACMD chair, Professor Sir Michael Rawlins, refused to criticise the home secretary, saying that the ACMD's recommendations were based entirely on harmfulness – but that the government had the right to consider other factors.
He said:

> We don't take into account 'the message', we don't take into account policing priorities; we are obliged by law only to take into account the harmfulness. The government may want to take into account other matters. That's their right; they are the government. We are only an advisory committee and from time to time governments, for their own reasons, may wish to ignore the advice.

Contrast this with the views of the 2009 ACMD chair, Professor Nutt in his Eve Saville Lecture 2009, already referenced in the early part of this chapter ('Estimating drug harms: a risky business?', Briefing, 10 October 2009, Centre for Crime and Justice Studies

<http://www.crimeandjustice.org.uk/opus1714/Estimating_drug_ harms.pdf>), who recognises the many competing influences on politicians but saw his role as chair of AMCD differently.

Make notes on what you feel you would decide if you were Home Secretary, e.g. Do we trust who we elect to make decisions based on more than scientific evidence, or do we trust the experts (who often disagree like all good academics) more?

Have a listen to Professor Nutt's own views on his comments and the relationship between scientific evidence and politics at:

● <http://www.youtube.com/watch?v=gwJ87LEsoec>
● Also see: 'Scientists line up to attack Alan Johnson over sacking of drug adviser', *Guardian*, 2 November 2009, <http://www.guardian. co.uk/politics/2009/nov/02/alan-johnson-drug-adviser-row>

## Task 2

How do you reconcile Professor Nutt's, and others' scientific advice with the experiences of victims (and their families) who suffer because of drugs? See:

● 'The big issue: Cannabis debate. Professor Nutt got it completely wrong', <http://www.guardian.co.uk/theobserver/2009/nov/08/big-issue-cannabis-debate>

You can use the following cases to discuss the victim perspective and bring in the themes debated in Chapter 9 on victims' and suspects' rights.

### Case 1

Tom Palmer, a knife-obsessed cannabis addict who was jailed for life for the brutal murders of two schoolboys:

● 'Schoolboys' murderer to serve at least 18 years', *Guardian*, 20 March 2007, <http://www.guardian.co.uk/drugs/Story/0,2038576,00.html>
● 'Drug user gets life for killing friends', *Guardian*, 21 March 2007, <http://www.guardian.co.uk/drugs/Story/0,2038696,00.html>

### Case 2

● 'Staff put killer's rights before public safety', *Daily Telegraph*, 17 November 2006, <http://www.telegraph.co.uk/news/uknews/1534382/ Staff-put-killers-rights-before-public-safety.html>

**The Killer: John Barrett** – 'He was a heavy *cannabis user* and specialist reports on him concluded that the *drug made him more psychotic*':

- 'Singer turned to life of crime', *Daily Telegraph*, 17 November 2006, <http://www.telegraph.co.uk/news/uknews/1534383/Singer-turned-to-life-of-crime.html>

**The Victim: Denis Finnegan** – 'he was killed doing something as ordinary as riding a bike in a park in Britain.':

- 'Great guy with a thirst for life', *Daily Telegraph*, 17 November 2006, <http://www.telegraph.co.uk/news/uknews/1534380/Great-guy-with-a-thirst-for-life.html>

## Case 3

Ezekiel Maxwell killed Carmelita Tulloch:

- 'Boy on skunk cannabis butchered a grandmother', *London Evening Standard*, 3 April 2007, <http://www.thisislondon.co.uk/news/article-23391305-boy-on-skunk-cannabis-butchered-a-grandmother.do>

## Case 4

Laurie Draper killed Paul Butterworth:

- 'Soldier killed friend's dad while having "cannabis-induced delusions"', *Daily Mail*, 29 August 2006, <http://www.dailymail.co.uk/news/article-402759/Soldier-killed-friends-dad-having-cannabis-induced-delusions.html>

### Film treatments

It is possible to set assessments based on a critique of relevant films. The following are suggestions that we think work well in this context.

## Drugs, crime control and due process

You can find a synopsis of the 2008 Brazilian film *Elite Squad* (Tropa de Elite) at <http://www.elitesquadmovi.eco.uk/#/Synopsis/>, about an elite anti-drugs squad in the late 1990s and, like *The Wire*, is based on real-life characters.

Try to relate the role that the police play back to the issues around crime control, due process, and the rule of law covered in Chapter 1.

What are the implications of enforcement against drug traffickers for the rest of the population?

You can carry out a similar exercise using the US Film *Bad Lieutenant* (1992). Similar themes of entrepreneurship in illegal markets and the role of law enforcement can be found in US/Mexico-based film *Blow* (2001) and in the UK-based *Layer Cake* (2004). For the heroin user perspective and hedonism (or desperate partying), look at *Trainspotting* (1996).

Other key films that can be recommended are:

- *Traffic* (2000)
- *Cookers* (2001)
- *Most High* (2006)
- *Nil by Mouth* (1997).

It is also worth visiting: <http://video.google.com/videoplay?docid=-6696582420128930236#> to see *Reefer Madness* (1936), directed by Louis J. Gasnier, for a historical perspective on concerns about the perceived threats that drugs posed and the extent to which official reactions were evidence-based in Anslinger's time.There are parallels to be had here with the 2009 spat between Professor Nutt and the Home Office, or more humorously with an updated public advice video on the Dangers of Drugs: <http://www.youtube.com/watch?v=7w_6oiR5IbE>

# References

Bean, P. (2005) *Drugs and Crime*. Cullompton: Willan.

Bennett, T. and Holloway, K. (2005) *Understanding Drugs, Alcohol and Crime*. Maidenhead: Open University Press.

Blackman, S. (2004) *Chilling Out: The Cultural Politics of Substance Consumption, Youth and Drug Policy*. Maidenhead: McGraw-Hill.

Bonnie, R. and Whitebread, C. (1974) 'The marijuana conviction'. Retrieved on 5 June 2006 from: <http://www.druglibrary.org/schaffer/library/studies/vlr/nationalmonster.htm>

Boyd, N. and Lowman, J. (1993) 'The politics of prostitution and drug control'. In K. Stenson and D. Cowell (eds) *The Politics of Crime Control*. London: Sage, pp. 109–26.

Brockes, E. (2005) 'Has any public figure not taken cocaine?' *Guardian*, 10 October.

Davenport-Hines, R. (2001) *The Pursuit of Oblivion: A Social History of Drugs*. London: Phoenix Press.

Department of Health (2002) *Drug Use, Smoking and Drinking among Young People in England 2001*. Retrieved on 5 June 2006 from: <http://www.dh.gov.uk/PublicationsAndStatistics/Publications/PublicationsStatistics/PublicationsStatisticsArticle/fs/en?CONTENT_ID=4010044&chk=KDwB0F>

Druglink (2001) 'The European School Survey Project'. *Druglink*, 16, 2: 6.

Drugscope (2006) *How Many People Die From Using Drugs?* Retrieved on 5 June 2006 from: <http://www.drugscope.org.uk/druginfo/drugsearch/ds_results.asp?file=%5Cwip%5C11%5C1%5C1%5C1%5Cdeaths.html>

Edwards, G. (1995) *Alcohol Policy and the Public Good*. Oxford: Oxford Medical Publications, pp. 75–106.

Farrell, G. and Thorne, J. (2005) 'Where have all the flowers gone? Evaluation of the Taliban crackdown against opium poppy cultivation in Afghanistan'. *International Journal of Drug Policy*, 16(2), 81–91.

GLADA (2004) 'An evidence base for the London crack cocaine strategy'. Retrieved on 5 June 2006 from: <http://www.westsussexdaat.co.uk/docs/London%20Crack%20Strategy%20evidence%20published%2029apr04.pdf#search='GLADA%20crack%20cocaine'>

Gossop, M. (2000) *Living with Drugs*. Aldershot: Ashgate.

Green, P. (1998) *Drugs, Trafficking and Criminal Policy: The Scapegoat Strategy*. Winchester: Waterside.

HMCPSI (n.d.) *Payback Time: Joint Review of Asset Recovery since the Proceeds of Crime Act 2002*. Retrieved on 5 June 2006 from: <http://www.hmcpsi.gov.uk/reports/PaybackPart1.pdf>

Home Affairs Select Committee (2002) *Third Report: The Government's Drugs Policy. Is it Working?* Retrieved on 5 June 2006 from: <http://www.publications.parliament.uk/pa/cm200102/cmselect/cmhaff/318/31802.htm>

Horgen, K.B. and Brownell, K.D. (1998) 'Policy change as a means for reducing the prevalence and impact of alcoholism, smoking, and obesity'. In W. Miller and N. Heather (eds) *Treating Addictive Behaviours: Applied Clinical Psychology* (2nd edn) New York: Plenum, pp. 105–18.

Inciardi, J. (1999) *The Drug Legalisation Debate*. London: Sage.

Jenkins, S. (1999) *Synthetic Panics: The Symbolic Politics of Designer Drugs*. New York: New York University Press.

Justice (2005) *Drugs Bill: Briefing on the Second Reading*. Retrieved on 5 June 2006 from: <http://www.justice.org.uk/images/pdfs/drugsbillsrl.pdf>

Kohn, K. (1992) *Dope Girls: The Birth of the British Drug Underground*. London: Granta.

Maguire, M., Morgan, R. and Reiner, R. (eds) (2007) *Oxford Handbook of Criminology* (4th edn). Oxford: Oxford University Press.

May, T., Warburton, H., Turnbull, P.J. and Hough, M. (2002) *Times they are A-changing: Policing of Cannabis*. York: Joseph Rowntree Foundation, available at: <http://www.jrf.org.uk/publications/policing-cannabis-class-b-drug>

Measham, F., Aldridge, J. and Parker, H. (2001) *Dancing on Drugs: Risk, Health and Hedonism in the British Clubs Scene*. London: Free Association Books.

Mill, J.S. (1986) *On Liberty*. New York: Prometheus.

Morgan, J. and Zimmer, L. (1997) 'The social pharmacology of smokeable cocaine: not all it's cracked up to be'. In C. Reinarman and H. Levine (eds) *Crack in America: Demon Drugs and Social Justice*. California: University of California. Retrieved on 5 June 2006 from: <http://www.druglibrary.org/schaffer/cocaine/crack.htm>

Morgan, R. and Liebling, A. (2007) 'Imprisonment: an expanding scene'. In M. Maguire, R. Morgan and R. Reiner (eds) *The Oxford Handbook of Criminology* (4th edn). Oxford: Oxford University Press.

Murphy, R. and Roe, S. (2007) 'Drug misuse declared: findings from the 2006/07 British Crime Survey'. Home Office Statistical Bulletin 18/07. London: Home Office. Retrieved on 16 May 2011 from: <http://www.drugslibrary.stir.ac.uk/documents/hosb1807.pdf>

Newburn, Tim (2007) *Criminology*. Cullompton: Willan.

Nurco *et al.* (1991) 'Recent research on the relationship between illicit drug use and crime'. *Behavioral Sciences & the Law*, 9(3) 219–370.

Parker, H., Aldridge, J. and Egginton, R. (2001) *UK Drugs Unlimited: Research and Policy Lessons on Illicit Drugs*. Basingstoke: Palgrave.

Parker, H., Measham, F. and Aldridge, J. (1998) *Illegal Leisure: Normalization of Adolescent Recreational Drug Use*. London: Routledge.

Pearson, G. (1987) 'Social deprivation, unemployment and patterns of heroin use'. In N. Dorn and N. South (eds) *A Land Fit for Heroin? Drug Policies, Prevention and Practice*. London: Macmillan.

Raistrick, D., Hodgson, R. and Ritson, B. (eds) (1999) *Tackling Alcohol Together: The Evidence Base for a UK Alcohol Policy*. London. Free Association Books.

Roe, S. (2005) 'Drug misuse declared: findings from the 2004/05 British Crime Survey'. Home Office Statistical Bulletin 16/05. London: Home Office. Retrieved on 16 May 2011 from: <http://www.compassunit.com/docs/hosb1605.pdf>

Schlosser, E. (2003) *Reefer Madness and Other Tales from the American Underground*. London: Allen Lane.

Shiner, M. and Newburn, T. (1999) 'Taking tea with Noel: drugs and discourse for the 1990s'. In N. South (ed.) *Drugs: Cultures, Controls and Everyday Life*. London: Sage.

South, N. (ed.) (1999) *Drugs: Cultures, Controls and Everyday Life*. London: Sage.

—— (2002) 'Drugs, alcohol and crime'. In M. Maguire, R. Morgan and R. Reiner (eds) *The Oxford Handbook of Criminology* (3rd edn). Oxford: Oxford University Press, Chapter 25, esp. pp. 923–44.

Taylor, I. (1999) *Crime in Context: A Critical Criminology of Market Societies*. Cambridge: Polity.

TheDEA.org (n.d.) 'In the beginning. It came. It was embraced. It was banned. But the final chapter has yet to be written'. Retrieved on 5 June 2006 from: <http://www.thedea.org/drughistory.html>

Trace, M. (2005) 'The Taliban and opium cultivation in Afghanistan'. *International Journal of Drug Policy*. 16, 79–80.

White, W.L. (1979) 'Themes in Chemical Prohibition'. In *Drugs in Perspective*. Rockville, MD: National Institute on Drug Abuse. Retrieved on 5 June 2006 from: <http://www.druglibrary.org/schaffer/History/ticp.html>

WHO (1955) 'Physical and mental effects of cannabis'. Retrieved on 5 June 2006 from: <http://members.aol.com/paladcampaign/whoquotes.htm>

Williamson, K. (1997) *Drugs and the Party Line*. Edinburgh: Rebel Inc.

Wincup, E., Buckland, G. and Bayliss, R. (2003) *Youth homelessness and substance use: report to the drugs and alcohol research unit*. Home Office Research Study 258. London: Home Office.

# 8 Capital punishment

## The case for and against

*Mark Button and Diana Bretherick*

---

- Read Garland, D. (2005) 'The cultural uses of capital punishment'. *Punishment and Society*, 4, 459–87.

---

In this chapter, one of the most contentious issues in criminal justice will be considered: the debate over the reintroduction of capital punishment for premeditated murder. Capital punishment was effectively abolished in the UK in 1964. Since then there have been periodic attempts in Parliament through private members bills to reintroduce capital punishment. This chapter will not explore those attempts at reintroduction; rather it will focus upon the debate and the arguments used for and against. The focus will be upon the UK; however, debates in the UK often utilise research and examples from other countries and therefore this chapter will do so too. Before we embark upon this, we first give a brief overview on the history and use of capital punishment in the UK and abroad.

## A brief history of capital punishment

Capital punishment (the execution of a person for a designated crime) has been used for as long as people have lived together in groups. England and Wales was no exception, apart from a brief period following William the Conqueror's successful invasion, when capital punishment was abolished in favour of mutilation. During the reign of Henry VIII (1509–47) it is estimated that 72,000 people were executed.

Most people think of capital punishment as being reserved for the most crimes such as murder. However, in the UK, crimes such as sodomy, impersonating a Chelsea Pensioner, striking a Privy Councillor and even damaging Westminster bridge have at some time carried the potential for execution. Methods of execution have included: beheading; boiling; burning; being hung, drawn and quartered; death by firing squad; and hanging.

In 1964, the death penalty was abolished in the UK, apart from cases of high treason. However, this has not dampened periodic calls for its re-introduction. e.g. Lord Stevens' calls for capital punishment for cop killers in 2005 following the murder of PC Sharon Beshenivsky.

Beyond Europe, however, capital punishment remains quite common. According to Amnesty International a total of 74 countries and territories still use the death penalty. During 2004, a total of at least 3,797 people were executed and 7,395 were sentenced to death. Some 97 per cent of all known executions took place in China, Iran, Vietnam and the USA (Amnesty International, n.d.). In some countries, capital punishment exists for offences that in most nations would not even be considered a crime. For example, in Iran people have been executed for simply engaging in homosexual activities. Now that the nature and extent of capital punishment have been considered, this unit will move on to consider the arguments for the reintroduction of the death penalty.

---

For more statistics on the death penalty worldwide go to:

- <http://web.amnesty.org/pages/deathpenalty-facts-eng>

Two gay teenagers, 16 and 17 years old, were executed in 2005 for conducting a homosexual relationship. See:

- <http://direland.typepad.com/direland/2005/07/iran_executes_2.html>

---

## The case for the reintroduction of capital punishment

This section will examine some of the many arguments used to argue for the reintroduction of capital punishment for premeditated murder. It will explore issues such as: murder is different; deterrence; the protection of society; the satisfaction of public outrage; the exemplary nature of capital punishment; the strong public support for reintroduction; the cruelty of long prison sentences; the religious justification; the safety of modern execution methods; and the weakness of some arguments against reintroduction.

## Murder is different

One of the first issues to note is that 'murder is different'. When a person is murdered they have no input into the punishment of their murderer. For the relatives and loved ones of the victim, no compensation will ever satisfy their loss. Murder is not like crimes of burglary, robbery or theft, where material losses can be replaced. Nor is it like crimes of assault or rape, where at least the person continues to exist (albeit possibly physically and mentally scarred for life). Life is the ultimate possession, and its loss can never be replaced. One of the fundamental roles of the modern state is the protection of the individual and, as such, the prevention of murder. Advocates of capital punishment argue that those that undertake the ultimate crime – murder – therefore deserve to face the ultimate punishment – death by execution.

### Deterrence

One of the most common arguments for the reintroduction of capital punishment is the potential deterrent effect. Rooted in the ideas of writers such as Becaria – that offenders are rational actors weighing up the potential costs and benefits of a crime – it is argued that if there is a penalty of death many potential 'capital' offenders will reconsider committing such a crime. As Sir James Fitzjames Stephen argued (cited in Baber, 1990: 21):

> No other punishment deters men so effectually from committing crimes as the punishment of death. This is one of those propositions difficult to prove, simply because they are in themselves more obvious than any proof can make them . . . No one goes to certain inevitable death.

These a priori views have also been supported with evidence of murder rates from studies of varying validity. For example, the number of police officers killed while on duty in the period 1946–64 was 0.6, a figure that rose to 1.8 in 1965–89; and in 1965–9 there was a 125 per cent increase in murders that would have attracted the death penalty (cited in Baber, 1994).

More detailed studies in America on the deterrence effect have produced varying results (see Sarat, 2005). Do an Internet search for some of the many studies – of varying quality – published on this subject.

There are also frequent calls for capital punishment to be attached to the murder of police officers in order to deter potential killers. When PC Beshenivsky was murdered in November 2005 by armed raiders, Lord Stevens (the former Commissioner of the Metropolitan Police), who had been a lifelong opponent of the death penalty, called for capital punishment for cop killers (see <http://news.bbc.co.uk/1/hi/uk/4457402.stm>).

## Capital punishment protects society

Linked to deterrence, advocates have also argued capital punishment offers greater protection to society. Primarily there is the fact that a murderer who is executed will never kill again – whether a fellow inmate, a prison guard or some other person. Indeed, in the period 1965–98, according to Home Office figures (Baber, 1994), there were 71 murders by people released from life sentences. As Thomas Aquinas argued (cited in Baber, 1994: 26):

> If a man be dangerous and infectious to the community, on account of some sin, it is praiseworthy and advantageous that he be killed in order to safeguard the common good.

Many murders provoke serious public outrage. The murder of eight-year-old Sarah Payne led to a press campaign against paedophiles that culminated in near riots in Paulsgrove in Portsmouth. Similar levels of outrage have occurred in the cases of notorious murderers such as the Yorkshire Ripper and Ian Huntley. In these cases life sentences – even though they mean life – often do not satisfy the public's demand for a punishment to fit the crime. It is argued that capital punishment would satisfy this public outrage and therefore bring calm to society when such crimes occur.

Another strand to the arguments that capital punishment protects society is that it is an exemplary penalty, which sends out a message to those in society considering committing such crimes that the state means to prevent and deal with these crimes with the ultimate punishment. It is argued that current 'life' sentences given to murderers – which can often mean prison terms in the 10- to 15-year bracket – only undermine public credibility in the criminal justice system. Statements relating to this argument are regularly made by judges when sentencing offenders to death. For example, in January 2006 when two Thai fishermen were sentenced to death for the rape and murder of Welsh student Katherine Horton, the judges said that 'the sentence would send a clear message to both Thai society and the international community' (*Guardian*, 19 January 2006, p. 3).

### Strength of public opinion

There are regular surveys of public opinion in the UK and they consistently show a majority in favour of the reintroduction of capital punishment. A poll for the *Observer* found that 67 per cent of those favoured the reintroduction of capital punishment (*Observer*, 2003). Most polls tend to show that the majority rises further when the murder of children is considered. It is therefore argued that, if we live in a democracy, then the democratic will of the people should be satisfied with the reintroduction of capital punishment.

---

Do a Google search to find examples of recent opinion polls on the issue of capital punishment.

*Life prison sentences are crueller*

Another strand to the case for the reintroduction of capital punishment is that alternative sentences are seen by some to be crueller. Primarily, a life sentence can be painful for a victim's family knowing that the killer is alive and may also be released to walk the streets again. Even if they are not released, the tabloid publicity surrounding some killers, e.g. Peter Sutcliffe, the Yorkshire Ripper, ensures that the pain of the bereavement continues for years to come.

Long prison sentences, it could also be argued, are crueller to the prisoner than capital punishment. As Sir Alexander Paterson, Commissioner of Prisons in 1930, stated (cited in Hitchens, 2003: 185):

> It requires a superhuman to survive 20 years of imprisonment with character and soul intact . . . I gravely doubt whether an average man can serve more than ten continuous years in prison without deterioration.

Long sentences are also very expensive for the taxpayer. With the average costs of imprisonment per prisoner over £40,000 a year, a life sentence of 20 years or more represents a significant ongoing cost. Furthermore, while the offenders are imprisoned they are still a risk to society – should they escape – and most significantly to fellow inmates and prison guards.

## Religious and moral justification

In American debates over capital punishment there are frequent religious justifications offered from the Bible. Other religions, such as Islam, also offer justifications from the Quran. We do not intend to go too deeply into the religious debates because theologians can often find conflicting evidence from religious sources. Nevertheless, two examples that are often used to illustrate the case for capital punishment from the Bible are presented below:

> Whoever sheds man's blood by man his blood shall be shed, for in the image of God, he made a man.
>
> (Genesis 9:6)

> Eye for eye, tooth for tooth, hand for hand, foot for foot, burn for burn, wound for wound, bruise for bruise.
>
> (Exodus 21: 24–25)

> Many Christian groups in America advocate the death penalty. Do a Google search to find some such groups and assess the strength of their arguments.

### A refutation of arguments against the reintroduction of capital punishment

One of the strongest arguments used against the reintroduction of capital punishment is that innocent people could be executed. The many examples of miscarriages of justice that have occurred in recent years are raised as innocent people who would have been executed if capital punishment had been available. However, with the emergence of DNA technology, miscarriages of justice are less likely in the future.

---

**Task**

Read the following article and make notes on how convinced you are of the above statement:

- Tracy, Paul E. and Vincent Morgan (2000) 'Big Brother and his science kit: DNA databases for 21st century crime control?', *Journal of Criminal Law & Criminology*, 90, 635–90.

---

Most significantly, however, some would argue that innocent people dying is not a strong enough argument in itself (Hitchens, 2003: 185–210). Hitchens argues that some politicians are quite content to authorise wars that lead to thousands of innocent deaths, but when capital punishment is considered they shy away. For example, a *Lancet* study of the Iraq war has suggested that more than 100,000 innocent victims have lost their lives. These – advocates of the war would argue – have been sacrificed for the greater good of Iraq. Surely, advocates of the death penalty like Hitchens would argue, the greater benefits of the reintroduction of capital punishment would justify the risk of a few innocent people being executed.

Many opponents of capital punishment have argued that execution methods such as hanging, the electric chair and the gas chamber are cruel and unusual punishments that lead to unnecessary harm and suffering to the prisoner. However, many advocates of modern execution methods argue that methods such as lethal injection address such concerns. Death by lethal injection simply requires a vein to be found enabling a combination of drugs to be injected that simply puts the prisoner to sleep before the lethal dose, which terminates the offender, is injected.

---

Those interested in the different methods used to execute prisoners should go to:

- <http://www.richard.clark32.btinternet.co.uk/contents.html>

## Conclusion

This section has considered the case for the reintroduction of capital punishment. It has illustrated the arguments used which are based upon murder being a different kind of crime, the deterrence effect, the protection it offers society, the strength of public opinion in favour, that life sentences are crueller, the religious justification and the weakness of some of the arguments used to argue against reintroduction. There are many groups – particularly in America – and many websites dedicated to the reintroduction of capital punishment. Those interested should consider the following web search. This unit will now consider some of the many arguments against the reintroduction of capital punishment.

---

For a website with extensive arguments for capital punishment go to:

- <http://www.prodeathpenalty.com/DP.html>

---

## The case against capital punishment

There are a number of arguments that are regularly put forward to justify the use of capital punishment. However these arguments are not as compelling as they may, at first, seem.

### Deterrence

Those who believe that deterrence justifies the execution of certain offenders bear the burden of proving that the death penalty actually is a deterrent. However this is not easy to do, because the overwhelming conclusion from many years of deterrence studies is that the death penalty is, at best, no more of a deterrent than a sentence of life in prison. In fact, it has been argued that the death penalty has the opposite effect in that society is brutalised by its use – thus increasing the likelihood of more murder. Studies from London and New York state have found an increase in homicides after highly publicised executions, rather than a decrease consistent with deterrence arguments (Bowers and Pierce, 1980). Most of America's leading criminologists believe that capital punishment does not contribute to lower rates of homicide (Radelet and Akers, 1996). Even most supporters of the death penalty now place little or no weight on deterrence as a serious justification for its continued use.

Those states in the US that do not employ the death penalty generally have lower murder rates than the states that do. The same is true when the US is compared to similar countries. The US, with the death penalty, has a higher murder rate than Canada or the countries of Europe, which do not use it.

The death penalty is not a deterrent because most people who commit murders either do not expect to be caught or do not carefully weigh up the differences between a possible execution and life in prison before they act. Frequently, murders are committed in moments of passion or anger, or by criminals who are substance abusers and who acted impulsively. As someone who presided over many executions in Texas, former Texas Attorney General Jim Mattox has remarked that 'It is my own experience that those executed in Texas were not deterred by the existence of the death penalty law. I think in most cases you'll find that the murder was committed under severe drug and alcohol abuse.' This was said after he had actually interviewed nearly all of the people executed in Texas between 1976 and 1988. He also concluded that the sentence of death never crossed their minds before their crime: <http://www.deathpenaltyinfo.org/php/article.php?did=545&scid=45> (Dugger, 1988).

There is no conclusive proof that the death penalty acts as a better deterrent than the threat of life imprisonment. This is borne out not only by the experience of Jim Maddox, discussed above, but also by that of Hugo Adam Bedau, the Austin Fletcher Professor of Philosophy at Tufts University. In his paper 'The case against the death penalty' (Bedau, 1997) he writes:

> Persons who commit murder and other crimes of personal violence either may or may not premeditate their crimes. When crime is planned, the criminal ordinarily concentrates on escaping detection, arrest, and conviction. The threat of even the severest punishment will not discourage those who expect to escape detection and arrest. It is impossible to imagine how the threat of any punishment could prevent a crime that is not premeditated . . .
>
> Most capital crimes are committed during moments of great emotional stress or under the influence of drugs or alcohol, when logical thinking has been suspended. In such cases, violence is inflicted by persons heedless of the consequences to themselves as well as to others . . .
>
> If, however, severe punishment can deter crime, then long-term imprisonment is severe enough to deter any rational person from committing a violent crime. The vast preponderance of the evidence shows that the death penalty is no more effective than imprisonment in deterring murder and that it may even be an incitement to criminal violence. Death-penalty states as a group do not have lower rates of criminal homicide than non-death-penalty states.

## Retribution

Supporters of the death penalty often assert that it is a just response for the taking of a life. However, we should be aware that the concept of retribution is simply another way of describing revenge. When somebody hurts us in some way our first instinct may be to respond with the infliction of immediate pain on them. However surely we, as a mature and supposedly civilised society, should require a more measured response. One cannot justify a system of capital punishment with all of its various problems and risks by a simple invocation of the emotional impulse for revenge. We should respect all life, even that of a murderer. We should hold higher principles than a life for a life, given our criminal justice system and laws. If we allow our basest motives of revenge to be encouraged, then the result will be more killing. Therefore, under these circumstances, the chain of violence is extended. If executions are permitted as part of our legal system then we are merely sanctioning the taking of a life as 'payback'. It is quite common for victims' families to denounce the use of the death penalty. They often assert that the use of an execution to try to right the wrong of their loss is an affront to them, and only causes more pain. For example, Bud Welch's daughter, Julie, was killed in the Oklahoma City bombing in 1995. Although his first reaction was to wish that those who committed this terrible crime be killed, he ultimately realised that such killing 'is simply vengeance; and it was vengeance that killed Julie . . . Vengeance is a strong and natural emotion. But it has no place in our justice system' (see http://deathpenaltycurriculum.org/student/c/about/arguments/argument26.htm).

The overall notion of an eye for an eye or a life for a life (*lex talionis*) is a simplistic one, which our society has never wholeheartedly endorsed. After all we do not allow torturing the torturer or raping the rapist. Taking the life of a murderer is a similarly disproportionate punishment, especially in light of the fact that the US executes only a small percentage of those convicted of murder, and these defendants are typically not the worst offenders but merely the ones with the fewest resources to defend themselves (see <http://www.teacher.deathpenaltyinfo.msu.edu/c/about/arguments/argument2b.htm>).

The views of the National Council of Synagogues and the Bishops' Committee for Ecumenical and Interreligious Affairs of the National Conference of Catholic Bishops endorse this opposition to retribution. Here is an excerpt from *To End the Death Penalty: A Report of the National Jewish/Catholic Consultation* (NJCC, 1999):

> Some would argue that the death penalty will teach society at large the seriousness of crime. Yet we say that teaching people to respond to violence with violence will, again, only breed more violence. 'We cannot teach that killing is wrong by killing.' We oppose capital punishment not just for what it does to those guilty of horrible crimes, but for what it does to all of us as a society. Increasing reliance on the death penalty diminishes all of us and is a sign of growing disrespect for human life. We cannot overcome crime by simply executing criminals, nor can we restore the lives of the innocent by ending the lives of those convicted of their murders. The death penalty offers the tragic illusion that we can defend life by taking life.

*Innocence*

The risk of executing the innocent precludes the use of the death penalty. Clearly, once the death penalty has been carried out it is irrevocable. One cannot bring someone back to life if an error has been made. And, of course, as we know from many previous cases of miscarriages of justice over the years, many mistakes have been made. For example, in the US since 1973 at least 88 people have been released from death row after evidence of their innocence emerged. During the same period, more than 650 people have been executed in the US. Thus, for every seven people executed, we have found one person on death row who never should have been convicted. These statistics represent an intolerable risk of executing the innocent (ibid).

Clearly, then, the use of capital punishment is essentially unreliable. A recent study by Columbia University Law School found that two-thirds of all capital trials contained serious errors. When the cases were retried, over 80 per cent of the defendants were not sentenced to death and 7 per cent were completely acquitted. Many of the releases of innocent defendants from death row came about as a result of factors outside of the justice system. Recently, journalism students in Illinois were assigned to investigate the case of a man who was scheduled to be executed, after the system of appeals had rejected his legal claims. The students discovered that one witness had lied at the original trial, and they were able to find the true killer, who confessed to the crime on videotape. The innocent man who was released was very fortunate, but he was spared because of the informal efforts of concerned citizens, not because of the justice system (ibid).

With the increasing use of DNA testing and other forensic evidence, we have seen many death row inmates exonerated. This is all well and good. However, initially the justice system had concluded that these defendants were guilty and deserving of the death penalty. We should remember that DNA testing only became available in the early 1990s, due to advances in science. If this testing had not been discovered until ten years later, many of these inmates would have been executed. One should also consider earlier cases, predating DNA testing, in the 1970s and 1980s, for example, where undoubtedly some innocent people were put to death in the name of justice. We should also be aware that not all defendants/death row inmates possess the resources to persuade the authorities to reopen their cases. Wrongful executions are a preventable risk. A sentence of life without parole is a suitable alternative whereby society's need to punish and protect can be met without running the risk of an erroneous and irrevocable punishment (ibid).

Here is an excerpt from a speech given in 1999 by Gerald Kogan, former Florida Supreme Court Chief Justice:

> [T]here is no question in my mind, and I can tell you this having seen the dynamics of our criminal justice system over the many years that

I have been associated with it, [as] prosecutor, defense attorney, trial judge and Supreme Court Justice, that convinces me that we certainly have, in the past, executed those people who either didn't fit the criteria for execution in the State of Florida or who, in fact, were, factually, not guilty of the crime for which they have been executed.

## Cases in the UK

In relation to the potential to execute the innocent we need only look at some past cases to remind us of how this has happened. Also, looking at some more contemporary cases, we can see how this might have happened today.

### Timothy Evans

The case of Timothy Evans was the first major post-war miscarriage of justice to capture public attention. Evans, of low intelligence, was damned by his own, false, 'confession' that he had murdered his wife and daughter. The bodies of the mother and child were found buried in a washroom at their flat in Notting Hill, west London, shortly after Beryl had told friends that she wanted to undergo an illegal abortion.

Three years after Mr Evans was hanged, John Christie, a neighbour in the house at 10 Rillington Place, confessed to strangling eight female victims – including Beryl and her baby daughter. He too was executed. The confession by Christie, which gripped post-war Britain with its grisly insight into the first mass murder of the era, uncovered one of the most notorious miscarriages of justice in British legal history. In the face of apparently overwhelming evidence gathered by two public inquiries that Christie had sent his neighbour to the gallows, Mr Evans received an official royal pardon in 1966.

### Derek Bentley

Derek Bentley (aged 19) and Christopher Craig (aged 16) broke into a London warehouse on 2 November 1952. Craig was armed with a revolver. The police were called and Craig shot one of them. This occurred when Bentley was already under arrest. Craig leapt from the roof onto the road thirty feet below. He landed badly, fracturing his spine and left wrist. Craig was then arrested.

It was clear that even if Craig was found guilty of murder, he could not be sentenced to death; being 16, he was below the minimum age for execution. However, Derek Bentley was over 18 years of age and could be sentenced to death despite having a mental age of 11. He was also illiterate and mentally subnormal. The jury took just 75 minutes to find both Craig and Bentley guilty of the murder of PC Miles. This was not surprising given

Judge Goddard's summing up, which was biased and misdirected the jury on a number of points of law. As Craig was not yet 18 at the time of the offence, he was sentenced to being detained at Her Majesty's Pleasure, while Bentley was sentenced to death. Various appeals – highlighting the ambiguous evidence, Bentley's mental age and the fact that he did not fire the fatal shot – were all rejected by the then Home Secretary. On 28 January 1953, Derek Bentley was hanged at London's Wandsworth Prison. Christopher Craig served ten years in prison before being released. On 30 July 1998, the Court of Appeal overturned the controversial conviction of Derek Bentley.

There are many other contemporary examples of miscarriages of justice – the Guildford Four, the Birmingham Six, Angela Canning, Sally Clarke – all of which show that our system of justice is far from infallible.

### Concluding thoughts

To sum up, the death penalty is not a just form of punishment. On the contrary, it is dangerously flawed, inhumane and ineffective. It brutalises our society and makes violence seem more acceptable. It does not provide a deterrent and is not a just response for the taking of a life. The risk of taking the life of an innocent person in error is too great to be ignored, as we are taught by past history. Capital punishment is inhumane and cruel, and the systems that support it are often guilty of the psychological abuse of prisoners due to the countless appeals that can be gone through and the last minute reprieves that often follow. Taking people to the brink of death and then bringing them back – often offering false hope – is just plain wrong in any decent society.

It is important that we are all aware of the reality of the death penalty. Therefore I have included below descriptions of the various methods used for executions in the US. They are taken from an article on a website run by the Death Penalty Information Centre (<http://www.deathpenaltyinfo.org/article.php?scid=8&did=479>). You may find some of the descriptions disturbing.

### Lethal injection

In 1977, Oklahoma became the first state to adopt lethal injection as a means of execution, though it would be five more years until Charles Brooks would become the first person executed by lethal injection in Texas, on 2 December 1982. Today, 37 of the 38 states that have the death penalty use this method.

When this method is used, the condemned person is usually bound to a gurney and a member of the execution team positions several heart monitors on his skin. Two needles (one is a back-up) are then inserted into usable veins, usually in the inmate's arms. Long tubes connect the needle through a hole in a cement block wall to several intravenous drips. The first is a harmless saline solution that is started immediately. At the warden's signal, a curtain is raised exposing the inmate to the witnesses in an adjoining room. Then, the inmate is injected with sodium thiopental – an anaesthetic, that puts the inmate to sleep. Next flows pavulon or pancuronium bromide, which paralyses the entire muscle system and stops the inmate's breathing. Finally, a flow of potassium chloride stops the heart. Death results from anaesthetic overdose and respiratory and cardiac arrest while the condemned person is unconscious.

Medical ethics preclude doctors from participating in executions. However, a doctor will certify the inmate is dead. This lack of medical participation can be problematic because often injections are performed by inexperienced technicians or orderlies. If a member of the execution team injects the drugs into a muscle instead of a vein, or if the needle becomes clogged, extreme pain can result. Many prisoners have damaged veins resulting from intravenous drug use, and it is sometimes difficult to find a usable vein, resulting in long delays while the inmate remains strapped to the gurney.

*Electrocution*

Seeking a more humane method of execution than hanging, New York built the first electric chair in 1888 and executed William Kemmler in 1890. Soon, other states adopted this execution method. Today, only in Nebraska is electrocution used as the sole method of execution.

For execution by electric chair, the person is usually shaved and strapped to a chair with belts that cross his chest, groin, legs and arms. A metal skullcap-shaped electrode is attached to the scalp and forehead over a sponge moistened with saline. The sponge must not be too wet, or the saline short-circuits the electric current; nor must it be too dry, as it would then have a very high resistance. An additional electrode is moistened with conductive jelly (Electro-Creme) and attached to a portion of the prisoner's leg that has been shaved to reduce resistance to electricity. The prisoner is then blindfolded.

After the execution team has withdrawn to the observation room, the warden signals the executioner, who pulls a handle to connect the power supply. A jolt of between 500 and 2,000 volts, which lasts for about 30 seconds, is given. The current surges and is then turned off, at which time the body is seen to relax. The doctors wait a few seconds for the body to cool and then check to see if the inmate's heart is still beating. If it is, another jolt is applied. This process continues until the prisoner is dead. The prisoner's hands often grip the chair and there may be violent movement of the limbs, which can result in dislocation or fractures. The tissues swell. Defecation occurs. Steam or smoke rises and there is a smell of burning.

US Supreme Court Justice William Brennan once offered the following description of an execution by electric chair:

The prisoner's eyeballs sometimes pop out and rest on [his] cheeks. The prisoner often defecates, urinates, and vomits blood and drool. The body turns bright red as its temperature rises, and the prisoner's flesh swells and his skin stretches to the point of breaking. Sometimes the prisoner catches fire. . . . Witnesses hear a loud and sustained sound like bacon frying, and the sickly sweet smell of burning flesh permeates the chamber.

(http://deathpenaltycurriculum.org/student/c/about/
methods/electrocution.htm)

At postmortem, the body is hot enough to blister if touched, and the autopsy is delayed while the internal organs cool. There are third degree burns with blackening where the electrodes met the skin of the scalp and legs. According to Robert H. Kirschner, the deputy chief medical examiner of Cook County, 'the brain appears cooked in most cases'.

### Gas chamber

In 1924, the use of cyanide gas was introduced as Nevada sought a more humane way of executing its inmates. Gee Jon was the first person executed by lethal gas. The state tried to pump cyanide gas into Jon's cell while he slept. This proved impossible because the gas leaked from his cell, so the gas chamber was constructed. Today, five states authorise lethal gas as a method of execution, but all have lethal injection as an alternative method. A federal court in California found this method to be a cruel and unusual punishment.

For execution by this method, the condemned person is strapped to a chair in an airtight chamber. Below the chair rests a pail of sulfuric acid. A long stethoscope is typically affixed to the inmate so that a doctor outside the chamber can pronounce death. Once everyone has left the chamber, the room is sealed. The warden then gives a signal to the executioner who flicks a lever that releases crystals of sodium cyanide into the pail. This causes a chemical reaction that releases hydrogen cyanide gas.

The prisoner is instructed to breathe deeply to hasten the process. Most prisoners, however, try to hold their breath, and some struggle. The inmate does not lose consciousness immediately. According to former San Quenton, California, Penitentiary Warden, Clifton Duffy, 'at first there is evidence of extreme horror, pain, and strangling. The eyes pop. The skin turns purple and the victim begins to drool' (http://deathpenaltycurriculum.org/student/c/about/methods/gaschamber.htm).

Caryl Chessman, before he died in California's gas chamber in 1960, told reporters that he would nod his head if it hurt. Witnesses said he nodded his head for several minutes. According to Dr Richard Traystman of John Hopkins University School of Medicine, 'The person is unquestionably experiencing pain and extreme anxiety . . . The sensation is similar to the pain felt by a person during a heart attack, where essentially the heart is

being deprived of oxygen' (http://deathpenaltycurriculum.org/student/c/
about/methods/gaschamber.htm). The inmate dies from hypoxia, the cutting-
off of oxygen to the brain.

At *post mortem*, an exhaust fan sucks the poison air out of the chamber,
and the corpse is sprayed with ammonia to neutralise any remaining traces of
cyanide. About 30 minutes later, orderlies enter the chamber, wearing gas
masks and rubber gloves. Their training manual advises them to ruffle the
victim's hair to release any trapped cyanide gas before removing the deceased.

### Firing squad

Firing squad remains a method of execution in Utah and Idaho, although
each allow lethal injection as an alternative method and only Utah allows
the inmate to choose this method. The most recent execution by this method
was that of John Albert Taylor. By his own choosing, Taylor was executed
by firing squad in Utah on 26 January 1996.

For execution by this method, the inmate is typically bound to a chair
with leather straps across his waist and head, in front of an oval-shaped
canvas wall. The chair is surrounded by sandbags to absorb the inmate's
blood. A black hood is pulled over the inmate's head. A doctor locates the
inmate's heart with a stethoscope and pins a circular white cloth target
over it. Standing in an enclosure 20 feet away, five shooters are armed with
.30 caliber rifles loaded with single rounds. One of the shooters is given
blank rounds. Each of the shooters aims his rifle through a slot in the
canvas and fires at the inmate.

The prisoner dies as a result of blood loss caused by rupture of the heart
or a large blood vessel, or tearing of the lungs. The person shot loses consciousness when shock causes a fall in the supply of blood to the brain. If
the shooters miss the heart, by accident or intention, the prisoner bleeds
to death slowly.

### Hanging

Until the 1890s, hanging was the primary method of execution used in the
US. Hanging is still used in Delaware and Washington, although both have
lethal injection as an alternative method of execution.

For execution by this method, the inmate may be weighed the day before
the execution, and a rehearsal is done using a sandbag of the same weight
as the prisoner. This is to determine the length of 'drop' necessary to ensure
a quick death. If the rope is too long the inmate could be decapitated, and
if it is too short the strangulation could take as long as 45 minutes. The
rope, which should be $^3/_4$-inch to $1^1/_4$-inch in diameter, must be boiled and
stretched to eliminate spring or coiling. The knot should be lubricated with
wax or soap 'to ensure a smooth sliding action', according to the 1969 US
Army manual.

Immediately before the execution, the prisoner's hands and legs are secured, he is blindfolded, and the noose is placed around his neck, with the knot behind the left ear. The execution takes place when a trap-door is opened and the prisoner falls through. The prisoner's weight should cause a rapid fracture-dislocation of the neck. However, instantaneous death rarely occurs.

If the inmate has strong neck muscles, if the inmate is very light, if the 'drop' is too short, or if the noose has been wrongly positioned, then the fracture-dislocation is not rapid and death results from slow asphyxiation. If this occurs the face becomes engorged, the tongue protrudes, the eyes pop, the body defecates, and violent movements of the limbs occur.

### The debates of others

You can refine your arguments from a legal perspective by viewing a mock trial (another form of debate?) which was organised by the legal charity Amicus and posted online by the *Guardian*, 13 May 2010, as 'The death penalty on trial':

> Former lord chief justice Lord Woolf presides over a trial of the US death penalty for perverting the course of justice. Two of Britain's leading criminal barristers cross-examine witnesses with intimate knowledge of the American justice system, including a mother who argued against the death sentence for her daughter's murderer.
>
> (<http://www.guardian.co.uk/law/video/2010/may/13/
> death-penalty-trial-law-video>)

For further information on capital punishment visit:

- The Centre for Capital Punishment Studies website at: <http://www.wmin.ac.uk/law/page-144>
- Amnesty International's website at <http://web.amnesty.org/pages/deathpenalty-index-eng>
- For extensive academic readings on capital punishment look at Sarat, A. (2005) *Capital Punishment*, Vols I and II. Aldershot: Ashgate.

Some other useful websites:

- <http://www.aclu.org/capital/general/10441pub19971231.html>
- <http://www.teacher.deathpenaltyinfo.msu.edu/c/about/arguments/argument2b.htm>
- <http://www.deathpenaltyinfo.org>
- <http://www.nytimes.com/2008/04/17/washington/17scotus.html?_r=1&th&emc=th&oref=slogin>

# References

Amnesty International (n.d.) 'Facts and figures on the death penalty'. Retrieved on 5 June 2006 from: <http://web.amnesty.org/pages/deathpenalty-facts-eng>

Baber, M. (1990) *Capital punishment.* House of Commons Background Paper 122. London: HMSO.

—— (1994) *Capital punishment.* House of Commons Research Paper 94/25. London: HMSO.

Bedau, H.A. (1997) 'The case against the death penalty'. Retrieved on 13 July 2006 from: <http://www.soci.niu.edu/~critcrim/dp/dppapers/aclu.antidp>

Blom-Cooper, L.J. (ed.) (1969) *The Hanging Question: Essays on the Death Penalty.* London: Duckworth.

Bowers, W. and Pierce, G. (1980) 'Deterrence or brutalisation: what is the effect of executions?' *Crime and Delinquency*, 26, 453–84.

Dugger, R. (1988) 'In the dead of the night'. *The Texas Observer*, 22 April.

Garland, D. (2005) 'The cultural uses of capital punishment'. *Punishment and Society*, 4, 459–87.

Hitchens, P. (2003) *A Brief History of Crime.* London: Atlantic Books, Chapter 6.

NJCC (1999) 'To end the death penalty', A Report of the National Jewish/Catholic Consultation, December (National Jewish/Catholic Consultation). Retrieved on 5 June 2006 from: <http://www.deathpenaltyinfo.org/article.php?scid=18&did=124>

*Observer* (2003) 'The Uncovered Poll': 27 April. Retrieved on 5 June 2006 from: <http://observer.guardian.co.uk/crime/_story/0,13260,942118,00.html>

Radelet, M. and Akers, R. (1996) 'Deterrence and the death penalty: the views of the experts'. *Journal of Criminal Law and Criminology*, 87(1), 1–16.

Sarat, A. (2005) *Capital Punishment, Vols I and II.* Aldershot: Ashgate.

Zimring, F.E. (2003) *The Contradiction of American Capital Punishment.* New York: Oxford University Press.

# 9 Victims' rights or suspects' rights?

*Chris Lewis and Jacki Tapley*

## Achieving justice for victims of crime: rebalancing the criminal justice process

If you became a victim of crime, would you expect to be:

- given recognition for the harm suffered?
- treated with respect by the police, the crown prosecutor and the courts?
- offered protection and support?
- provided with timely and accurate information about the criminal justice system and the progress of your case?
- compensated for the injuries and losses suffered?
- given support to help return to the same psychological and physical well-being you enjoyed before the offence?

> Consider for a moment what your expectations as a victim would be. What types of service and support would you like or expect?

If you believe that as a victim of crime you should be provided with the support and services listed above, then we can agree that victims should be entitled to certain rights that ensure they are treated fairly and with respect. However, until very recently, victims of crime were not being accorded such recognition and respect. As a consequence of the professionalisation of the criminal justice system over the last two centuries, the role of victims in the criminal process became increasingly marginalised. From being once the main protagonist, victims became a legal non-entity, the 'forgotten figure of crime' (Shapland *et al.*, 1985: 176). The overriding issues of deterrence, detection, prosecution, punishment and reform usurped the once prominent role of the victim as a complex modern criminal justice system evolved (Tapley, 2003). In such a system, crime generates a debt to society rather than any obligation to the victim, and once the offender is punished by way of legitimate sanctions by the state, the debt is considered repaid.

No consideration is given to the needs of the victim, only the wider needs of the offender, the state and society.

It was not until the 1960s that increasingly well-organised groups began to campaign on behalf of victims and became commonly described as the 'victim's movement'. The development of feminist groups in the 1970s was a significant contribution to the movement and began to reveal the true extent of female and child victimisation, previously unchallenged by a society dominated by patriarchal values and beliefs (Stanko, 1985; 1988; Temkin, 1987). As a consequence, increasing criminological concern for the victims of crime grew steadily during the 1980s in both the US and the UK. This was fuelled by the ascendance of national and local victimisation surveys. These popular surveys indicated that, whilst official statistics are able to provide useful insights into the extent and distribution of crime, they fail to accurately represent the amount of crime actually committed and, thus, do not reflect the true extent of victimisation (Hough and Mayhew, 1983; Zedner, 1994). In particular, academic research emerging during the 1980s began to highlight the acute stress and adverse physical, practical and financial effects suffered by many victims of crime (Zedner, 1994), and began to provide evidence that the pendulum had swung too far in favour of the offender (Maguire and Bennett, 1982).

As a result, these studies began to reveal the true extent of victim dissatisfaction and the loss of public confidence in the criminal justice system. Ashworth (1983) argued that the relationship between the offender and the state had come to dominate all developments in criminal justice prosecution, punishment and rehabilitation over the last century, to the exclusion of the relationship between the victim and the state. Victims' experiences of the criminal justice process began to indicate a real need to redress what appeared to be an imbalance of power between victims and offenders. Whereas offenders as citizens were entitled to the rights of a defendant against the power of the state, victims as citizens appeared to have no redress from the state and no right to participate in the proceedings to restore the harm done. In essence, there was a growing realisation that society was more concerned with rehabilitating the offender than with rehabilitating the victim (van Dijk, 1988). Whilst the reform period of the 1960s and 1970s had done much to ensure better rights for the defendant, based predominantly on a welfare model of justice, they occurred without any consideration for the victim. Subsequently, research discovered that victims were being exposed to insensitive treatment by the criminal justice process, resulting in what has now become commonly termed as 'secondary victimisation' by the system itself (Tapley, 2005a).

It was not until the 1990s, following the demise of the rehabilitative ideal and the increasingly punitive ideology of a far-right conservative government, that supporting victims of crime became politically expedient. Thus, the 1990s witnessed a plethora of initiatives and reforms aimed at improving the services and support offered to victims, including the publication of the first *Victim's Charter* (Home Office, 1990) and a revised *Victim's Charter* (Home Office, 1996). However, these reforms were not supported by legislation or additional resources to assist with their implementation and, therefore, did not lead to an improvement in the treatment of victims and witnesses (Tapley, 2003). Instead, whilst recent years had seen a number of developments which had given rise to the notion that in some sense victims have 'rights', these were seriously misleading 'merely providing minimal, inexpensive and unenforceable entitlements' (Fenwick, 1995: 845). This included the introduction of Victim Personal Statements (VPS, and not to be confused with Victim Impact Statements used in other jurisdictions) in the UK in 2001. The purpose of the VPS scheme is to allow victims to let the police and prosecutors know how a crime has affected them, in order for the agencies to take this information into account when considering charges, bail and prosecution decisions. Its purpose is not to give victims an opportunity to say what should happen to the defendant if found guilty. However, research has indicated that VPSs are not being implemented consistently, due to a lack of appropriate training and resources (Tapley, 2005b) and the Home Office has indicated that the VPS scheme will have to be re-launched (Home Office, 2003a).

Evidence that the reforms and initiatives have not been successfully implemented supports the arguments of those who argue that the politicisation of victims' issues has been a relatively cheap and convenient ploy to divert attention away from the other failings of the criminal justice system. However, whilst this may have been the original motivation, the ploy has certainly backfired over recent years due to an increased demand for victims to be accorded legislative rights. Instead of pacifying victim advocates, the increasing focus on victims has drawn even greater attention to the distinct imbalance between the rights of defendants and the absence of rights of victims (Tapley, 2005c).

A significant turning point came when research began to indicate that, despite statistical evidence that overall crime rates are falling, fear of crime among individuals and communities remains high (Dodd *et al.*, 2004). This is further evidenced by a number of research studies that indicate public confidence in the criminal justice system is continuing to decline (Mirrlees-Black, 2001; Institute of Public Policy Research, 2001; Audit Commission, 2003). Thus, despite a plethora of initiatives and reforms introduced to improve the services offered to victims of crime, victims continue to feel unsupported and alienated by the process, illustrating that whilst possible solutions have been produced *rhetorically*, these have not resulted in an increased responsiveness to victims' needs *in reality* (Tapley, 2005c).

As a consequence, the true extent of victim and witness dissatisfaction has finally been acknowledged, together with the realisation that the Criminal Justice System (CJS) relies on the goodwill of members of the public and, in particular, victims, to apprehend, prosecute and punish those who commit criminal offences. The now apparent unwillingness of victims and members of the public to participate in the criminal justice process has necessitated an acknowledgement of the importance of their role, finally recognised in the objectives outlined in the *Criminal Justice System Strategic Plan 1999– 2002* (Home Office, 1999: 1):

> The criminal justice system stands or falls on whether it jointly meets what people can reasonably expect of it – victims, witnesses, jurors and the wider public – whose confidence and trust need to be earned, and interests respected.

Addressing the needs of victims and witnesses is now routinely recognised as a central objective of the criminal justice system, outlined by Tony Blair in his foreword to *Cutting Crime, Delivering Justice: A Strategic Plan for Criminal Justice 2004–08* (Office of Criminal Justice Reform, 2004a: 5):

> We start with one overriding principle – that the law abiding citizen must be at the heart of our criminal justice system. For too long, that was far from the case. The system seemed to think only about the rights of the accused. The interests of victims appeared to be an afterthought, if considered at all. This whole programme amounts to a modernising and re-balancing of the entire criminal justice system in favour of victims and the community.

Thus, it can be argued, that steadily declining public confidence in the ability of the criminal justice system to deal effectively with crime and, in particular, to assist those most affected by it, acted as the catalyst for the state to reflect quite intently upon the aims of the criminal justice system and the role of victims and witnesses within the criminal process. This led to a number of reports being published that focused on the reform of different parts of the criminal justice system, including the Narey Report (1997), the Glidewell (1998) report, the Halliday (2001) Report and the report by Lord Justice Auld (2001). Importantly, Auld (2001) acknowledged that whilst the rights of the defendant as a citizen must be protected, the current system pursues this without due consideration for the rights and protection of the victim.

In addition to these wider attempts to modernise the criminal justice system, reports have also been published focusing specifically on victims and witnesses. One report in particular has culminated in the introduction of a number of special measures aimed at assisting vulnerable and intimidated victims and witnesses to give their best evidence in court. The *Speaking Up for Justice Report* (Home Office, 1998) published the findings of a working group and made seventy-eight recommendations for improvements to the system, including the reporting of crime, identification of vulnerable and intimidated witnesses and measures to assist witnesses before, during and after the trial. Twenty-seven of the recommendations required legislation and some of these were introduced as part of the Youth Justice and Criminal Evidence Act 1999 and others were introduced and expanded by later legislation (see below).

In an attempt to address some of the problems identified in the reports, the government published the White Paper *Justice for All* (Home Office, 2002: 1), which promised to 'rebalance the system in favour of victims, witnesses and communities'.

> This phrase can be considered quite emotive and illustrates the use of political rhetoric to ensure that the government is seen to be doing something for victims of crime and, more importantly, to improve public confidence in the CJS.
>
> However, do we want a system that goes from being in favour of the offender to being in favour of victims?

To assist in implementing some of the ideas raised in the White Paper, the government published a national strategy to deliver improved services to victims, entitled *A New Deal for Victims and Witnesses* (Home Office, 2003a). The strategy incorporated two Public Service Agreement targets for the criminal justice agencies: to narrow the 'justice gap' by bringing more offenders to justice; and to improve public confidence. Improving services to victims and witnesses were stated as key to delivering both of these targets (Tapley, 2005c). To achieve these objectives, and as part of its wider process of reforms to modernise the criminal justice system, the government published a national framework document in 2003 entitled *Improving Public Satisfaction and Confidence in the Criminal Justice System* (Home Office, 2003b). The document identified five key aspects that affect satisfaction and confidence and outlined five performance areas that Local Criminal Justice Boards were given responsibility for improving. Improving victim and witness satisfaction was again reiterated as one of these key aspects (Tapley, 2005c).

One initiative aimed at improving victim and witness satisfaction was the introduction of Witness Care Units nationally in December 2005, following five pilot studies under the *No Witness, No Justice* project (Office of Criminal Justice Reform, 2004b). The main aim of the Witness Care Units is to provide one point of contact for prosecution victims and witnesses who are required to attend court to ensure that their needs are accurately assessed and met, to enable more victims and witnesses to give evidence. However, the Witness Care Units only contact victims and witnesses once a decision to prosecute has been made by the Crown Prosecution Service and when the defendant has entered a 'not guilty' plea. Therefore, Witness

Care Units only meet the needs of a very small percentage of victims whose cases actually reach the prosecution stage. Witness Care Units are based within the co-located departments of the police and the Crown Prosecution Service, which were introduced as part of the Criminal Case Management Programme (Office of Criminal Justice Reform, 2004b).

Central to achieving the objectives of improving public confidence have been a number of legislative changes that impact upon the interests of victims and witnesses. Part 11 of the Criminal Justice Act 2003 came into force on 15 December 2004 and allows evidence of bad character of the defendant to be admitted. The definition of bad character is wide enough to apply to conduct arising out of a conviction or conduct where there has been an acquittal.

---

This has caused some controversy, however; defence barristers are allowed to bring up the previous convictions and medical history of victims, whether relevant or not, in order to discredit their evidence and portray them as untrustworthy and undeserving victims.

Is it fair to be able to attack the character of victims and witnesses, but not to disclose relevant previous convictions of the defendant?

---

The Criminal Justice Act 2003 introduced the rule of double jeopardy, so that where someone has been acquitted of certain serious offences, cases can be re-tried where compelling new evidence comes to light. Also, in cases of serious offences, victims or victims' families who feel that a sentence passed by the Crown Court is unduly lenient can refer it to the Attorney General who can then ask the Court of Appeal to consider changing the sentence. All of these measures have attracted some controversy, contributing further towards the victims' rights debate. However, it should be remembered that legislative rights are not a finite entity, therefore affording rights to one group (for example, victims) does not automatically lead to the taking away of rights of another group (for example, offenders). Instead, the introduction of rights for victims should assist in the effective pursuit of justice for both victims and defendants.

Legislation of particular significance to victims of crime has been the Domestic Violence, Victims and Crime Act 2004 (Home Office, 2004a), which outlines a number of legislative rights in the form of a Code of Practice. The Act has culminated from a review of the Victim's Charter in 2001, the White Paper *Justice for All* (Home Office, 2002) and the domestic violence consultation document *Safety and Justice* (Home Office, 2003c). When introducing the bill to the House of Commons, the then Home Secretary David Blunkett hailed it as the biggest overhaul of domestic violence law in thirty years, heralding tough powers for the police and the courts to protect victims and prosecute abusers (Home Office, 2004b). Some of the key provisions introduced by the Act are listed below:

● common assault is an arrestable offence;
● breach of a non-molestation order is a criminal offence;
● imposing restraining orders for any offence, not just harassment or causing fear of violence;
● restraining orders for defendants not found guilty;
● anonymity of victims;
● register of offenders; and
● access to law for same-sex couples and non-cohabiting couples.

The Act also establishes domestic homicide reviews and, following concerns with the way in which the partial defence to murder of provocation has worked in the past, in 2005 the Sentencing Guidelines Council published new guidelines on manslaughter by reason of provocation (Criminal Justice System, 2005a). It is now recognised that provocation can be cumulative, particularly where the offender has suffered from domestic violence over a long period of time. It also recognises the necessity to examine the balance of power between one party and the other, resulting in the offender being the weaker or vulnerable party. This will hopefully redress the current imbalance whereby males who murder their partners can plead manslaughter by reason of provocation resulting in a lesser sentence, whereas females who kill a male partner after suffering years of abuse cannot claim provocation and face charges of murder resulting in a life sentence. The Sentencing Guidelines Council (Criminal Justice System, 2005a) has also reviewed what constitutes provocation and offers guidelines on assessing the degree of the provocation as shown by its nature and duration as the critical factor in the sentencing decision.

The Guidelines now recognise that infidelity on the part of a partner does not necessarily amount to high provocation. It also now acknowledges the nature of the conduct, the period of time over which it took place and its cumulative effect. How will this assist in fairer sentencing, particularly in cases involving domestic violence?

Part 3, Section 13 of the Domestic Violence, Crime and Victims Act 2004 places responsibility upon the Secretary of State to issue a Code of Practice for victims of crime. This places legislative responsibilities upon the criminal justice agencies to provide a standard minimum service for victims. Under the code, vulnerable or intimidated victims and witnesses, as defined by the Youth Justice and Criminal Evidence Act 1999, will receive an enhanced service. This enhanced service also includes the introduction of special measures to assist intimidated and vulnerable victims and witnesses to give evidence in court (Hamlyn *et al.*, 2004). The Act establishes an independent Commissioner to safeguard and promote the interests of victims, to encourage good practice and to review the Code of Practice. The importance of the Victim's Code of Practice is that it replaces the Victim's Charter and for the first time places victims' rights on a statutory footing. If dissatisfied with the service received by any of the criminal justice agencies under the code, victims can first take their complaint to the agency involved and if the matter is not resolved satisfactorily, can take their case to the Parliamentary Ombudsman.

A copy of the final draft of the Code is available on the Criminal Justice System online website and is to be implemented from April 2006. For more information go to:

- <http://www.cjsonline.gov.uk>

Whilst some controversy still exists regarding the rights of victims and what their role in the criminal justice process should be, the significant shift in focus towards a more victim-centred criminal justice process is now clearly evident. This has required criminal justice agencies to work and consult more widely with victims, victims' families and witnesses, resulting in significant changes to professional cultures. The probation service has established victim contact units, the police service now has a range of specialist officers working with victims and victims' families and the Crown Prosecution Service is now required to communicate directly with victims regarding charging decisions and to take into account the concerns of victims and witnesses when giving evidence at court. The responsibilities of prosecutors towards victims and witnesses have now been clearly defined in a ten-point *Prosecutors' Pledge*, launched by the Attorney General, Lord Goldsmith in October 2005 (Criminal Justice System, 2005b). The *Prosecutor's Pledge* sets out how the prosecutors will protect the interests of victims from the point of charge right through to appeal. This will include considering the impact of the crime on the victim and their family when charging a defendant; clear and early information if a charge is withdrawn or the charge is substantially changed and protection from unwarranted character attacks by the defendant's lawyer during the trial. This signifies an unprecedented shift in the role of the Crown Prosecution Service, which was once able to distance itself from victims and witnesses by defending its role as an independent prosecutor for the state.

The end of 2005 also saw the publication of a number of consultation documents focusing on victims and witnesses. One that has given particular rise to controversy has been the government's plans to give the bereaved relatives of murder and manslaughter victims a say in criminal proceedings (Criminal Justice System, 2005c). The aim is to allow relatives to make a personal statement in court before sentence on how they have been affected by the crime. Relatives could address the courts themselves, or through a lawyer or suitable representative – a victim's advocate. However, the proposal to pilot the use of victims' advocates is facing strong opposition from the judiciary, who are concerned that it would alter the adversarial basis of the trial and falsely raise victims' expectations of being able to influence the sentence (Gibb, 2005). However, the government is determined to introduce a number of pilot schemes, so it will be interesting to follow how the plan to introduce victims' advocates progresses.

To support further its acknowledgement of the important role that victims and witnesses play in the criminal justice process (Home Office, 2003a), the government has also published a consultation document regarding plans to introduce a Witness Charter. The aim of the Charter is to set out the standards of service that all witnesses, whether or not they are also victims, can expect to receive at every stage in the process. The Charter forms part of the government's 'respect' agenda, recognising that (Criminal Justice System, 'The Witness Charter', 2005d: 1):

> when witnesses come forward they are playing their part in tackling crime and bad behaviour and in building a culture of respect, so that justice is done and society is made safer for them, their family and friends and the community in which they live.

Finally (or at least at the time of writing), the government published its latest Green Paper *Rebuilding Lives: Supporting Victims of Crime* (Home Office, 2005). In this, the government outlines quite clearly the progress made to date and what it wants to do in the future to assist victims and witnesses, and ultimately improve public confidence in the criminal justice system. One of the main intentions of the Green Paper is to reconsider the purpose and aims of the criminal injuries compensation scheme, an issue which is continually revisited by successive governments. The Green Paper also considers proposals for introducing Victim Care Units in order to improve the delivery of services and support to victims of crime. A number of different models are put forward for consideration of how this can best be achieved.

Whilst it can be argued that a number of political motivations underpin the range of different proposals currently under review (in particular, an acknowledgement of the need to improve public confidence in the criminal justice system), it cannot be denied that significant progress is beginning to be made. However, still more needs to be done if any of the above is to have any impact on the actual experiences of victims and witnesses. Whilst legislation is a step in the right direction, for legislation to be effective it has to be implemented. Professional cultures and attitudes are changing, but new policies and initiatives must be supported with adequate resources and appropriate training. Policies and initiatives need to be monitored and evaluated, particularly from a victim's perspective, as it is only by improving the victims' and witnesses' experiences of the criminal justice process, that satisfaction will be improved and public confidence restored. As has been discussed above, an effective and efficient criminal justice system relies on the goodwill and cooperation of victims, witnesses and the public. To achieve a system that truly seeks justice, victims need to be responded to as valued participants and accorded rights to support and protect them, whilst continuing to respect the rights of defendants.

It will be interesting to follow how criminal justice policy progresses in the light of these consultation procedures and to keep up to date with new initiatives that may be introduced in the future. All the documents referred to above can be found on the Criminal Justice System website:

- <http://www.cjsonline.gov.uk>

This website is very useful for keeping up to date with new policies, legislation and publications. Click on the 'What's New' site regularly. Also check the Home Office website for new publications by the Home Office Research Directorate.

Literature and research in victimology is expanding and there have been a number of new books published. One that will be very useful to students studying victimology is Goodey (2005). Goodey's book makes helpful links between academic victimology, victim advocacy and the development of social policy, linking in an accessible way how theory and practice interact. Williams (2005) also offers an evaluation of the development of victim-centred policies, focusing on community justice and restorative justice, drawing upon evidence and experiences from the UK and around the world. The *British Journal of Community Justice* has also published a special issue on victims of crime (Tapley, 2005b). Most criminology texts now also contain a chapter that focuses on victims of crime and witnesses.

## Suspects' rights

Pete was a 20-year-old student living in a rented room in Peckham. His landlady and her teenage daughter seemed pleasant enough but he kept to himself. After a year there he was short of money so moved back in with his parents. Soon after the police called and accused him of sexual grooming and rape of the teenage daughter. This was the last thing he expected, since he had barely noticed the girl and certainly never touched her. He could not plead mistaken identity: the girl had chapter and verse of each occasion; in fact she had kept a 'diary' of what went on. She showed this to her mother, who reported it to the police. When questioned, the mother could throw no further light on the accusation but admitted that she was often out until late. Her daughter had been pretty taciturn during the last year, but she had put this down to her age.

Pete had no alibi. He usually ate at college and studied in his room at night while the mother went out to a cleaning job, and the daughter was in the front room watching TV. He said this was fantasy land and the girl had made all this up. The police said they had to take all such charges seriously. One of them reminded Pete he had been arrested before as a teenager and cautioned for affray and cannabis smoking. Although they released him on police bail, they implied the case was strong enough to go to the CPS and current CPS policy was to prosecute to avoid having to explain to the victim why they had not brought a charge.

Sure enough, after three months, Pete was charged. From his solicitor he found there was no eyewitness or other evidence. The girl said she had been too frightened to tell anyone. Pete assumed she had been dumped by a boyfriend and wanted to get her own back on men generally. The case was to be heard at Crown Court eight months after the charge was brought. Pete's mother was supportive but his father was not sure of his innocence. His studies suffered. He failed his exams, got very depressed and gave up college. The case itself was postponed from week to week, mainly, his solicitor said, because CPS was short-staffed.

The actual hearing lasted three days, being delayed by legal arguments in court. His accuser was confused and inconsistent. No one corroborated what she said, although several witnesses spoke of her honesty. He denied the charges and witnesses spoke of his honesty. The jury retired for three hours and found him not guilty of all charges: the judge told him he could go.

This case is not untypical: in fact it is a real case with names and circumstances slightly changed. The girl may or may not have been a victim. But Pete was a victim. The case could have resulted in a long term of imprisonment, but even if it had been a case of mistaken identity involving minor theft, the suspect and his family go through a significant ordeal. The victim is entitled to a supportive police response and could apply for compensation or sue her attacker in a civil court. However, the suspect could only do that if it could be proved – which is exceptionally difficult – that there was malice on the part of the victim or the police.

Pete felt that he had lost his rights as a citizen, in the same way as if he had been a victim of a crime. He had not realised how far the rights of victims and suspects could interact. He felt that undermining suspects' rights, as his had been, could only lead to a loss of trust in the CJS, to juries refusing to convict, and to governments becoming less concerned with civil liberties.

### Suspects and victims

Let us consider things more generally. Although some people feel suspects get treated too kindly, things can be far more complicated. Look at the following possibilities (Table 9.1). They show that the circumstances which are considered *normal* by the public are not the only possible outcomes.

There is a strong likelihood that there are a large number of 'non-normal' outcomes each year, both because of the fallibility of CJS staff and because 'victims' are themselves fallible, for example as poor witnesses, liars, or simply overcome by the court situation.

Most suspects are found guilty, but until then they are innocent. It is therefore improper reasoning to suggest or hint that suspects are less deserving of respect and protection than the rest of us. Indeed they deserve more because they can also be victims of the criminal justice investigatory process, systems of trial and the balance of power between the various players within the system and sometimes things really go wrong. With a miscarriage of justice, we should also ask if the rights of the person wrongly convicted are strong enough? The sums paid to prisoners wrongly convicted sound attractive but, spread over the years of wrongful imprisonment, are they anywhere near adequate compensation for loss of earnings, pleasures or opportunities? How much do you think would be adequate compensation for ten years' wrongful imprisonment? And, of course, there is no compensation for persons 'wrongly accused and found innocent'. Perhaps there should be: it would be interesting to see if the CPS brought fewer cases if they had to compensate suspects who were found innocent after trial.

### Suspects have too many rights: we need to convict more people

Victims feel aggrieved when nobody is prosecuted for the crime they experienced or they see the person they think responsible found 'not guilty'. But, if people are found 'not guilty' in our justice system, this implies a reasonable doubt

*Table 9.1*

| What actually happened | Suspect found guilty in court | Suspect acquitted by court |
|---|---|---|
| Suspect committed offence | 'Normal' circumstance | |
| Suspect committed an offence but not the one charged | | Suspect 'got away with it' |
| | Miscarriage of justice | |
| Suspect did not commit any offence | | 'Normal' circumstance |

and the system is thus working properly! However, recently this has proved to be unacceptable and lobbyists, particularly the police, aided and abetted by the popular press, have sought for suspects' rights to be reduced. A weak government has allowed many such changes through and more suspects' rights are likely to go soon: a list is given in Table 9.2.

It is difficult to argue that suspects should have more rights when, as this table shows, successive governments have salami sliced away the rights that still exist. Let us look at some in more detail.

### The right to silence

This has virtually gone! Those arrested are warned that if they do not answer police questions then this may be used against them when they get to court. Those who know their way around 'the system' may still refuse to answer questions, knowing, from prior experience that police need interviews for information and evidence. On the other hand, innocent suspects are liable to be frightened into speaking and incriminating themselves.

### Prior convictions

Over the centuries, English Common Law developed a range of rules of evidence to protect against miscarriages of justice. The courts realised that juries must be discouraged from making erroneous assumptions, inferences and from using poor reasoning (Roberts and Zuckerman, 2004; Doak and McGourlay, 2005). To ensure that people were only tried for the crime accused, and not for what they had already been punished for, suspects' prior criminal records could not be mentioned in court, except in some special circumstances. However the Criminal Justice Act 2003 abolished the old common law rules and introduced new tests, which make it easier to introduce evidence of prior convictions, particularly in relation to sex offences (Roberts and Zuckerman, 2004; Doak and McGourlay, 2005).

### Hearsay evidence

In the past, Common Law judges developed rules to limit evidence when one person wants to say what they heard someone else say. So a court will not be allowed to hear that Bill told Alan that he saw Chris stab Dennis. Why not? Well, what are we really concerned about; that Bill told Alan or that Chris stabbed Dennis? If we are concerned with the attack on Dennis then proof that Alan is telling the truth about what Bill told him is not evidence, let alone proof, either that Chris stabbed Dennis or that that is what, if anything, Bill saw. There are many reasons that Bill might have said what he did. Perhaps he was trying to get Chris into trouble; was psychotic and totally misinterpreted what he saw; or mistook Chris for Edward,

*Table 9.2*

| | |
|---|---|
| Issue of fixed penalty notices | Police can now issue fixed penalty notices, not only to traffic offenders, but to those who plead guilty to public order offences or even shoplifting. Those who plead guilty, and many do, to avoid a lengthy involvement with an uncertain legal process, thus lose their rights to a fair trial and to having their defence publicly stated. It also gives the police the right to be accuser and judge at the same time, something most jurisdictions avoid as unethical practice. |
| Powers of arrest | The concept of the arrestable offence was abolished by the Serious Organised Crime and Police Act 2005 which came into force on 1 January 2006. The Terrorism Act 2000 abolished the need for 'reasonable' suspicion. |
| Length of detention | This has been increased from 24 to 36 hours for indictable offences. For those suspected of being terrorists (itself a concept widened over the last few years so that 'terrorism' is now defined as what the government of the day wishes) detention has now been increased to 42 days without charge under certain stringent circumstances. |
| Right to legal advice | Lawyers do not give enough importance to suspects' rights and work with the police to discourage suspects exercising their right to it. As a result, suspects exercise their right to request legal advice in less than a half of cases. |
| Right to silence | This no longer exists and an inference can be made by the court if a suspects refuses to answer police questions. Perhaps 10 per cent of suspects still refuse to answer questions and hence are open to possibly inaccurate inferences by the court. However, confessions by suspects are still admissible. |
| Right to protection from particular types of evidence | Prior convictions can be announced in court in a greater number of circumstances. Hearsay evidence is no longer excluded as an absolute right. |
| Right to 'neutral' prosecution | The AG's Code now requires the police to seek, retain and exchange 'negative' as well as 'positive' evidence, which disproves innocence as well as proving guilt. |
| Plea-bargaining | Pressure to remove practice of giving sentencing discounts for guilty pleas. |
| Disclosure of evidence | The Criminal Cases Review Committee says that non-disclosure of evidence is a common reason for cases being referred to it as miscarriages of justice. |
| Choice of venue | CJ authorities want to take more cases at lower courts, where they are heard more quickly and hence are cheaper. Suspects are persuaded to agree to this because of possibly lower penalties but lose out on having a jury trial. |
| Jury trial | There is constant pressure by the government on Parliament to remove jury trial for some cases. |
| Witness evidence | Judges have quashed guilty verdicts based upon the evidence of anonymous witnesses, without the chance of being challenged effectively. This is leading to the likelihood that new legislation will be passed to allow witnesses to give their evidence anonymously. |

amongst many other explanations, including that it actually happened as he said it did. These and other rules of evidence are progressively being diluted (Roberts and Zuckerman, 2004).

### Labelling of suspects

One of the unfortunate consequences of the last decade in the way suspects are treated is that there has been significant extension of the way that once people are 'labelled' they can be treated more severely.

One example has been suspects labelled as possible terrorists. This has led to their rights being further restricted. From 2005 politicians tried to hold in prison some suspected of terrorism although they were not yet charged with an offence. Judges ruled this illegal, so 'Control Orders' were set up to deal with such people, leading to 'house arrest under severe restrictions'. A 2009 Law Lords Judgement banned their use to limit the freedom of three Libyan terrorist suspects without a trial by ruling the use of secret evidence breached human rights legislation. Although the Law Lords said that 'The trial procedure can never be considered fair if a party to it is kept in ignorance of the case against him', the Home Secretary called the ruling 'Extremely disappointing [which] would make it more difficult to protect the public from terrorism.' A typical press comment was 'The English judiciary has now pretty well completed its attempt to destroy altogether Britain's ability to defend itself against terrorism. By their ruling, the Law Lords made it clear that the rights of the individual thus trumped the rights of citizens to be protected from terrorism' (Melanie Phillips in *Spectator* (<http://www.spectator.co.uk/melaniephillips/3690341/the-law-lords-make-britain-unsafe-yet-again.thtml>)). This line of argument sets a specific right, that of the suspect, against a more general right, that of the citizen.

Other labelling developments include:

- the way that the several million volunteers wishing to work with children have to prove their innocence of any crime by obtaining an expensive certificate from the government;
- the way that the government has expanded the size of the police DNA database to include all those connected with a criminal case, despite there being no evidence of any guilt in many cases; and
- the November 2009 judgement against Guantanamo Bay ex-detainees who are suing UK security intelligence agencies for 'unlawful acts, negligence and conspiracy' in a London civil court. It has been decided that 'secret intelligence information can remain hidden'.

### Search for truth?

It is sometimes said that English law does not allow a 'search for truth' as other systems do and that suspects' rights are better defended in such systems and this amounts to a condemnation of aspects of our adversarial trial system. However, it is not as simple as that. The English system involves a court hearing, and deciding between allegation and counter-allegation. Other systems involve a legally supervised inquiry into what happened. However, it is wrong to conclude that the English system is not an inquiry into the truth! As Lord Devlin (1979) a very experienced English judge, commented in 1979:

> The English say that the best way of getting at the truth is to have each party dig for the facts that help it; between them they will bring all to light. Two prejudiced searchers starting from opposite ends of the field will between them be less likely to miss anything than the impartial searcher starting in the middle.

Other facts are that the adversarial system is much stricter on what evidence is allowed than other systems and that, for various reasons, many foreign jurisdictions are moving towards the English systems, e.g. the Japanese are introducing a quasi jury system called Saiban-in from 2009.

The key points are motivation and rigour. There can be no denying it; a trial is a contest. It does not matter where in the world it takes place. Having someone duty bound to work for you and use every legitimate tool, just as the CPS will, is our best protection against error. So tying a lawyer's hands by restricting suspect's rights, is not just a threat to justice but involves a misunderstanding of our trial system. Getting the truth requires more, not less, freedom.

However, the fact that a suspect's rights can be eroded, as they have been in the last few years, says a lot about the ability of any English government to change the law fundamentally over a short period, something that other jurisdictions, with firm Constitutions or strong Supreme Courts of judiciary, are proof against. This feature of English law makes it even more important that trends such as the erosion of suspect's rights should be commented on widely and not be accepted as a 'natural consequence' of a global fight against terrorism, or fears about rising violent crime.

### Suspects should have more rights

We could argue that suspects should have more rights. For example, what redress has Pete, wrongly accused of rape, got from the police or the CPS? None, in the absence of proof of malice! The police are 'only doing their job'. They are empowered to arrest and question us. The CPS is 'only doing its job to protect victims'. It is empowered to prosecute offences. It is not just that there is always a risk that someone like Pete will be wrongly convicted but that some people, who are actually innocent, plead guilty (Gudjonsson, 2003). Indeed this problem is liable to increase given that the courts have recently instituted procedures to make the advantages of pleading guilty at an early stage more explicit (*Goodyear (Karl)*, [2005] 3 All ER 117). Suspects, although knowing that they are innocent, may pessimistically fear that everything is stacked against them, that the courts will not believe them and that it is more sensible to plead guilty and gain a reduction in sentence for an early plea. Indeed, Pete was encouraged to plead guilty by the CPS to avoid the girl having to appear in court and to get a lower sentence: he even considered this for a short time, but was encouraged by friends to stick to the truth.

What redress did Pete have from the courts? After all, he was found 'not guilty'. The court did not proclaim to the world – let alone apologise to Pete for the inconvenience – that he was positively innocent in fact and/or in law. They simply announce the negative; they did not find Pete guilty. Is it reasonable to expect his neighbours to believe there was no fire when there evidently was sufficient smoke to justify a prosecution; or would a local employer be likely to give him a job, once the local press had reported his 'acquittal'.

### Surely it doesn't matter that much?

Why shouldn't victims be given more information about when trials are going to take place, and what giving evidence in court is like? No good reason. But what about protecting some witnesses, calling them 'vulnerable', and letting victims tell courts about the effect the crimes have had upon them? Again it sounds sensible. But it is so seductive, slipping in changes here and there to a legal system developed over centuries. Yes, giving evidence is difficult and anxiety provoking. But it should be! Someone's future is at stake. If you are going to lie then you should do it in public, so that the consequences will be obvious. Judges can, and should, protect certain witnesses after making individualised assessments of what is appropriate. However, the category of 'vulnerable' witness is liable to keep expanding until we forget why we had a different system in the first place.

Victim Impact Statements also sound like a good idea. They may also buy electoral advantage by mollifying a pressure group. It is so much easier to concede an apparently 'reasonable' law reform than to engage in careful analysis of the need for, and consequences of, particular reform. So now we have arrangements for courts to hear statements about the effects of a crime (Ashworth and Redmayne, 2005). However, that statement may not influence the punishment the court specifies. That is decided on different principles. Nevertheless the victim is heard. It is a symbolic gesture (Gusfield, 1963) rather than a substantive measure. Victims are being palmed off with gestures. It would be more appropriate to give them the right to confront those who offended against them after sentence and as part of the punishment designed to ensure that offenders realise the individuality of their victims and the reality of the harm caused (Umbreit, 2001).

## Conclusion

It is wrong to restrict suspects' rights. It is critically important that they be protected (Kennedy, 2005). It is too easy to let others care, to reason lazily that suspects' rights do not matter. Each time a police car goes past, just wonder whether it might be stopping for you. Do you wish to be a victim because suspects' rights were not thought important? It is also interesting that, by and large, these removals of suspects' rights has been in response to the pressures from the middle classes of British Society, who are less likely to commit the types of crime which these suspects are accused of. These are the same group who would cry foul, if the restrictions on rights had been concentrated on those committing more 'white-collar' crimes, such as insider trading, money laundering, creative accounting, tax avoidance, recreational drug use or environmental crimes. After all, as Sanders and Young (2007: 971) argue: 'Arguably, major advances in liberty are only ever secured in the UK when the middle classes are threatened.' The last 10 years have seen a very effective action to ensure government keeps its eyes averted from the crimes the middle classes are likely to commit.

## Bibliography

ACPO (2002) Press release: 'The game is up for criminals'. Retrieved on 7 June 2006 from: <http://www.acpo.police.uk/news/2002/q1/02acrimjust.html>
—— (2004) Press release: 'ACPO welcome for new Criminal Justice Act'. Retrieved on 7 June 2006 from: <http://www.acpo.police.uk/news/2004/q1/New_criminal_Justice_act.html>
Ashworth, A. (1983) *Sentencing and Penal Policy*. London: Weidenfeld & Nicholson.
Ashworth, A. and Redmayne, M. (2005) *The Criminal Justice Process* (3rd edn). Oxford: Oxford University Press.
Audit Commission (2003) *Victims and Witnesses: Providing Better Support*. London: Audit Commission.
Auld, Lord Justice (2001) *Review of the Criminal Courts*. Retrieved on 5 June 2006 from: <http://www.criminal-courts-review.org.uk>
Criminal Justice System (2005a) 'New sentencing guidelines launched on manslaughter by reason of provocation and robbery'. Retrieved on 5 June 2006 from: <http://cjsonline.gov.uk/the_cjs/whats_new/news-3257.html>
—— (2005b) 'Victims' needs must be a priority for prosecutors'. Retrieved on 5 June 2006 from: <http://cjsonline.gov.uk/the_cjs/whats_new/news-3234.html>
—— (2005c) 'Hearing the relatives of murder and manslaughter victims'. Retrieved on 5 June 2006 from: <http://cjsonline.gov.uk/thecjs/whats_new/news-3204.html>
—— (2005d) 'The Witness Charter: new standards of care for witnesses in the criminal justice system'. Retrieved on 5 June 2006 from: <http://www.cjsonline.gov.uk/downloads/application/pdf/The%20Witness%20Charter%20Consultation.pdf>
Davies, M., Croall, H. and Tyrer, J. (1998) *Criminal Justice: An Introduction to the Criminal Justice System in England and Wales* (2nd edn). London: Longman, Chapter 11, pp. 373–85.
Davies, P., Francis, P. and Jupp, V. (eds) (2003) *Victimisation: Theory, Research and Policy*. Basingstoke: Palgrave Macmillan.

Devlin, D. (1979) *The Judge*. Oxford: Oxford University Press.

Doak, J. and McGourlay, C. (2005) *Criminal Evidence in Context*. Exeter: Law Matters Publications.

Dodd, T., Nicholas, S., Povey, D. and Walker, A. (2004) *Crime in England and Wales 2003/2004*. Home Office Statistical Bulletin 10/04. London: Home Office.

Fenwick, H. (1995) 'Rights of victims in the criminal justice system: rhetoric or reality?' *Criminal Law Review*, 843–53.

Gibb, F. (2005) 'Judges set against plans for victims' advocates'. *The Times*, 24 December, p. 4.

Glidewell, I. (1998) *The Review of the Crown Prosecution Service: A Report*. Cmnd. 3960. London: HMSO.

Goodey, J. (2005) *Victims and Victimology: Research, Policy and Practice*. Harlow: Pearson.

Gudjonsson, G. (2003) *The Psychology of Interrogations and Confessions: A Handbook*. Chichester: Wiley.

Gusfield, J.R. (1963) *Symbolic Crusade: Status Politics and the American Temperance Movement*. Urbana, IL: University of Illinois Press.

Halliday, J. (2001) 'Review of sentencing'. Retrieved on 7 June 2006 from: <http://www.homeoffice.gov.uk/documents/halliday-report-sppu/>

Hamlyn, B., Phelps, A., Turtle, J. and Sattar, G. (2004) *Are Special Measures Working? Evidence from Surveys of Vulnerable and Intimidated Witnesses*. Home Office Research Study 283. London: HMSO.

Hill, J. and Wright, G. (2004) 'Victims, crime and criminal justice'. In J. Muncie and D. Wilson (eds) *Student Handbook of Criminal Justice*. London: Longman, Chapter 8, pp. 105–122.

Home Office (1990) *Victim's Charter: A Statement of the Rights of Victims*. London: HMSO.

—— (1996) *Victim's Charter: A Statement of Service Standards for Victims of Crime*. London: HMSO.

—— (1998) *Speaking Up for Justice*. London: HMSO.

—— (1999) *Criminal Justice System Strategic Plan 1999–2002*. London: Home Office.

—— (2002) *Justice for All*. London: Home Office.

—— (2003a) *A New Deal for Victims and Witnesses*. London: Home Office.

—— (2003b) *Improving Public Satisfaction and Confidence in the Criminal Justice System*. London: Home Office.

—— (2003c) *Safety and Justice*. London: HMSO.

—— (2004a) *Domestic Violence, Crime and Victims Act 2004*. London: HMSO.

—— (2004b) 'Putting victims first: the Domestic Violence, Crime and Victims Bill'. Available at: <http://www.homeoffice.gov.uk>

—— (2005) *Rebuilding Lives: Supporting Victims of Crime*. London: Home Office.

Hough, J.M. and Mayhew, P. (1983) *The British Crime Survey: First Report*. Home Office Research Study 76. London: Home Office.

Institute of Public Policy Research (2001) *Reluctant Witness*. London: Institute of Public Policy Research.

Justice Gap Task Force (2002) *Narrowing the Justice Gap: Framework*. London: Home Office.

Kennedy, H. (2005) *Just Law: The Changing Face of Justice – and Why it Matters to Us All*. London: Vintage.

Maguire, M. and Bennett, T. (1982) *Burglary in a Dwelling*. London: Heinemann.

Mirrlees-Black, C. (2001) *Confidence in the Criminal Justice System: Findings from the 2000 British Crime Survey*. Home Office Research, Development and Statistics Directorate, Research Findings 137. London: Home Office.

Narey Report (1997) *Review of Delay in Criminal Justice System*. Available at <http://www.nationalarchives.gov.uk/ERO/records/ho415/1/cpd/pvu/crimrev.htm>

Office of Criminal Justice Reform (2004a) *Cutting Crime, Delivering Justice: A Strategic Plan for Criminal Justice 2004–08*. London: HMSO.

—— (2004b) *No Witness, No Justice*. London: HMSO.

Roberts, P. and Zuckerman, A. (2004) *Criminal Evidence*. Oxford: Oxford University Press.

Sanders, A. and Young, R. (2002) 'From suspect to trial'. In M. Maguire, R. Morgan and R. Reiner (eds) *The Oxford Handbook of Criminology* (3rd edn). Oxford: Clarendon Press, Chapter 28.

—— (2007) *Criminal Justice* (3rd edn), Oxford: Oxford University Press.

Shapland, J., Willmore, J. and Duff, P. (1985) *Victims in the Criminal Justice System*. Aldershot: Gower.

Stanko, E. (1985) *Intimate Intrusions: Women's Experience of Male Violence*. London: Virago.

—— (1988) 'Fear of crime and the myth of the safe home: a feminist critique of criminology'. In K. Yllo and M. Bograd (eds) *Feminist Perspectives on Wife Abuse*. London: Sage.

Stevens, J. (2002) 'The search for truth in the criminal justice system'. Speech to Convocation/Haldane Law Lecture at University of Leicester, 6 March. Retrieved on 7 June 2006 from: <http://www.reform.co.uk/filestore/pdf/The%20Search%20for%20Truth%20in%20Criminal%20Justice,%20John%20Stevens.pdf>

Tapley, J. (2003) 'From "good citizen" to "deserving client": the relationship between victims of violent crime and the state using citizenship as the conceptualising tool'. Unpublished PhD Thesis, University of Southampton.

—— (2005a) 'Political rhetoric and the reality of victims' experiences'. *Prison Service Journal*, 158, March, 45–52.

—— (2005b) 'Public confidence costs: criminal justice from a victim's perspective'. *British Journal of Community Justice*, 3(2), 25–37.

—— (2005c) 'Confidence in criminal justice: achieving community justice for victims and witnesses'. In F. Pakes and J. Winstone (eds) *Community Justice: Issues for Probation and Criminal Justice*. Cullompton, Devon: Willan.

Temkin, J. (1987) *Rape and the Legal Process*. London: Sweet and Maxwell.

Umbreit, M.S. (2001) *The Handbook on Victim Offender Mediation: An Essential Guide for Practice and Research*. San Francisco, CA: Jossey-Bass.

van Dijk, J. (1988) 'Ideological trends within the victims movement: an international perspective'. In M. Maguire and J. Pointing (eds) *Victims of Crime: A New Deal?* Milton Keynes: Open University Press.

Williams, B. (2005) *Victims of Crime and Community Justice*. London: Jessica Kingsley.

Zedner, L. (1994) 'Victims'. In M. Maguire, R. Morgan and R. Reiner (eds) *The Oxford Handbook of Criminology* (2nd edn). Oxford: Clarendon Press.

—— (2002) 'Victim'. In M. Maguire, R. Morgan and R. Reiner (eds) *The Oxford Handbook of Criminology* (3rd edn). Oxford: Clarendon Press, Chapter 13, especially pp. 428–48.

# 10 Sex offender notification

*Andy Williams and Mike Nash*

## Introduction

The debate concerning whether the general public should have access to personal information about sex offenders living in their local community is an emotive one. In recent years this debate has been controlled by lead agencies within the criminal justice and legal systems. There are strong arguments on both sides of the debate, most of which are qualitatively similar. For example, advocates *against* public notification often state the human rights of the offender as a justifiable reason as to why the United Kingdom should not (or cannot) have such a system in place (Power, 2003: 76–86). Likewise, those who believe that the general public *should* have the right to know if there are sexual offenders living next door to them often use the human rights of people and victims of sexual offences as a reason for why public notification should be allowed. This chapter examines arguments for and against allowing the creation of public notification legislation. In the first instance arguments *against* public notification will be considered. In section two we turn our attention to the arguments *for* public notification. The final section summarises the main points from both sides of the argument presented and places these arguments within the criminal justice models of due process and crime control. The final two sections contain a number of exercises and suggestions for further reading that will be of interest to the reader.

## Public notification of sex offenders – the arguments against

Those who argue for the public notification of the whereabouts of sex offenders often do so on the basis that they have a *right* to know. This right is essentially predicated upon a view that the right of the public to protection outweighs any rights that the offender might have, for example to privacy. It could be argued that the issue is therefore one of competing rights (Floud and Young, 1981; Hudson, 2001, 2003). Any student of criminology will know that when it comes to rights, offenders often sink near the bottom of the list, and sex offenders probably below it. Therefore, to frame the discussion in a rights box may not be appropriate, or at least should not constitute the whole argument. For even if we support the 'for' lobby, the real question should be – what will public notification actually achieve? This is perhaps the most important issue.

## What does public notification entail?

There is already provision for public notification of sex offenders in the UK; indeed there is a requirement that it be considered in all cases which are assessed as posing a serious risk of harm (NOMS PPU, 2007, S. 4.2). The police, in consultation with other public protection agencies, can and do engage in a form of limited public notification. This might include the use of local newspapers, television channels and the Internet as well as leaflets and posters in public buildings. However, this form of action remains rare and is usually concerned with a sense of real and imminent risk and perhaps the loss of contact with the offender. It is likely that disclosure when it does take place is to a very specific audience. That such information release remains rare should lead to an obvious conclusion. And that is that the relevant authorities do not, as a rule, feel the need to inform the public of the location and other details of convicted sex offenders. On the whole it appears as if they are content with present arrangements. The high compliance rate for those on the sex offenders' register (in the region of 97 per cent in the UK and much higher than American registers), indicates that the whereabouts of sex offenders is known and they can be monitored according to their level of assessed risk. These are professional judgements that appear to work well. Yet those who support public notification appear to play along with the idea that knowledge is power and greater safety can be guaranteed. The media pillorying of professionals involved in those cases that do go wrong lend credence to this view (Nash and Williams, 2008).

Supporters of public notification systems appear to go beyond the scope of professional judgement and discretion. The debate is contextualised in personal terms – for example, parents have the right to protect their children. It appears as if there is a lack of trust in professional judgement; no doubt largely due to the fact that this judgement is only presented negatively (when it goes wrong) in the media. How then would notification improve public protection and reduce the numbers of serious further offences?

If we examine the American experience of notification we can gain an idea of how the process would look in practice. Levels of risk (or serious harm) were the original and primary driver of the extent and scope of notification – in other words how much information is given to whom. Level 1 (the lowest level of risk) meant that people could gain access to the information held on the sex offenders' register. Even this release should be restricted to those with a legitimate interest, for example parents, crèche owners, youth club leaders, swimming pool managers and so on. In other words, those people who have responsibility for children can find out information to help protect those children. The information disclosed will give name, address (if within one mile of requester – or will name those on specific streets), working address, offence and conviction dates, age, race, height, eye and hair colour, and possibly a photograph (although this may be at a cost).

Of course the real issue here is not perhaps the right of such people to know of this information, but is more about who gets to know. There can be no guarantees that this information will rest with those having a legitimate interest. It can, and does, easily fall into the hands of those with other interests. Sporadic vigilante attacks, at times fatal, bear testimony to the old adage about information falling into the wrong hands.

Level 2 notification shifts the emphasis from a public right to know to a professional duty to inform. In this scenario the police, within two days of receiving information, must advise public authorities such as schools, day care facilities, other eligible organisations and individuals. Theoretically there is still a cap on those people who can obtain this information, but it is a wider group than level 1 and is automatic rather than on request. It is clear here that there is tremendous scope for information spread. For example, if a children's nursery is informed that a registered sex offender lives in the vicinity, what do they do with that information? Presumably all staff would be informed, but what about parents? In a blaming culture, with the ever-present threat of legal action, who would keep such information to themselves? The information would therefore likely as not find itself 'out there' very quickly.

Level 3 notification concerns those offenders regarded as posing the most serious and imminent risk of further offending. It can include advertisements in local newspapers, public notices in public buildings such as libraries, websites, the prisoner being required to give all addresses in given locations prior to release. In a more extreme example, the offender's house or their vehicle might be marked. In the US, a state representative from Cleveland has proposed bright pink number plates on sex offenders' cars to attract the attention of children. In Phoenix, AZ the sheriff makes male prisoners wear pink underwear. Identifying offenders by a colour mark, like the old scarlet lettering, remains a live issue in parts of the world. When Garland (2001: 181) talks about 'public marking' of offenders, this serves as a graphic illustration of how this scenario can unfold. The following extract from a US radio report illustrates the point:

'Sex offenders face life in prison, castration under bill'

The Minnesota House has overwhelmingly passed a wide-ranging public safety bill that would place tough new sanctions on sex offenders. The bill contains longer prison sentences, the possibility of castration for paedophiles and license plates that would identify sexual predators.

(Minnesota public radio, 28 April 2005)

However, the focus upon 'risk' as a determining factor has proved difficult in the United States. In New Jersey, home of the murdered child Megan Kanka by a released sex offender and home to Megan's Law, the system of public notification has proved anything but the widespread process of notification envisaged by British supporters. Corrigan (2006) found that 'risk' was predicated upon a predominantly 'stranger/danger' perception, and for example, that far more common (and often equally damaging) familial or acquaintance abuse, was scored lowly and generally negated a need for public notification (32 per cent). She also claimed that so many prisoners disputed their risk score with a legal challenge (24 per cent) that in effect, of all convicted sex offenders eligible for registration, 8,760 in total, only 362 (2 per cent) were at level 3, which is that normally understood to represent Megan's Law notification.

## What are the downsides of public notification?

Although not strictly 'notification', the banning of sex offenders from certain areas is another form, in a sense, of identifying them by association. For example in 2006 in Oklahoma, USA, a new law was introduced that effectively banned convicted sex offenders from living within 2,000 feet of day care centres, parks and schools. In a report in the newspaper *The Oklahoman* (Coppernoll, Dean and Sutter 2006), it was noted that a graduate at the University of Oklahoma and the father of a 6 year old, was effectively barred from living in any of the available college accommodation because as a younger man he was convicted of indecent exposure. A local parole officer claimed that sex offenders would effectively be driven from urban areas and said: 'There is no doubt in my mind that what the legislators have done has put the community at risk,' said Mark Pursley, a parole officer who supervises sex offenders. 'They want to pass things that make constituents feel good and it's going to have the opposite effect. Residential restrictions actually increase recidivism.' Pursley said his research shows that removing sex offenders from the conveniences of urban areas – housing, jobs, treatment and public transportation – makes them more likely to reoffend. Pursley said the law is based on irrational fears, not fact. This echoes Corrigan's findings cited above.

What research such as that just cited confirms is that we (society) react to a standardised, stereotypical image of the sex offender, what Edwards and Hensley (2001: 85) describe as a 'master status' that obscure the 'variety and diversity of the offender's other behaviours and identities'. They argue that notification laws actually operate to increase risk by negating an offender's ability to reintegrate into society or even to obtain the most basic of human needs such as accommodation, work, social contact etc. Edwards and Hensley (2001: 89) suggest that relapse in sex offenders may be related to triggers such as stress and isolation, situations likely to be exacerbated by laws which isolate, shame and reject. They suggest that these offenders become 'nomadic lepers' and that notification also manages to shame families whilst denying positives such as employment as organisations would become involved in the naming process. It should also be remembered that victims might also find themselves identified as part of the offender's notification process. For example, recent federal guidelines in the United States require all convicted sex offenders' names and addresses to be posted on the Internet. In the case of incest cases this also serves the purpose of identifying the families. A side effect of this process has been an increase in *under-*reporting of familial abuse. A failure to comply with this policy may result in a loss of central criminal justice funding – this really does appear to be a case of conflicting goals and very fragmented thinking.

The emerging evidence from the United States is therefore of a 'global' approach to sex offender restrictions, such as the common adoption of the '1,000 feet rule' (child molesters must live 1,000 feet from schools or places where children congregate, including, in certain places, school bus stops). Levenson and Cotter (2005) argue the paradox of these exclusion rules when citing a sex offender in Florida, 'You don't want me to live near a school where the kids are when I'm at work. The way it is now, when I get home from work, they're home too – right next door.' The argument here surely is that you cannot guarantee safety by exclusion zones, which, when they overlap, would effectively confine sex offenders to ghettoes where any support mechanisms would be absent (as Edwards and Hensley, 2001 suggest) and they would be an easily identified target for those wishing to do them harm. In similar vein, notification laws would simply make people aware of offenders living in their locality and give them the choice of whether or not they take the risk of their children going into that area. The combinations of exclusion zones and notification information would effectively debar children from large parts of their urban neighbourhood. Is that a way to live?

The idea of the 'wrong' people accessing personal information has already been mentioned. For example, a man admitted killing two recently released sex offenders in Washington State in September 2005. He claimed to have found the information on a sex offenders' website, and there would have been a third victim had he not been at work at the time of the killing. The American system of notification does try to nullify the possible vigilante effect through a policy of public education. Public meetings precede release and may include information on various types of risk and offender as well as offering crime prevention advice. On the whole this appears to work satisfactorily, but the intermittent attacks on sex offenders indicate that they remain at risk.

Doubts must remain, however, about how discriminating the public would be if it gained access to information. For example, in early 2005 a public furore erupted over convicted sex offenders teaching in schools. In some cases the incidents were over two decades old and there had been no reported concerns in the interim. The demand was for all such offenders to lose the right to work with children and in most cases this is what will happen. The man in question has, for the moment, been allowed to continue teaching, but one must question how much longer he can do so in the gaze of the media spotlight. The point here is that the label of sex offender is to be applied for life, with little, *if any*, hope of redemption. The 'public' are unlikely to want to differentiate between offenders too much when the label has already been applied – that in itself is enough.

The potential risk to the offender increases beyond that of physical attack. If their whereabouts become common knowledge there is every chance that employment opportunities will disappear or be severely restricted. Even those employers who may offer help to ex-offenders may think again if the public get to know that they are employing sex offenders. No job will mean lots of free time and will undoubtedly increase opportunities for further offending. Formal and informal social control through work and professional supervision must afford more protection than an offender disappearing or going underground. Yet widespread public notification amplifies the risk of losing contact with offenders or creates ghettos where they may feel safer.

It is almost as if punishment rather than protection is at the heart of the demand for public notification. Protecting vulnerable people has to be the main ambition of managing sex offenders in the community. The Sarah Payne case, so prominent in this particular claim, emphasises some of the inherent difficulties. A known sex offender killed Sarah when she was visiting her grandparents. She actually lived a considerable distance from the attack and it must be questioned where the notification of the killer's details would have started and stopped. Would they have been circulated in Sarah's home area? Would her grandparents have paid much attention if they did not normally have children in their home? Would any of this stop offenders moving around the country? Can we really expect that parents can hold images and details of all offenders in their heads?

The simple truth is that no system is foolproof, and unless all children are forever to be kept indoors then tragedies will happen – that sadly is human nature. The question for society is whether professional oversight of known offenders offers greater protection than offenders running scared and disappearing?

Perhaps the final issue is where would notification actually stop? The case of Ian Huntley serves as an example. Huntley gained employment in a school and ultimately murdered two girls. The issue focused on a number of allegations made against Huntley, in another part of the country, which people argued should have been made public and thus prevented him from working in schools. In fact he did have an actual conviction, not for a sexual offence, but in another name. Had the police sorted this out, he would most likely not have been employed. The issue of allegations is another matter. We still operate a policy of innocent until proven guilty.

Not only would acting on allegations prevent people finding work but, if notification schemes were to be expanded, then people would come to public notice as a result of an allegation, which may well have been malicious. This is a fundamental issue of rights but, as we know, the debate on sexual offenders and rights has been virtually foreclosed.

## Public notification of sex offenders – arguments for public disclosure

This section reviews the key arguments *for* allowing public notification. Indeed it highlights the fact that the UK already has in place a basic notification system, but more needs to be done to develop this. It argues that as long as it is done with adequate care and attention, allowing the public access, if they so desire, to information pertaining to sex offenders in their local communities is *another* preventative measure that can greatly reduce future risk of harm (HMIP, 2006) from sex offenders.

There are a number of precursors for arguing *for* public notification of sex offenders. Firstly, sex offending is complex and multi-determined which means it is difficult to reduce this type of behaviour merely to statistical probabilities; something which occurs during risk assessment, the current dominant method used within the official discourse *against* public notification. Furthermore, there are such a large range of sexual offences that can be placed on a seriousness continuum between low-level and high/extremely serious, that to place all these types under one 'control umbrella' potentially creates problems with monitoring these offenders.

Secondly, sexual offences take place in the real world – not clinical or prison settings, where risk assessment and monitoring protocols have largely developed. Therefore, it is important that we constantly critically assess and develop the received wisdom relating to the types of offences and offenders, social-psychological characteristics of offenders, victims, and perhaps most importantly relating to this debate, the potential criminogenic risk factors leading offenders to reoffend. Public notification can play a part not only in crime prevention, but also potentially adding to the stock of knowledge on the subject. Thirdly, there is no such thing as a risk free environment (Kemshall, 2003; Nash, 2006). Therefore, it is imperative that a range of different monitoring and surveillance measures are made available and to not close off the possibility of developing new innovative ideas for reducing sex offending. One thing that must be stressed is that public notification is about increasing vigilance and creating consciousness of the criminogenic dynamics of sex offending (Ward, Polaschek and Beech, 2006) in order for the general public to be able to identify the signs of this type of criminal behaviour.

In order to argue *for* public notification it is first necessary to outline and critically assess the arguments *against* having public disclosure; for it is within these criticisms that the arguments *for* are born.

## Assessing arguments against public notification

The key arguments *against* public notification, which may appear to adhere to the 'new penology' (Nash, 1999) or the current Government discourse, which replaces the 'language of rehabilitation' with the 'language of surveillance and control through information' (Worrall and Hoy, 2005: 173), actually rest upon evidence created by populist punitiveness. Therefore, arguments against public notification are problematic and need to be reconsidered before, as Worral and Hoy (2005: 173), and Williams and Thompson (2004b: 203–4) argue, the debate is foreclosed and becomes too entrenched. The key problem areas can be generically identified as:

- using populist arguments to gain support;
- confuses *naming and shaming* with *public notification*;
- lack of systematic research into types of offenders and offences, risk assessment, societal responses, and potential notification strategies;
- largely based on an emotive topic which has been 'hijacked by the forces of prejudice and misinformation' (Silverman and Wilson, 2002: 1);
- based on what the offender wants/claims.

## Populist penology

The common arguments as to why public notification is a bad idea are threefold and rest on populist notions that such a policy would: *increase vigilante activity*, *force paedophiles underground*, and increase the likelihood of *innocents being targeted and attacked* (Williams and Thompson, 2004b). These arguments will be discussed in greater detail below, but for now it is important to identify that these three areas tend to be placed within the framework of the rights of the offender, reducing a complex issue to 'not so much a balancing of rights as a decision as to whose rights are the most important' (Nash, 1999: 188).

There are a number of problems with using populist arguments to gain support for social policy. Firstly, it is always the most extreme and rare cases highlighted in the media that are utilised, ignoring the large range of behaviours and offenders. For example, practically every single academic article or book on the subject uses the events in Paulsgrove, in August of 2000, or the release of the notorious 'paedophile' Sidney Cooke in 1998, as evidence to support the claim that public notification would lead to vigilante activity (Williams, 2004). A small point on the Cooke case is that he is *not* a paedophile he's a hebophile, meaning he has a sexual proclivity towards teenage boys (Howitt, 1995). This information is never introduced and would obviously reduce fear amongst say those parents who have prepubescent boys or have daughters, as this type of offender wouldn't be interested in abusing their child (even though it sometimes happens it is still rare that child sex offenders like a mixture of genders or ages, as they tend to stick to a particular type).

Another major problem with using these examples is that they are not only *rare* examples, but they have also been decontextualised. The release of Sidney Cooke led to demonstrations outside Broadbury police station, *not* because of naming and shaming/public notification but because it was 'proposed that he should be placed at the Brigstocke bail hostel in St Paul's, Bristol, which was close to two schools, two nurseries and a brand new adventure playground' (Williams, 2004: 235). So it was the *lack of community involvement* in the decision-making process, as well as making the ridiculous decision to house a child sex offender in areas frequented by children, which was the main reason why there were demonstrations. What is more concerning is that the Sidney Cooke incident also flared up because for many years local residents raised concerns over the level of security offered by Brigstocke. Living approximately half a mile away from the hostel for a number of years, I even witnessed such concerns about Brigstocke on numerous occasions. It took until 2006 for such concerns to be taken seriously when *Panorama* broadcast their findings from an undercover operation undertaken in two hostels in Bristol – with Brigstocke being one of them. The programme identified a lack of supervision and monitoring of child sex offenders in these hostels. As a result of this programme, the then Home Secretary John Reid ordered Her Majesty's Chief Inspector of Probation, Andrew Bridges, to undertake a review of the hostels involved. In March 2007 *Not Locked Up But Subject To Rules* was published. It found that despite the fact that overall supervision of offenders was effective, there were key cases of poor supervision and management of offenders that needed to be addressed (HMIP, 2007: 78–82).

Moving on to Paulsgrove, I have argued elsewhere that the events in Paulsgrove were not a result of naming and shaming, which was the dominant discourse presented at the time (Williams, 2004; Williams and Thompson, 2004a and 2004b). In August 2000 residents of the Paulsgrove estate in Portsmouth demonstrated outside the home of a convicted child sex offender. Victor Burnett had been 'named and shamed' in the *News of the World*, as part of their 'For Sarah' campaign, which was started after the horrific abduction and murder of Sarah Payne in July 2000. Ever since the events in Paulsgrove, a simplistic and reductive analysis by academics (e.g. see Silverman and Wilson, 2002; Evans, 2003) has created the impression that the residents were a bunch of unintelligent, ill-informed, uncouth ruffians who were overreacting to reading something in a tabloid newspaper. Such notions of the residents of Paulsgrove have of course become common amongst academics and social commentators, who tend not to live in areas where there is a high propensity of sex offenders living, or the various social problems faced by these individuals on a day-to-day basis. Indeed, this attitude can often be quite patronising. In the section above on the downsides of public notification, one of the current authors echoes the widespread condescension often seen in accounts through the simple suggestion that people cannot hold images and details of all offenders in their heads. My own experience of these people is that they are more than capable of researching, memorising, and organising information about such offenders (Williams, 2004). Some even have far superior logical and critical faculties than many of the academics and social control agents I've met.

The claims about these residents are based solely on newspaper reports of events rather than any research undertaken. As I found in my ethnographic research, the residents in Paulsgrove were not simply reacting to the *News of the World* but because of the perceived failure of the police and council to take seriously official complaints made against a child sex offender who was about to go 'active'. These complaints were made 18 months prior to the *News of the World's* naming and shaming of the offender, suggesting a non-symbiotic link between the two events (Williams, 2004).

A second reason to be dubious about arguments against public notification placed within an anti-vigilante framework is that in one of the key academic works on the subject, the evidence utilised to support the argument is based upon popular fiction. Kemshall and Maguire (2003: 111) claim that:

> From 1996 onwards there have been several major outbreaks of vigilante actions, exacerbated by a feeling of siege in some communities, especially council house tenants on 'sink estates' who have come to feel that they are being asked to accept a disproportionate level of risk.

The 'evidence' used to support this argument was taken from Minnette Walters appallingly stereotypical crime novel *Acid Row*. It seems a tad non-academic and simplistic to use a work of fiction as evidence to support professional and ideological agendas. It would be preferable for social policy to be constructed using evidence generated within a systematic, scientific framework.

## Naming and shaming OR public notification

The second key framework to consider is that arguments against public notification use naming and shaming to mean the same as public notification. This confuses naming and shaming with properly organised and controlled public notification. There is a world of difference between the two. Why does public notification have to take the form of media induced naming and shaming? The answer is it doesn't, and, if properly conceptualised and operationalised, it could be structured so as to provide a well-monitored and controlled system of public protection.

Public notification is not about the very visible disintegrative shaming (Braithwaite, 1989: 55) of a newspaper campaign; it's about allowing the public access to basic descriptive and criminogenic information relating to potentially dangerous individuals within their local communities.

*Research issues – knowing the sex offender*

Another area that needs to be addressed is the issue of risk assessment and identifying criminogenic risk factors. Despite the abundance of actuarial research (Craissati, 2004: 16–39), more research is needed to profile the different types of offenders and offences. One of the fundamental arguments for not having public notification is that it is not needed due to the development in risk assessment and monitoring protocols within the criminal justice system. For example, the much praised prison sex offender treatment programme (SOTP), introduced in 1991, and based on cognitive-behavioural techniques, has created the belief that if these offenders 'pass' the programme they are 'safe' to return to society, or at least are deemed to be of low risk of becoming a recidivist. A key problem with this, identified by Grubin (1998), is that treatment for sex offenders is most effective if there is long-term follow-up and support. Long-term assessment is something that is often not provided routinely in the UK. Furthermore, in a recent study by Seto (2003: 131–3), it was discovered that those offenders who 'passed' the SOTP had higher recidivism rates than those who had not performed well in the programme, indicating that sex offenders were working out how to gain high scores in order to obtain early release, and therefore be able to go on to reoffend. The key point here is that, despite the best intentions of the criminal justice system, its practitioners and the sophisticated methods used, no system is infallible. We have found similar issues in our work on serious further offences (Nash and Williams, 2008). Public notification could be utilised not only as a system check (i.e. to identify when the system is failing) but also as another preventative measure. Of interest perhaps is that, despite Burnett being deemed a 'low-risk' by Hampshire police between 1999 and 2000, in 2004 a police officer from another Hampshire town phoned up one of the Paulsgrove residents whose child had been going into Burnett's flat, to ask her if she would make a statement outlining what the offender had been doing. When asked why, she was informed that Burnett was apparently up to his 'old-tricks' in Andover, and was causing concern in the local community. It is amazing that four years after the event, we had still not learned the lessons of Paulsgrove.

*Deconstructing the myths*

One of the central reasons for this inability to learn from past mistakes is that official discourse surrounding what happened in Paulsgrove has been dominated by the professional ideologies of the police and probation services. They have highlighted that the issue relating to public notification rests on preventing *vigilante activity*, which would lead to *offenders going 'underground'*, thereby making monitoring of offenders difficult if not impossible, and finally, reducing the likelihood of *innocents being targeted*.

These three arguments are weak and tend to be built more on the rhetoric of the professional agencies disseminating them, than actual evidence.

## Vigilante mob action

Let's take the idea that allowing public notification would lead to an increase in vigilante activity. There is no evidence to suggest that this would be the likely outcome. As Johnston (1996: 220) has noted, there have been few attempts to conceptualise vigilantism and that 'everyone has an opinion on what vigilantism is, but no one has taken the trouble to define it'. For Johnston, there are three main characteristics of a typical vigilante activity: the identification and pursuit of deviants and their behaviour; righting the wrongs of this behaviour through violent or informal means; and leaving a warning to other likeminded offenders (Johnston, 1996: 220). This relates to the issue of 'policing vacuums' identified from the only study into the Paulsgrove demonstrations (Williams, 2004). Following from the social-psychological and sociological literature (Smelser, 1963; Gilje, 1987; Rudé, 1981; and Van-Ginneken, 1992) there is compelling evidence that the 'vigilante-crowd' in Paulsgrove formed when a policing vacuum existed after a number of residents had made previous complaints to the police and council about the offender who, 18 months later, was named and shamed by the *News of the World*. There was a build up of anxiety over a given perceived threat – a child sex offender hanging out with their children – which created fear. The lack of communication from the council and police regarding the complaints heightened the residents' fear and anxiety. It is perhaps telling that anyone who ever met the residents of Paulsgrove would have a completely different perception of these individuals. For example, a *Dispatches* journalist from the pulled documentary said 'but they're not vigilantes, are they?' This is not to suggest that vigilante activity could never occur. There will always be occasions where individuals take the law into their own hands. The point here is that the risk of this occurring is still relatively low.

## Offenders going underground

The second argument against public notification is that the increased vigilante activity would lead offenders to go underground. Again the evidence for this is sparse and it seems striking that in many discussions with various police and probation officers the key evidence supporting this claim comes from anecdotal evidence provided by the offenders themselves. In the end, whether it comes from the official discourse of the police or probation services, or from the offenders it has become a tautological argument.

A counter-argument to this claim is that it's difficult to go 'underground' if the general public are notified and are more vigilant. An excellent example to illustrate this point is that in 2002, Bob McLachlan, the then head of the Paedophile Squad at Scotland Yard, gave details to the *News of the World* and *Sun* newspapers of four high risk sex offenders who had 'disappeared' after ineffective monitoring by the police. Due to the visibility of the issue, these offenders were located and monitored within a week. There was no outcry, no vigilante activity, and it certainly did not result in innocents being wrongly identified and attacked.

### Innocents attacked

The 'innocents attacked' argument rests on the idea that innocent individuals who look the same, have similar names and live in the same location will be wrongly targeted and attacked. In terms of probability that is highly unlikely, and although there have been one or two examples where this has happened it is still a rare occurrence. This argument is often closely tied to the events in Paulsgrove; however, what the official discourse fails to mention is that the 'innocents' on the Paulsgrove estate were not actually attacked and the five families used the demonstrations to secure council house moves that they had previously been denied (Williams and Thompson, 2004a). A further erroneous example from Paulsgrove is the infamous 'fire-bomb' incident in which an innocent family's house was burnt down when they were wrongly targeted. Again, what the official discourse fails to mention is that this had nothing to do with the protestors, but was undertaken by the local drug gang, who was owed money by members of the family who lived at that address. They used the demonstrations as cover, enabling them to torch the property. The police were far too busy blaming the protestors to investigate this crime properly.

The key lessons of Paulsgrove are clear: Paulsgrove was not a result of the *News of the World*'s naming and shaming campaign but as a result of the perceived failure of the official monitoring protocols of Hampshire and the Isle of Wight's Multi-Agency Public Protection Arrangements; previously complaints were seen by the residents as not to have been taken seriously creating a policing vacuum in which the protests developed; the fact that despite the Government's initiatives into community crime prevention, there is still an atmosphere of silence surrounding such offenders and if there is a lack of communication between the control agencies and the community that will potentially increase fear and anxiety, and ultimately the likelihood of vigilante activity.

### Whose rights?

One of the more difficult issues relating to the public notification debate is the issue of balancing the rights of offenders and victims. The issue of rights should not restrict control agencies' ability to undertake their primary role – protecting the public and preventing crime. Therefore, public notification could become an active social policy, with any challenges relating to human rights going through the normal channels – the Court of Appeal, House of Lords or the Court of Justice of the European Communities. Indeed, there is legal precedent where a decision to notify the public was upheld by the Court of Appeal. The High Court in *R* v. *Chief Constable of North Wales Police*, ex parte AB & CD, rejected the complaint of two defendants and upheld the decision of North Wales police to inform the local community that two individuals living on a local caravan site had convictions for child sexual offences. The couple sought a judicial review but the decision was upheld in order to 'prevent crime' and 'alert the public to a potential risk'.

### Thinking outside the box

There are a number of possible forms that community notification could take. These are tentative suggestions but ones that could seriously be considered. Public Notification *could* include:

- access – *if requested* – to basic information pertaining to the offender (not their address as is often assumed);
- public meetings to educate local communities regarding:
  - types of offender;
  - social-psychological characteristics of offending behaviour;
  - monitoring arrangements – i.e. MAPPA;
  - risk assessment protocols;
  - criminogenic risk factors – so the public are aware of potential risk and abusive situations;
  - trained police liaison officers in local communities as a direct contact for concerned members of the public.

Put simply, knowledge empowers communities, creating stronger bonds, enabling parents to become more vigilant, making their children aware of potential risk situations, and ultimately aids grassroots crime prevention (Williams and Thompson, 2004b).

### Current developments

Finally, it is perhaps pertinent to briefly mention a number of important developments within the criminal justice system over the last five years that have began to move towards allowing public notification of sex offenders under particular circumstances. Indeed, since the height of the debate in 2000, things have moved on, albeit slowly. In the UK we are moving more towards public notification and attitudes that were once opposed (to the point of being downright hostile) to the idea, are now moving towards an acceptance that some sort of system needs to be put in place.

In April 2006, the Child Exploitation and Online Protection (CEOP) Centre was launched. CEOP Centre works across the UK and combines police powers, knowledge and personnel with the expertise of business sectors, government, specialist charities and other interested organisations. The key aim is to tackle child abuse 'wherever and whenever it happens' across the world (<http://www.ceop.gov.uk/what_we_do.asp>). One of the first issues that CEOPs dealt with was public notification. In 2006 they took the bold step of creating a 'most wanted' page on their website. This page, similar to the publicly available sex offender databases across America, listed the pictures and profiles of sex offenders that had breached the requirement to register as a sex offender. For two years now this has been in operation and at the time of writing, four offenders had failed to register and were listed on the most wanted site (see <http://www.crimestoppers-uk.org/ceop/>). As far as we are aware this has not resulted in an increase in vigilante attacks; nor have innocent individuals been mistaken for these individuals and attacked. The fact that these offenders were already 'underground' is perhaps telling that public notification is perhaps useful for tracing those that do breach the notification requirement.

A second development that has been more subtle, but none the less significant has been the aforementioned changes to MAPPA guidance (as discussed above). In section 4.2 of the current version of MAPPA guidance, it is a presumption that disclosure to third parties will be made:

> All level 2 and 3 MAPP meetings must consider disclosure with the presumption being that it will take place if an offender presents a risk of serious harm to any identified person(s), particularly children, unless there are defensible reasons not to do so. This is essential at the initial MAPP meeting and must form part of each review. Where disclosure is not to take place, the reasons why must be fully recorded in the MAPP meeting minutes.
>
> (NOMS PPU, 2007: 34)

This is a dramatic change in policy considering that only a few years ago public notification was very rare, not even discussed and was very tightly managed by the police and probation services. The fact that MAPPs now have to justify why they *haven't* allowed public disclosure is testament to the change in attitudes towards public notification in such a short period of time.

Finally, at the time of writing the public notification argument seemed to come full circle when Portsmouth local newspaper *The News* published a story entitled 'Sarah's Law is a step closer' (*The News*, 8 February 2008). It was suggested that Hampshire may become one of the three areas chosen for a Home Office pilot scheme that would test new laws 'designed to let parents know if people in contact with their children are paedophiles' (ibid.: 3). At the time of writing, details were yet to be finalised and it is clear that such laws would fall short of a full-blown 'Sarah's Law'. However, as with the previous two developments briefly mentioned above, it would appear that over the last eight years there has been a slow, yet steady change in attitude towards developing a policy of public notification.

## Summarising the key arguments

This section provides a summary of both sides of the public notification debate and considers whether a notified public is a better protected one.

### Arguments against public notification

The public notification of sex offenders is popular with the public and certainly supported by parts of the mass media. Each new incident of a sex offender attack on a vulnerable person increases the demands for it. Yet it is really unclear how it would enhance the protection of the public. The public at present appear to be unable or unwilling to differentiate the risk posed by different offenders. As such, many people would be included in notification and those posing low risk or having spent a long time away from offending may find themselves caught up in public denunciation and hounding, with potential loss of job, accommodation and family. This hardly represents protection, certainly not of the wider community, but is punitive. In such cases the punishment extends way beyond that originally meted out by the court.

Public protection should be and is a priority for public agencies. Where necessary and appropriate they will engage with the public and pass on information in cases where danger is clear and imminent. It is their job to assess the risk and, although they cannot be expected to get it right every time, they are likely to be better than people fuelled by spectacular media reporting. The public are much less likely to exercise this judgement on risk and therefore there is a strong likelihood that more and more people would be notified. The recent history of vigilante attacks is not promising, and the high numbers of 'lost' sex offenders in the US certainly shows the downside of notification processes. Agencies need to work with the community but equally the community needs to have trust in its experts. There is little evidence to suggest that existing systems are not working effectively but plenty of evidence to suggest that the alternative may be very damaging.

Perhaps the final word should rest with the police, who not only have significant responsibilities for the monitoring of sex offenders in the community but also an absolute duty to protect all citizens at risk of harm (including offenders). In refusing to disclose information regarding sex offenders whose whereabouts were currently unknown, Surrey Police suggested that pieces of information released about registered sex offenders could be pieced together like a jigsaw. Their concern was that such information could be used by those determined to take vigilante action and that not only sex offenders, but wrongly identified 'innocent' members of the public could also be harmed. They concluded:

> Opposed to the somewhat minor benefits in disclosure is the key negative of public safety. We can never be entirely sure what effect information disclosure may have. As far as the police service is concerned, the protection of the community must and will always take precedence over information provision. We would be failing in our duty to protect all members of the public, regardless of who they are, should one person suffer as a result of disclosure under this legislation.
>
> (Surrey Police, 2007)

### For public notification

To summarise the key points: arguments *against* public notification are problematic as they are based upon penal populism; lack systematic research and are largely based upon prison and clinical populations; and thus, are based on the claims made by the offender as well as professional discourse of the police, probation and prison services, which as Cohen (1985) noted have an underlying agenda to dominate and maintain their professional organisations, which often restricts development of adequate policy.

Arguments *for* public notification are simple: they should be based upon firm evidence and a greater understanding of the criminogenic risk factors of such behaviour; individuals should have the right to be able to make informed decisions relating to potential lifestyle risks; equally, parents should be given the right to adequately protect their children. Furthermore, there is huge public support in favour of public notification.

Ultimately, public notification, if structured and controlled correctly, fits in with grassroots community policing and crime prevention. The main difference with this strategy as opposed to the current policy is that it actually involves the community.

### Is a notified public an informed public?

Deciding upon issues which touch upon raw nerves is always difficult. Emotions run very strongly throughout this debate and many would sympathise with a view that parents have a right to protect their children from danger. Yet those very emotions may also get in the way of seeing the reality of the effectives or ineffectiveness of public notification schemes. In this chapter we have suggested that in the United States there is good evidence that such schemes have had a negative impact in terms of public protection but have also suggested that a well organised scheme will empower and involve communities in their own law enforcement and crime prevention.

# References

Braithwaite, J. (1989) *Crime, Shame, and Reintegration*. Cambridge: Cambridge University Press.

Brown, M. and Pratt, J. (eds) (2000) *Dangerous Offenders: Punishment and Social Order*. London: Routledge, Chapter 6.

Cohen, S. (1985) *Visions of Social Control: Crime, Punishment and Classification*. Cambridge: Polity Press.

Conrad, P. and Schneider, J. (1992) *Deviance and Medicalization: From Badness to Sickness*. Philadelphia: Temple University Press, Chapters 1, 2 and 6.

Coppernoll, C., Dean, B. and Sutter, J.D. (2006) *The Oklahoman*. Retrieved 1 February 2008 from: <http://www.nacdl.org/sl_docs.nsf/freeform/sex_offender008? OpenDocument>

Corrigan, R. (2006) 'Making meaning of Megan's Law', *Law and Social Inquiry*, 31(2), 267–312.

Craissati, J. (2004) *Managing High Risk Offenders in the Community*. Hove: Brunner-Routledge.

Critcher, C. (2003) *Moral Panics and the Media*. Buckingham: Open University Press, Chapter 7.

Edwards, W. and Hensley, C. (2001) 'Contextualising sex offender management legislation and policy: evaluating the problem of latent consequences in community notification laws'. *International Journal of Offender Therapy and Comparative Criminology*, 45(1) 83–101.

Evans, Jessica (2003) 'Vigilance and vigilantes: thinking psychoanalytically about anti-paedophile action'. *Theoretical Criminology*, 7(2) 163–89.

Floud, J. and Young, W. (1981) *Dangerousness and Criminal Justice*. London: Heinemann.

Garland, D. (2001) *The Culture of Control*. Oxford: Oxford University Press.

Gilje, P. (1987) *The Road To Mobocracy: Popular Disorder in New York 1763–1834*. London: University of North Carolina Press.

Grubin, D. (1998) *Sex Offending Against Children: Understanding the Risk*. Police Research Series, Paper 99. Policing and Reducing Crime Unit. London: Home Office.

Grubin, D. and Prentky, R. (1993) 'Sexual psychopath laws'. *Criminal Behaviour and Mental Health*, 3, 381–92.

HMIP (2006) *An Independent Review of a Serious Further Offence Case: Anthony Rice*, London: HMIP.

—— (2007) *'Not Locked up but Subject to Rules': An Inquiry into Managing Offenders in Approved Premises (hostels) following the Panorama Programme Broadcast on 8 November 2006*, London: HMIP.

HMIP and HMIC (2005) *Managing Sex Offenders in the Community: A Joint Inspection on Sex Offenders*. London: Home Office.

Holmes, R. and Holmes, S. (2002) *Profiling Violent Crimes: An Investigative Tool*. London: Sage.

Howitt, D. (1995) *Paedophiles and Sexual Offences Against Children*. Chichester: Wiley.

Hudson, B. (2001) 'Human rights, public safety and the Probation Service: defending justice in the risk society', *The Howard Journal*, 40(2) 103–13.

—— (2003) *Justice in the Risk Society*. London: Sage Publications.

Jenkins, P. (1998) *Moral Panic: Changing Concepts of the Child Molester in Modern America*. New Haven, CT: Yale University Press.

Johnston, L. (1996) 'What is vigilantism?' *British Journal Of Criminology*, 36(2), 220–36.

Kemshall, H. (2003) *Understanding Risk in Criminal Justice*, Maidenhead: Open University Press.

Kemshall, H. and McIvor, G. (2004) *Managing Sex Offender Risk*. London: Jessica Kingsley.

Kemshall, H. and Maguire, M. (2003) 'Sex offenders, risk penality and the problem of disclosure to the community'. In A. Matravers (ed.) *Sex Offenders in the Community, Managing and Reducing the Risks*. Cullompton, Devon: Willan.

Knock, K., Schlesinger, P., Boyle, R. and Magor, M. (2002) *The Police Perspective on Sex Offender Orders: A Preliminary Review of Policy and Practice*. Police Research Series, Paper 155. London: Home Office.

Levenson, J.S. and Cotter, L.P. (2005) 'The impact of sex offender residence restrictions: 1,000 feet from danger or one step from absurd?', *International Journal of Offender Therapy and Comparative Criminology*, 49(2) 168–78.

Matravers, A. (ed.) (2003) *Sex Offenders in the Community: Managing and Reducing the Risks*. Cullompton, Devon: Willan.

Nash, M. (1999) *Police, Probation and Protecting the Public*. London: Blackstone.

—— (2006) *Public Protection and the Criminal Justice Process*. Oxford: Oxford University Press.

Nash, M. and Williams, A. (2008) *The Anatomy of Serious Further Offending*. Oxford: Oxford University Press.

NOMS PPU (2007) *MAPPA Guidance 2007: Version 2.0*. London: NOMS PPU.

Petrunik, M. (2003) 'The hare and the tortoise: dangerousness and sex offender policy in the United States and Canada'. *Canadian Journal of Criminology and Criminal Justice/La Revue canadienne de criminologie et de justice pénale*, 45(1) 43–72. Retrieved 24 May 2011 from: <http://utpjournals.metapress.com/content/h7l7101708l08885/>

Power, H. (2003) 'Disclosing information on sex offenders: the human rights implications'. In A. Matravers (ed.) *Sex Offenders in the Community: Managing and Reducing the Risks*. Cullompton, Devon: Willan.

Rudé, G. (1981) *The Crowd in History: A Study of Popular Disturbances in France And England 1730–1848*. London: Wiley.

Seto, M. (2003) 'Interpreting the treatment performance of sex offenders'. In A. Matravers (ed.) *Sex Offenders in the Community: Managing and Reducing the Risks*. Cullompton, Devon: Willan.

Silverman, J. and Wilson, D. (2002) *Innocence Betrayed: Paedophilia, the Media and Society*. Cambridge: Polity Press.

Smelser, N. (1963) *Theory of Collective Behaviour*. London: Routledge.

Surrey Police (2007) 'Freedom of Information Request No: 165-06-504'. Retrieved 5 February 2008 from: <http://www.surrey.police.uk/FOI_View.asp?ID=31>

Thomas, T. (2000) *Sex Crime: Sex Offending and Society*. Cullompton, Devon: Willan, Chapter 7.

—— (2003) 'Sex offender community notification: experiences from America'. *The Howard Journal*, 42(3), 217–28.

Van-Ginneken, J. (1992) *Crowds, Psychology and Politics, 1871–1899*. Cambridge: Cambridge University Press.

Ward, T., Polaschek, D., and Beech, A. (2006) *Theories of Sexual Offending*, Chichester: John Wiley & Sons Ltd.

Williams, A. (2004) ' "There ain't no peds in Paulsgrove": social control, vigilantes and the misapplication of moral panic theory'. Unpublished PhD thesis, University of Reading.

Williams, A. and Thompson, B. (2004a) 'Vigilance or vigilantes: the Paulsgrove riots and policing paedophiles in the community, part 1: the long slow fuse'. *The Police Journal*, 77, 99–119.

—— (2004b) 'Vigilance or vigilantes: the Paulsgrove riots and policing paedophiles in the community, part 2: the lessons of Paulsgrove'. *The Police Journal*, 77, 199–205.

Wilson, R.J., Picheca, J.E. and Prinzo, M. (2007) 'Evaluating the effectiveness of professionally-facilitated volunteerism in the community-based management of high-risk sexual offenders, Part Two: a comparison of recidivism rates'. *The Howard Journal*, 46 (4), 327–37.

Worrall, A. and Hoy, C. (2005) *Punishment in the Community: Managing Offenders, Making Choices*. Cullompton, Devon: Willan.

# Index